Printed in the United States of America

All Bible quotations are taken from the King James [Authorized] Version. All italics in Scripture quotations reflect the author's emphasis.

Reformed Free Publishing Association
1894 Georgetown Center Drive
Jenison MI 49428
616-457-5970
www.rfpa.org
mail@rfpa.org

Cover design by Erika Kiel
Interior design by Katherine Lloyd / theDESKonline.com

ISBN: 978-1-944555-99-3
ISBN: 978-1-7368154-0-3 (ebook)
LCCN: 2022900976

The Savior's Farewell

comfort from the upper room

Martyn McGeown

REFORMED
FREE PUBLISHING
ASSOCIATION
Jenison, Michigan

I prepared this book, based on sermons that I preached for the Limerick Reformed Fellowship in Limerick, Ireland, between December 2018 and June 2019, while my wife and I waited for approval from the authorities to immigrate to the USA (April 2020 to August 2021). I dedicate it to the congregation of Providence Protestant Reformed Church in Hudsonville, Michigan, to "the church that waited."

I thank my God upon every remembrance of you,
always in every prayer of mine for you all making request
with joy, for your fellowship in the gospel from the
first day until now; being confident of this very thing,
that he which hath begun a good work in you will
perform it until the day of Jesus Christ.
(Phil. 1:3-6)

Contents

Part Three
Warnings and Encouragement about the Future

Introduction

In John 13 Jesus eats a final meal with his twelve disciples. The end of the Passion Week, the week of his sufferings, is fast approaching. Jesus has been very busy over the previous days. He had entered Jerusalem on a donkey to the acclaim of an excited crowd of Passover pilgrims, who viewed his entrance as signifying the coming of a king. They were right, of course, but the king was not the one they expected. Instead of a mighty warrior riding triumphantly into the holy city on a white steed, a king appeared who is "just, and having salvation; lowly, and riding upon an ass, and upon a colt the foal of an ass" (Zech. 9:9). When the people cried out, "Hosanna to the Son of David: Blessed is he that cometh in the name of the Lord; Hosanna in the highest" (Matt. 21:9), a cry echoed by the little children, then Jesus' enemies, the chief priests and scribes, were "sore displeased" (v. 15) and commanded Jesus to restrain his disciples' praises.

Hosanna means "Give salvation now," "Salvation now, please," or "Save us now, we pray." The people of Jerusalem did not understand that the salvation Jesus was bringing was not political emancipation from the hated Romans, but spiritual deliverance from the guilt, pollution, and power of sin, which Jesus would accomplish by his sufferings and death on the cross. In fact, the loud Hosannas turned into cries of "Away with him, crucify him" by the end of the week when Jesus, as John the Baptist had prophesied, became "the Lamb of God, which taketh away the sin of the world" (John 1:29). Indeed, the Passover pilgrims might well have been bemused when, instead of overthrowing the Roman occupiers of Jerusalem, Jesus wept over the doomed city (Luke 19:41–44). These are hardly the actions of a military commander coming to deliver them from the heathen oppressor!

Jesus spent much of the Passion Week teaching the people for the last time, as well as instructing his disciples privately. Many of these events are well known to the reader of the New Testament gospel accounts. Jesus cursed the barren fig tree as a sign of the doom of fruitless, hypocritical professors of faith not only in Israel but in every age. Jesus cleansed the temple of ungodly and avaricious buyers, sellers, and money changers. Jesus confounded the Pharisees, scribes, lawyers, and Sadducees who tried to tempt him with difficult questions and dilemmas. Jesus told a number of important parables: the laborers in the vineyard (Matt. 20), the pounds (Luke 19), the wicked husbandmen (Matt. 21), and the king's wedding feast (Matt. 22). Jesus pronounced woes upon the scribes and Pharisees (Matt. 23), and he gave instruction to his disciples on the signs of his coming and warned them to be watchful (Matt. 24–25).

Jesus' instruction and behavior during the Passion Week also intensified the conflict between him and the religious leaders of Jerusalem, who already hated him and sought his destruction. About halfway through the week, one of the twelve, Judas Iscariot, approached the enemies of Jesus. Alienated in his wicked mind against the Master, and also greedy of gain, he offered to betray Jesus to the chief priests, who, glad for his offer, "covenanted with him for thirty pieces of silver" (Matt. 26:15). Now the treacherous Judas waited for an opportunity to commit his foul deed, but "not on the feast day," urged his co-conspirators, lest there be an uproar among the people. Nevertheless, Christ our passover must be sacrificed, not according to the timetable proposed by Jesus' enemies, but according to the decree of Jesus' sovereign Father.

Jesus, mindful of all these things, readied himself for the last supper, sending some of his disciples to make preparations for the meal in an undisclosed location. Having gathered the disciples into an upper room in Jerusalem, Jesus acts in ways that greatly unsettle the disciples. He washes the disciples' feet, which was an act of great, unparalleled humility, as well as an act that humbled the disciples in their foolish, self-seeking pride. Peter, as might be expected, reacted impetuously, first refusing to permit Jesus to wash his feet, and then insisting that Jesus wash his feet, his hands, and his head (John 13:6–9). In connection with the foot washing, Jesus warned the disciples that one of their number was not washed from his sins: "Ye are clean, but not all" (v. 10), something the disciples did not immediately understand.

Following the foot washing, the disciples ate the Passover meal with their lord, at which meal Jesus revealed that one of the disciples would betray him. Although he gave Judas Iscariot the sop (a piece of bread dipped in a bitter sauce) and charged that wicked man, "That thou doest, do quickly" (John 13:27), the other disciples did not grasp the significance or even identify the traitor until he appeared in the Garden of Gethsemane hours later. They imagined that Jesus had sent him on an errand for the relief of the poor (v. 29).

After Judas departed into the night (v. 30), Jesus instituted the Lord's supper, which is recorded not in the gospel according to John, but in the synoptic gospels (Matt. 26:26–30; Mark 14:22–26; Luke 22:17–20). Words such as "This is my body" and "This is my blood" (Matt. 26:26, 28), while comforting to us, were deeply disturbing for the eleven disciples, who could scarcely comprehend what Jesus could mean by the eating of his body and the drinking of his blood.

Jesus begins his actual farewell in John 13:31: "Now is the Son of man glorified, and God is glorified in him," and he continues speaking, with occasional interruptions, until the end of chapter 16. Nevertheless, since John 14–16 constitutes a unit, I do not deal with the final verses of chapter 13 in this book, nor do I treat the sublime prayer of chapter 17, traditionally known as Christ's high priestly prayer. Instead, this book is an exposition of chapters 14–16, often identified as the upper room discourse.

Two things, however, are important to mention by way of introduction to chapters 14–16. First, in John 13:33 Jesus begins to explain his departure, which is the major theme of chapters 14–16, especially chapter 14: "Little children, yet a little while I am with you. Ye shall seek me: and as I said unto the Jews, Whither I go, ye cannot come; so now I say unto you" (John 13:33). Peter especially objects to these words, demanding to know where Jesus is going and why he cannot follow, and proudly boasting that he will die as a martyr for Jesus's sake rather than be separated from him (v. 37). In response to Peter's foolish boast, Jesus utters a warning, recorded in more detail in the synoptic gospel accounts, which is the second important thing that must be mentioned: "Wilt thou lay down thy life for my sake? Verily, verily, I say unto thee, The cock shall not crow, till thou hast denied me thrice" (v. 38).

Jesus is departing. Peter will deny Jesus three times. One of the disciples will betray Jesus. No wonder that at the beginning of John 14 the disciples' hearts are troubled. It is to soothe the disciples in their trouble, and to prepare them for the future, that Jesus utters the words of this most sublime of discourses.

The three chapters, John 14–16, that make up the upper room discourse can be neatly divided. In chapter 14 Jesus, having introduced the subject of his imminent departure in chapter 13:33, begins to explain and apply that truth to the disciples' troubled hearts. Jesus' approach is to comfort his anguished disciples by explaining to them the advantages that accrue to them because of his departure. What they view as the greatest misery is, in fact, the source of their greatest blessedness: Jesus goes away in order to secure everlasting salvation for his disciples. Therefore, the theme of chapter 14 is "The Disciples' Advantage in Jesus' Departure." In chapter 15 Jesus introduces a different subject, having temporarily dropped the subject of his departure. The new subject is "Spiritual Fellowship with Jesus Christ," illustrated by the relationship of branches to a vine, which, by virtue of their union with the vine and the divine husbandman's care, bring forth fruit to the Father's glory. Jesus urges his disciples to abide in him, in his word, and in his love, and he warns against the hatred of the world. Finally, in chapter 16 Jesus develops further the relationship between his disciples, the persecuting world, and the Holy Spirit. In this final chapter the theme is "Warnings and Encouragement about the Future."

The teaching of John 14–16 is so profound that a preacher or writer can scarcely do justice to it. Two thousand years of commentators have not plumbed its depths of meaning. The cry of one man, awed by Jesus, is appropriate: "Never man spake like this man" (John 7:46). In this discourse are words that have comforted Christians for some two thousand years. Pastors have read these words to dying saints, many of whom have mouthed them from their deathbeds. These words have often been used in funeral messages to comfort the bereaved. God's afflicted saints have rejoiced in these truths in every circumstance of life. Profound theological truth is clothed in the simplest of language, and yet who can fully comprehend the meaning! Let us, then, sit at the feet of Jesus to hear his instruction, receive his exhortation and encouragement, heed his warnings, and appropriate his comfort through faith.

PART ONE

The Disciples' Advantage in Jesus' Departure

Chapter 1

Jesus Comforts His Disciples' Troubled Hearts

(John 14:1–3)

1. Let not your heart be troubled: ye believe in God, believe also in me.
2. In my Father's house are many mansions: if it were not so, I would have told you. I go to prepare a place for you.
3. And if I go and prepare a place for you, I will come again, and receive you unto myself; that where I am, there ye may be also.

At the beginning of John 14 Jesus' disciples need comfort and reassurance. They are like frightened little children, bewildered and confused. It seems that their world is coming to an end and that everyone on whom they relied is crumbling beneath their feet. For three and a half years these eleven men (Judas Iscariot had already departed into the night, and they did not understand why) had been Jesus' closest companions. They were his disciples or students, while he was their lord and master. They had listened to, and tried to imbibe, his teachings. They had closely observed, admired, and even worshiped him. For his sake they had forsaken everything: some of them had left their nets, Matthew had left the receipt of custom, and Jesus had promised to make them fishers of men. For his sake they had endured the opposition and suspicion of the religious leaders. They were sincere when they, with Peter, vowed to die as martyrs for his cause. They were looking forward to the revelation of his kingdom and glory.

But on that evening Jesus brought troubling tidings: he was going away. What did this mean? How could this be so? Where was he going? How would this affect them? Questions crowded in upon their minds, which served only to unsettle and even to horrify them.

Jesus, noticing their troubled expressions, spoke directly to their hearts: "Let not your heart be troubled" (v. 1). When we are troubled through the manifold trials of our lives, Jesus speaks the same soothing words to us, words that we always need to hear. These words contain a wealth of beautiful, profound comfort. Let us embrace them by faith.

THE TROUBLED HEARTS

Jesus perceives that his disciples are troubled in heart. To be troubled in heart is to be in the grip of deep distress. Sometimes troubles are superficial or on the surface of our lives. That is true with most of our everyday trials and irritations. By the grace of God we can continue to live in the world and to fulfill our calling in the home, workplace, school, state, and church. But at other times trouble strikes at the very heart, as is the case here.

When the heart is troubled, everything is troubled. The heart is the spiritual center of a person. It is the rational center of man: we would use the word "mind." From the heart our thoughts proceed, because before we speak a word or perform an action, we conceive a thought in our hearts. Jesus recognized this in Mark 2:8: "Why reason ye these things in your hearts?" The Pharisees were reasoning evil things about Jesus in their hearts. The heart is also the emotional center of man: we use the word "heart." Not only do we think with our hearts (or minds), we feel with our hearts because emotions such as love, fear, or anger proceed from our hearts. Our hearts are the source of our affections: our heart yearns after some object so that we desire it, or our heart is repelled by some object so that we detest it. Finally, the heart is the motivational or volitional center of man: we use the word "will" or "plan" or "ambition." Why do we undertake certain actions and avoid other things? The main reason is our heart, for our heart determines our preferences. That is why Solomon urges his son, "Keep thy heart with all diligence; for out of it are the issues of life" (Prov. 4:23).

The hearts of the disciples of Jesus were troubled. That Jesus says, "Let not your heart be troubled," presupposes this. The Lord does not mean, "Do not start to be troubled in heart," but "Stop being troubled in heart." We could liken the hearts of the disciples to the sea. Sometimes, even often, the sea is calm: the sun shines upon it, perhaps there is a gentle breeze, and everything is pleasant and at peace. But suddenly and often without warning the winds whip the waters of the sea into a frenzy so that everything is agitated, stirred up, and stormy. That is the word here translated "troubled." Let not your hearts be agitated, confused, stirred up, perplexed, disquieted, and restless.

Jesus could see the state of the disciples' hearts. Certainly he could read their hearts, and undoubtedly fear and perplexity were etched on their faces. Inside the hearts of the disciples stirred a maelstrom of emotion: their thoughts were running to and fro in confusion, they did not know what to think or how to react, and their emotions were all over the place. The disciples were like frightened, confused little children.

Jesus knew their thoughts and he cared for his disciples. Although Jesus had enough to think about, he took upon himself their fears and sorrows. "In all their affliction he was afflicted, and the angel of his presence saved them: in his love and in his pity he redeemed them; and he bare them, and carried them all the days of old" (Isa. 63:9). Our Savior has not changed: at the right hand of God, as he governs the entire universe, he never forgets his people, but he bears our burdens and understands our sorrows, even sympathizing with us in them. "For we have not an high priest which cannot be touched with the feeling of our infirmities; but was in all points tempted like as we are, yet without sin. Let us therefore come boldly unto the throne of grace, that we may obtain mercy, and find grace to help in time of need" (Heb. 4:15–16).

The reason for the disciples' troubled hearts was simple: Jesus was leaving them. In fact, Jesus would be leaving them that very night. Jesus had said upsetting things that evening. He had warned of imminent betrayal by one disciple and denial by another, but the worst thing he predicted was in John 13:33: "Little children, yet a little while I am with you. Ye shall seek me: and as I said unto the Jews, Whither I go, ye cannot come; so now I say to you." The disciples were troubled and confused at his saying, for they did not know what he meant, and they did not know where he was going. In addition, they did not know how he would go, why he would go, why they could not follow him, and how or whether he would return. Or perhaps they did know, but they did not like the answer, and they desperately tried to explain the words of Jesus away. Their beloved Lord had spoken often and repeatedly of his suffering and death. Shortly before this, he had given them bread and called it his body, and he had passed around wine and called it his blood. He had spoken of his broken body and shed blood. It was all so confusing and troubling.

And yet Jesus takes the time to comfort them. Take note: *they* do not comfort him, but *he* comforts them. The troubles of Jesus were greater than the troubles of his disciples. The Lord would be arrested, tried, condemned, and crucified. Jesus would suffer the wrath and curse of his Father on the cross, and he would die. Yes, this would be traumatic for the disciples, but it would be much worse for Jesus. Yet Jesus is more concerned about the troubled hearts of his disciples than his own sorrows.

Into the disciples' troubled hearts Jesus speaks the soothing words of verse 1, words that have cheered believers for generations: "Let not your heart be troubled." This is not a suggestion but an imperative or a command. It is not a command to start doing something but a command to stop doing something. Jesus says, "I perceive that your hearts are troubled; let that trouble cease." Or Jesus says, "I perceive that your thoughts are confused, your emotions are in disarray, and your spiritual center is in turmoil. Let there be no more confusion, disarray, or turmoil: let that trouble cease."

Notice, too, that the command is not to the disciples, but to their hearts. Jesus does not say, "Do not be troubled," but "Let not *your heart* be troubled." In this way, Jesus speaks directly to the source of the disciples' trouble. The issue is not the external circumstances, which are troubling. The issue is the disciples' response, which is the troubling of their heart. Do not react, Jesus says, to the difficult circumstances of your lives with a troubled heart. Instead, trust, believe, and be at peace. He repeats the command in verse 27: "Peace I leave with you, my peace I give unto you: not as the world giveth, give I unto you. Let not your heart be troubled, neither let it be afraid."

Jesus speaks the same words to believers today and to his church in every age. We hear the benediction, "Grace, mercy, and peace be granted unto you." We could rephrase that, "Let not your heart be troubled, neither be ye afraid." When we face sudden, devastating blows, our natural response is to be troubled. Our hearts are filled with fear, confusion, and agitation. Perhaps we receive a phone call from the doctor's office. Our test results confirm that we have a very serious disease so that our hearts are troubled. Perhaps we lose a loved one in death: as we make arrangements for the funeral, our hearts are troubled. Perhaps our loved one is dying, and for many days our heart is troubled, agitated, and confused. Other sorrows trouble our heart: a wayward child, the apostasy of a church member, the sudden loss of a job, the persecution by the ungodly, and especially our own sins. Our hearts are filled with disquieting thoughts, and we sense turmoil within and feelings of panic and helplessness. What shall we do? Where shall we go? How shall we cope? Our hearts are troubled.

Then Jesus speaks these words of peace. Gently he assures us, "Let not your heart be troubled" (v. 1). Do not continue to be troubled in heart, but let the trouble of your heart cease. As we put down the phone and contemplate our future treatment options, Jesus says, "Let not your heart be troubled." As we sit by the bedside of a loved one, Jesus says, "Let not your heart be troubled." As we bury a loved one, Jesus says, "Let not your heart be troubled." To the saint in the lonely dungeon or the martyr mounting the scaffold Jesus has said: "Let not your heart be troubled." When antichrist rages and the future for the church looks bleak, Jesus will say, "Let not your heart be troubled." If Jesus can calm the troubled sea, he can, and he will, calm our troubled hearts.

THE COMFORTING PROMISES

To comfort the disciples further, Jesus explains something about the cause of their trouble, namely, his departure. First, Jesus explains the reality of his departure. He *is* leaving. They misunderstand his destination and the purpose, but it is true: he is going away. In verses 2–3 he affirms what they had feared. In verse 2 he says, "I go," or "I am going away." In verse 3 he repeats it, "And if I go," or "And if I go away." In verse 4 he adds, "Whither I go ye know, and the way ye know."

Jesus therefore speaks of a departure or of a parting: he is going away, but the disciples are not going with him. This parting will be difficult. The disciples had been his closest companions for about three and a half years. They had rarely, if ever, left his side, but now he was leaving. They would no longer be physically together in the same place. Jesus was not going on an ordinary journey. He was not departing to a strange city or to a foreign country. He was not traveling to the Gentiles. Instead, he was going on a very long journey, a journey to heaven. To reach his celestial destination he would walk a very difficult path through suffering and death. After death he would take the path of resurrection and ascension to the Father's right hand. And he would be away for a long time: in fact, Jesus has been away for some two thousand years, and we do not know the day or the hour of his return to us.

Second, Jesus describes his destination, which is the Father's house. The Father's house is the place that the Father with Jesus Christ, the eternal Son, calls home. The Father in this text is the triune God. In many places in the New Testament the Father is a reference to the triune God, not to the first person of the Trinity.

We know this because he is the Father of the incarnate Son, who is the mediator of the covenant. In the being of the Trinity the first person is the Father of the second person, while in the Incarnation the triune God is the God and Father of our Lord Jesus Christ. To this triune Father the Son prays; this triune Father the Son obeys; this triune Father the Son worships. He is the God and Father of our Lord Jesus Christ, and he is our Father, for we are his adopted children. We will return to this point often because the upper room discourse contains profound theology about the Trinity, the relationship between the Father and the Son, and the Holy Spirit.

Jesus presents a beautiful, homely conception of heaven: heaven is where the triune Father dwells in glory and majesty. Heaven is where the children of God (first Jesus, and then believers adopted in Jesus) will also dwell. Heaven is not a terrifying place but a place of love, light, joy, holiness, beauty, and glory. It is a place without sorrow, fear, trouble, or sin. It is, Jesus says, "my Father's house." Jesus used to live there, and he is returning there to be with his Father whom he loves.

This Father's house, says Jesus, is roomy and spacious: "In my Father's house are many mansions" (v. 2). The English word "mansion" might give the wrong impression to the reader, for in modern English a mansion is the house of a very wealthy person. The word that Jesus uses is better translated as "dwelling place" or "abode." The same word is found in verse 23: "We will come unto him, and make *our abode* with him." The emphasis is not on the luxuriousness of the dwellings ("mansions"), but on the permanence of the dwellings, for the word comes from the Greek verb "to stay," "to remain," or "to abide": "many abiding places." Do not be troubled, says Jesus, at my departure: my Father's house is spacious, roomy, and even vast. There is more than enough room for you, for those who believe in me, and for the entire church of all ages. There is room there for the Old Testament saints and the New Testament saints and for you, believing reader. What a beautiful depiction of heaven! It is a house, a home, the Father's home, the place where we fellowship with God in Christ, and a place of many rooms, many abiding places.

In addition, Jesus comforts the hearts of his disciples by describing the purpose of his departure, for his departure is preparatory. "I go to prepare a place for you," he says (v. 2). It is wonderful to hear about heaven, which is the Father's house, but the disciples might wonder, "What does the Father's house have to do with us?" The answer is that Jesus is not going to heaven in order to dwell alone, and he is not going to heaven merely to be with the Father again. And it is certainly not God's purpose that his many mansions should be unoccupied. Rather, he will bring the disciples to heaven.

To reassure them Jesus says in verse 2, "If it were not so, I would have told you." These words could be a question: "If it were not so, would I not have told you?" If there were no such place as heaven, Jesus would have told them. If heaven were not the Father's house, Jesus would have told them. If there were only a few places in heaven, Jesus would have told them. And if there had not been room for the disciples, Jesus would have told them. The reality of heaven rests on the truth of Jesus' words, and the roominess of heaven rests on Jesus' words. Certainly, we can trust in Jesus' words. What peace for troubled hearts! Contemplate heaven, think about the Father's house, dwell upon the many rooms, meditate on these things often, and trust the word of Jesus concerning them.

Nevertheless, if the disciples are to reach the Father's house, and if we are to reach the Father's house, preparation is required. The disciples were not yet ready for the Father's house, and the Father's house was not yet ready for their arrival. "I go to prepare a place for you" (v. 2). The disciples were sinners. How could they dwell in the Father's house? One of them (Peter) would deny Jesus three times before the next cockcrowing, while the rest of them would flee when Jesus would be arrested. All of them would prove to be cowards in the face of persecution.

Besides, the disciples were guilty of many sins and were by nature totally depraved. They would defile the Father's house by their presence. Better to let a dirty pig sleep in your bed than a filthy sinner defile the Father's house! The same thing is true of us. Shall guilty, filthy sinners take up their abode in the Father's house? Shall those who have broken God's commandments enter heaven? Of course not! Therefore, Jesus must prepare a place for us.

That preparation is twofold: Jesus prepares dwelling places for his disciples (and for us) and Jesus prepares us for our place, for the particular mansion assigned to us. First, Jesus prepares a place for us by his sufferings and death: that is really the first part of the meaning of "I go." In those little words "I go" there is a wealth of meaning, and in those little words "I prepare" is also a wealth of significance.

"I go," says Jesus, "to the garden of Gethsemane. There I will sweat great drops of blood while I agonize in prayer to my Father."

"I go," says Jesus, "to the hall of Annas and Caiaphas, the high priests, to be tried before the Sanhedrin: they shall beat me, spit in my face, and label me a blasphemer worthy of death."

"I go," says Jesus, "to Pilate's hall of judgment. Although he will find no fault in me, the Roman governor will hand me over to his soldiers to be scourged, mocked, beaten, crowned with thorns, and crucified."

"I go," says Jesus, "to Calvary, where I will be nailed to a cross and left to die in agony. God's wrath and curse shall fall on me and I will die."

"And I go," says Jesus, "to Joseph's tomb, where my body shall lie under the power of death for three days."

Why must Jesus go in that way? Because of sin! The guilt of sin must be removed, the pollution of sin must be washed away, and the power of sin must be broken. Jesus shall pay the full price of sin on the cross for his disciples. That is the first step in order to prepare a place for us.

Second, Jesus prepares a place for us by his resurrection, ascension, sitting at the right hand of God, and outpouring of the Spirit. Even if the disciples' sins are forgiven, they are still not fit for heaven. They might be justified or free from guilt, and they might even be sanctified or cleansed of pollution, but to live in heaven the disciples need new life: they need heavenly, spiritual life. Jesus gives that life by virtue of his resurrection, ascension, and sitting at the right hand of God, so that he gives the Holy Spirit. Only one pardoned of all sin, cleansed of all sin, and filled with the Holy Spirit can dwell with God in the Father's house. That, too, is the work of Jesus.

Third, Jesus prepares a place for us by returning to take us to be with him: "And if I go and prepare a place for you, I will come again, and receive you unto myself; that where I am, there ye may be also" (v. 3). Jesus comes for the believer at the point of death: at that point heaven is ready for our souls and our souls are ready for our particular place in heaven. The Bible teaches that when the believer dies his soul is immediately taken up to glory. But at the point of death our body is not yet ready and the new creation is not yet ready for our body. Therefore, our body rests in the dust of the earth under the power of corruption until the last day or the day of the bodily resurrection. Jesus will not be satisfied, and his work will not be complete, until he returns on the clouds of heaven to take us bodily to heaven. He does not merely want us to be in heaven (perhaps in some room somewhere), but the great desire of his heart is that we be with him: "I will come again, and receive you unto myself; that where I am, there ye may be also" (v. 3).

Now the disciples should understand, and we should understand too, that Christ's departure is necessary, that it is temporary, and that it is good. What the disciples see as a heart-troubling disaster, they should see rather as a blessing: "Let not your heart be troubled" (v. 1).

THE CALL TO FAITH

We have seen the disciples' troubled hearts, we know our own troubled hearts, and we have seen Jesus' comforting promises. What is the answer? Heart trouble can be soothed in only one way: by faith alone in God's promises. Jesus makes that point in verse 1: "Ye believe in God, believe also in me."

There are various ways to translate these words because of the ambiguity or flexibility of the Greek language: the Greek could be either indicative or imperative depending on the context. Indicative expresses a statement of fact: "You believe" is indicative. Imperative expresses a command: "Believe" is imperative. There are four possible translations therefore. First, it could be two indicatives: "Ye believe in God; ye believe also in me." Second, it could be two imperatives: "Believe in God; believe also in me." Third, it could be an indicative followed by an imperative, as in the KJV: "Ye believe in God; believe also in me." Fourth, it could be an imperative followed by an indicative: "Believe in God; ye believe also in me." The best translation is two imperatives: "Believe in God; believe also in me." That fits best with the context. Jesus commands them not to let their hearts be troubled; then he commands them to believe in God and to believe in him.

Moreover, the imperatives are present imperatives, where the meaning is a continuation of the command: "Continue to believe in God; continue also to believe in me." "Keep believing in God; keep also believing in me." In other words, Jesus is not speaking to unbelievers: he is not commanding the disciples to believe for the first time. He is commanding them to continue to believe. Only by continuing to believe will they deliver their hearts from troubling, disquieting thoughts. Jesus says this because he sees that the faith of the disciples is wavering: the troubling realities that Jesus is describing are shaking the disciples' faith, so that they doubt. These words encourage the disciples not to lose heart in the battle of faith, but to press on in full assurance of faith as the day approaches.

Notice, too, how Jesus equates faith in God with faith in himself: "Believe in God and believe also in me," or "Trust in God and trust also in me." Without faith in Jesus Christ there is no faith in God, for the only true and living God is the God and Father of Christ.

Thus we see that the soothing answer to the disciples' troubled hearts is faith. Faith is certain knowledge and assured confidence in God through Jesus Christ. Through faith we have a vital or living connection to Jesus Christ in heavenly glory. Faith lays hold of the promises of God concerning Christ's going away, concerning his preparation, concerning the house of many mansions, and concerning Christ's coming again. Faith says, "I believe. I believe that these marvelous blessings are for me." Reader, do you believe that? Believe in God and believe in Jesus Christ: when your heart is troubled, cling to Christ by faith. Through faith alone you shall receive comfort.

Chapter 2

Knowing the Way to the Father

(John 14:4–6)

4. And whither I go ye know, and the way ye know.
5. Thomas saith unto him, Lord, we know not whither thou goest; and how can we know the way?
6. Jesus saith unto him, I am the way, the truth, and the life: no man cometh unto the Father, but by me.

One thing troubled the disciples' hearts: Jesus was leaving them. Therefore, Jesus takes the time in his instruction in the upper room to comfort them. He explains the purpose of his departure: he is going to the Father's house to prepare a place for them, and he assures them that there is room for them there. He encourages them with the truth of the roominess of his Father's house: it has many mansions. He promises to return to them; he will come again to take them to be with him in heavenly glory.

In light of those promises, Jesus urges his disciples not to be troubled in heart, but rather to believe: "Believe in God, believe also in me" (v. 1). In addition, he gives further assurance in verse 4: "And whither I go ye know, and the way ye know." In other words, "You know where (whither) I am going, and you know how to get there (the way)." There is no reason to be troubled; it is not as if Jesus is abandoning his disciples to travel to an unknown location from which he will never be returning. The disciples who are already believers know that Jesus is going to the Father's house, and they know that the way to the Father's house is through faith in Jesus. Therefore, the truth that they already possess should be more than enough to bring peace to their troubled hearts.

To that explanation one of the disciples, Thomas, responds in verse 5: "Lord, we know not whither thou goest; and how can we know the way?" Thomas is confused: he thinks that he does not know the way because he does not know where Jesus is going. The reason is not that Thomas does not know, but that Thomas does not realize what he knows. That is often the trouble with us: we know the truth, but we do not realize that we know the truth. Often our preconceived notions and prejudices blind us to the truth that we already know. That is even more problematic when we are in an emotional state, as were the disciples. When our emotions cloud our judgment, we panic, we are afraid, and we forget how to apply the comforting truths of the gospel to our hearts and lives.

Therefore, for the benefit of Thomas, for the comfort of the other disciples, and for the peace of the church of all ages, Jesus patiently explains: "I am the way, the truth, and the life." These words are simple, yet profound. They are also highly offensive words in our modern, tolerant, ecumenical, and pluralistic age. In these words, Jesus identifies himself in the sixth of the seven famous "I AM" sayings. He identifies himself as the only, the exclusive way to the Father, something that Thomas already knew, although in his blindness he failed to grasp it.

WHO IS THE WAY?

The heart of the text is verse 6: "Jesus saith unto him, I am the way." We begin with that idea, "the way." Obviously, Jesus is using a figure of speech or a metaphor here. In fact, Jesus employs metaphors frequently to describe spiritual realities. The metaphor here is the word "way" because a way is a path, a road, or a journey. A way is the distance between the starting point and the destination, and it includes every step that a man takes on his journey.

The Bible uses the word "way" frequently. Sometimes the meaning is a literal pathway, but often the meaning is a way of life or a manner of life. In Proverbs 16:25 we read, "There is a way that seemeth right unto a man, but the end thereof are the ways of death." In Jeremiah 6:16 the prophet proclaims, "Thus saith the LORD, Stand ye in the ways, and see, and ask for the old paths, where is the good way, and walk therein, and ye shall find rest for your souls. But they said, We will not walk therein."

Jesus teaches in the sermon on the mount about two ways with two very different destinations: "Enter ye in at the strait gate: for wide is the gate, and broad is the way, that leadeth to destruction, and many there be which go in thereat: because strait is the gate, and narrow is the way, which leadeth unto life, and few there be that find it" (Matt. 7:13–14). In other words, there are evil ways, evil ways of life, which lead to evil destinations; and there are good ways, good ways of life, which lead to good destinations. Only one way leads to heavenly glory.

A way has a starting point, a path, and finally a destination at the end of the way. In a certain sense the starting point of a man's way is the beginning of his life, even in his mother's womb, but I want to apply the metaphor specifically to *the Christian life*. The unbeliever is on the broad road that leads to destruction, while the believer is on the narrow way that leads to life. The starting point is the point at which an individual begins the Christian life. For many in the established church they began to be on the way in their childhood; in fact, they cannot remember ever not being on the way. Their parents were on the way, and they were taught to be and remain on the way from earliest infancy. Others, usually on the mission field, began on the broad way, but after years wandering in sin and unbelief, they were born again or regenerated, they were converted, they believed in Christ and repented of their sins, and they have been on the narrow way ever since.

Nevertheless, for all believers, whether beginning in infancy or later in life, the way of the Christian life began for them when they were regenerated. The same was true for the disciples in John

14. Although they were confused about the way, they should have known that they were actually already on the way. The Spirit had already regenerated them, and they were already believers, walking on the way.

The destination or goal for the one walking on this way is the Father's house with its many mansions or dwelling places, or even simply the Father himself. That is clear from the context: in verse 2 Jesus refers to his Father's house, while in verse 6 he declares, "No man cometh unto the Father, but by me." When Christ places us on the way, that is, when he regenerates us, the goal is to bring us step by step along a path to the Father's house. The way ends with us arriving in heaven and enjoying everlasting and blessed fellowship with the triune God in Jesus Christ. Moreover, the destination is guaranteed: we do not begin on the way but fail to reach the Father's house. Certainly, if we were left to our own powers, we would wander out of the way and perish, but Christ preserves us in the way until we enter glory.

We might think, then, that if the beginning of the way is regeneration or the new birth and the end of the way is the Father's house, the way *itself* is the Christian life or the Christian's activity of walking and even struggling toward heaven. But Jesus does not say that. Instead, Jesus makes an astounding claim: "*I am* the way." With these words Jesus distinguishes himself from all prophets and religious leaders, whether true or false. A prophet or religious leader will say, "I will show you the way," or "I will give you advice for walking on the way." But Jesus says, "*I am* the way." In other words, Jesus says, "I am the beginning, I am the destination, I am the pathway, and I am every step along the pathway."

He adds, "No man cometh unto the Father, but by me." In other words, "No man can enjoy any fellowship with the triune God except through me. No man can enter heaven except through me. All other ways are dead ends, for I alone am the way."

The meaning of "way" requires further explanation. If Jesus is the way, he is the distance between two points or he is the means by which we move from point A to point B. We are by nature at point A (which is sin, misery, and spiritual death), and Jesus brings us to point B (which is life, joy, salvation, fellowship, and peace).

Think of the enormous distances that must be spanned in order to bring us from point A to point B. The first distance that must be spanned is the distance between the creature and the Creator; the second is the distance between earth and heaven; and the third is the distance between the sinner and the holy, just God. Jesus had just explained to his disciples that he was departing for this purpose: to prepare a place for them in the Father's house. We could express it in these terms: Jesus was going away in order to bridge the gap between the disciples and the triune God; between earth and heaven; and between sinners and the holy, just God.

The distance between those three sets of points—between the creature and the Creator; between earth and heaven; and between sinners and the holy, just God—is impossible for anyone else to cross. Many people in the past have attempted it, but each of them has failed miserably. History is littered with the writings of religious thinkers and philosophers who have attempted to reach the divine, who have attempted to reach heaven, and who have attempted to overcome sin. All such writers, thinkers, and philosophers have perished. Plato, Aristotle, and Socrates perished; Buddha, Mohammed, and Confucius perished; Charles Taze Russell and Joseph Smith (the founders of the Jehovah's Witnesses and the Mormons) perished; and people without Jesus still perish today. They perish because, instead of acknowledging Jesus as the only way to the Father and to the Father's house, they seek salvation and fellowship with God in their works, in their religious deeds, or in their speculations and ideas.

Only Jesus Christ is the way because he has accomplished three works that no one else could perform, which have spanned the distance between the creature and the Creator; earth and heaven; and the sinner and the holy, just God. First, Jesus has spanned the distance between the creature and the Creator. He did that in the incomprehensible wonder called the Incarnation. John describes that wonder in John 1:14: "And the Word was made flesh, and dwelt among us." The Word is not a creature, for the Word was with God and the Word was God (v. 1). The Word is the second person of the blessed Trinity, who became flesh and dwelt among us. Since only the Son (Jesus) became incarnate or took upon himself a true, complete, sinless, weakened human nature (which the Bible calls "flesh"), only he bridges the distance between the infinite Creator God and the finite creature man. If Jesus is not the divine Son of God, he cannot bridge that distance between man and God. Then he would not be, and could not be, the way.

Second, Jesus has spanned the distance between the sinner and the holy, just God. Jesus did that in his lifelong sufferings and atoning death on the cross. Our sins make us obnoxious to the holy, just God. God is too holy to look on sin with favor, while God is too righteous to overlook sin without punishment. But God is also merciful, and since he desired and determined our salvation, he forgives our sins and blesses us. But God does that only because Jesus paid the penalty for our sins in our place. Furthermore, only Jesus was qualified to make satisfaction for our sins to the justice of God, for only he has the power to lay down his life, only his death has infinite value in the sight of God, and only he has the sinless human nature (body and soul) in which to suffer God's wrath against sin.

Third, Jesus has spanned the distance between earth and heaven. Jesus did that by his glorious resurrection from the dead and his ascension into heaven. Only Jesus has conquered the power of sin and death. Only by the Incarnation, cross, and resurrection could we, who by nature languish under sin and death, be raised to new life in order to dwell in fellowship with the living God in heavenly glory. Paul explains:

9. [God] hath saved us, and called us with an holy calling, not according to our works, but according to his own purpose and grace, which was given us in Christ Jesus before the world began,

10. But is now made manifest by the appearing of our Saviour Jesus Christ, who hath abolished death, and hath brought life and immortality to light through the gospel. (2 Tim. 1:9–10)

Only Jesus has overcome, even abolished, death. Every thinker, religious leader, and philosopher has died, and they remain dead. While they philosophized about death, their tombs are testimony to their powerlessness before death. Therefore, Jesus by his Incarnation, sufferings and death on the cross, and glorious resurrection is the way to the Father. He alone brings earthbound, sinful creatures to the Creator and Father in heaven.

HOW IS HE THE WAY?

Jesus is the way because he is also the truth and the life. Jesus is the truth: "I am…the truth" (v. 6). "Way" is a metaphor, while "truth" is an abstract noun, and an abstract noun that is not easy to define. An abstract noun is a word that describes something intangible, something that cannot be known through the senses. An abstract noun differs from a concrete noun, therefore. *Table* is a concrete noun: you can see and touch a table. *Truth* is just as real as a table, but you cannot see or touch truth. It is an abstract noun.

Truth is, first, that which corresponds to reality. The ultimate reality is God: because God is, everything else is. Without God, there is nothing else. Since Jesus is the truth, he is the perfect, complete, final revelation of God. What God is, Jesus is. What God reveals, Jesus reveals. What God speaks, Jesus speaks. And what God does, Jesus also does. In fact, because Jesus is the truth, it is impossible to know the true, living, ever-blessed God without him.

Truth is, second, that which is solid, firm, trustworthy, or reliable. That follows from the first aspect of the definition of truth. Because truth corresponds to, or accords with, reality, it is perfectly reliable. You can trust the truth, but you cannot trust the lie. You cannot rely upon fiction or falsehood, but the truth is faithful. Therefore,

Jesus can say, "Believe also in me." Why should the disciples believe in Jesus? Because he is the truth. Since Jesus is the truth, he speaks that which is reliable and trustworthy, his actions are always reliable and trustworthy, and he never deceives or disappoints those who put their trust in him. To follow anyone else other than Jesus or to follow one who disagrees with or contradicts Jesus is to follow lies and falsehoods, and ultimately to suffer disappointment and damnation.

Truth is, third, that which is binding or authoritative. If truth corresponds with reality, and if it is solid or reliable, then of course it has authority. You should, and you must, believe what is true, and you must reject what is false. What Jesus says must be believed because he is the truth, and what Jesus commands must be obeyed because he is the truth. Moreover, Jesus is *the* truth: he is not one truth among many truths. He is not the truth only for some, and he is not merely one version of the truth. He is *the* truth, and the only truth.

If a person refuses to believe in Jesus, he perishes in his sin. Jesus is still objectively the truth even if the majority of people refuse to believe in him and even if they scoff at his claim to be the truth. Jesus declared this to Pilate: "Every one that is of the truth heareth my voice" (John 18:37), to which Pilate responded with a sneering question, "What is truth?" (v. 38). Everyone that is of the lie hears the voices of others (who are liars, and whose father is Satan), but everyone that is of the truth hears the voice of Jesus, for he is *the* truth.

It is significant that Jesus added the word "truth" to his self-designation, for it shows us that the Christian life is not a journey with an undefined, indefinable Jesus, but with the Son of God who is the way, the *truth*, and the life. Some professing Christians describe their life as an undefined, indefinable relationship with Jesus. Such professing Christians prefer not to define the nature of the Jesus whom they claim to know. Instead, they will say, "Jesus is my personal friend and Savior"—they rarely mention "Lord." But they are reluctant to define Jesus in doctrinal terms. In the worst case, they will speak of a journey with Jesus but without a Bible, and even of a journey with Jesus without necessarily being a Christian at all. According to some, everyone is on a journey with Jesus and, since each person's journey is unique, it is immaterial what you believe.

Jesus does not permit us to think of Christianity in terms of such a vague religious journey because he is not only the way, but also the truth. If you are on a journey with Jesus, you must be with the right, true Jesus. There are other versions of Jesus on the religious market, but they are false. Paul warns about this in 2 Corinthians 11:4: "For if he that cometh preacheth another Jesus, whom we have not preached, or if ye receive another spirit, which ye have not received, or another gospel, which ye have not accepted, ye might well bear with him." Not just any Jesus will do: he must be the true Jesus. Jesus is the way to the Father, and he is also *the truth*. He is the truth as the true God reveals the truth in holy Scripture: "This is the true God, and eternal life" (1 John 5:20).

Jesus is also the life: "I am…the life" (v. 6). Life, like truth, is another abstract noun, and it is also difficult to define. The only life that the world knows is earthly life, but that is not the meaning in this text. In the Bible earthly life is *bios*, from which we get our word *biology*. Biology is the study of life. But the word "life" in verse 6, which occurs over 130 times in the New Testament, is an entirely different word and is usually designated "eternal life." A man might live for one hundred years, and throughout his youth he might be vibrant, agile, and healthy, so that in an earthly sense he is full of life, but if he does not have eternal life, he is dead.

What, then, is the difference between earthly life and true, eternal life? First, we should remember that Adam and Eve before the fall had earthly life, but not eternal life. At least, they did not enjoy life in the fullest, richest sense, for Christ brought greater life than Adam ever knew.

Second, the life of the text is divine, for it has its source in God: only God possesses life in the absolute sense, and only God is able to give it. That is because God is the living God, who does not merely exist, but he lives. God lives a life of perfect blessedness: therefore, to have true life is to have life with God. "And this is life eternal, that they might know thee the only true God, and Jesus Christ, whom thou hast sent" (John 17:3). Life is the knowledge of the one true God in Christ: it is to know him, to have fellowship with him, to enjoy him, and to live with him. Adam and Eve had fellowship with God, but the life of which the New Testament speaks is fuller and richer than anything that our first parents enjoyed. In fact, the Son of God had to become incarnate, suffer, die, and be resurrected in order for sinners to enjoy that life in its fullness.

Jesus makes the astounding claim: not only is he the way (the only way), and the truth (the only truth), but also he is the life (the only life). This means that Jesus possesses the very life of God, for he is (as to his person) the second person of the holy Trinity. In eternity the Son of God dwells in the bosom of the Father. Even as the incarnate Savior Jesus enjoys perfect fellowship with the triune God. The life of Jesus is not derived from another external source. It was not given to him, but it is his by divine right: "For as the Father hath life in himself; so hath he given to the Son to have life in himself" (John 5:26). In fact, Jesus *is* the life. "For the life was manifested, and we have seen it, and bear witness, and shew unto you that eternal life, which was with the Father, and was manifested unto us" (1 John 1:2); and "This is the true God, and eternal life" (5:20). Indeed, the work of Jesus is to give eternal life to sinners: "As thou hast given him power over all flesh, that he should give eternal life to as many as thou hast given him. And this is life eternal, that they might know thee the only true God, and Jesus Christ, whom thou hast sent" (John 17:2–3).

Religious leaders and teachers can give instruction, and godly members of the church can give advice, but only Jesus can *give life*, because only he is the life. Outside of Jesus Christ sinners are dead: Paul writes that they are "alienated from the life of God through the ignorance that is in them, because of the blindness of their heart" (Eph. 4:18). We are by nature enemies of the life of God and strangers to the life of God. We cannot impart life to our souls, and we cannot bring about our resurrection from the dead. Therefore, as long as we remain dead in our sins, we must perish. Jesus lived, obeyed, died, and rose again in order to give us life. It is because of the cross and resurrection of Christ that we have the right to life and that we possess everlasting life, which consists in knowing God in love.

What, then, is the relationship between these ideas? Jesus is the way, and the truth, and the life, but are these three separate things or is there a connection between them? The connection is expressed in the use of a hendiadys, which is a figure of speech. The word *hendiadys* comes from two Greek words and translates as "one through two." In a hendiadys two or more ideas are connected by means of the conjunction *and*. We often use such figures of speech in English: "I went to the shop and bought bread" is a hendiadys. "I went to the shop *in order to* buy bread" is the meaning.

"I am the resurrection, and the life" (John 11:25) is another hendiadys. "I am the resurrection *because* I am the life" is the meaning. "I am the way, the truth, and the life" is a hendiadys. "I am the way *because* I am also the truth and the life" is the meaning. How, then, does Jesus bring us to the Father's house? He is the way by turning us from darkness and lies to the truth, by enlightening our hearts and causing us to believe the truth; he is the way by resurrecting us from death to life; and he is the way and he is every step of the way by bringing us through his own work alone by grace alone to the Father's house above.

HOW DO WE KNOW HE IS THE WAY?

At the beginning of verse 5 Thomas was confused about the way, so he asked, "Lord, we know not whither thou goest; and how can we know the way?" Thomas asked this question in response to Jesus' assertion in verse 4, "And whither I go ye know, and the way ye know." Thomas seems to contradict Jesus. Jesus says, "And whither I go ye know." Thomas responds, "We know not whither thou goest." Jesus says, "And the way ye know." Thomas retorts, "How can we know the way?" If the destination ("whither I go") is unknown, how can the way be known?

But Thomas did not realize what he knew, for if he had given it a moment's reflection, he would have realized that he did, in fact, know. The reason Thomas claimed not to know is that his mind was filled with wrong notions about Jesus' mission. Although all the disciples labored under the same misconceptions, this was especially typical of Thomas.

The personality of Thomas can best be described as melancholy. Recall his reaction in John 11 on hearing that Jesus intended to return to Judea. The other disciples expressed severe misgivings about the idea of returning to Judea because of earlier attempts on Jesus' life by the Jewish leaders. When Jesus explained his intention to wake Lazarus (who had actually died) from sleep, Thomas replied, "Let us also go, that we may die with him" (John 11:16). Jesus had spoken of something wonderful, of raising Lazarus from the dead. Thomas completely missed the point and gloomily concluded that he, Jesus, and the other disciples would die. Yet Thomas expressed courage to be willing to die with Jesus. In addition, after the resurrection it was Thomas who was absent from the other disciples (probably because he wanted to be alone given the traumatic events that had just occurred), and it was Thomas who adamantly refused to believe that Jesus was alive until he saw Jesus with his own eyes. Here also, Thomas is gloomy: "Lord, we know not whither thou goest; and how can we know the way?"

Thomas reflects the misunderstandings and the foolish notions of the disciples. They dreamed of an earthly kingdom, which did not fit with the reality of Jesus going away. In Thomas' mind and in the minds of the other disciples Jesus was supposed to stay: he was not supposed to go away. He should set up a kingdom in Jerusalem, and Thomas hoped, with the others, to have a prominent place in that kingdom. In that kingdom Jesus would be king, Israel would have peace and prosperity, and Herod and the Romans would be banished.

Despite this dream, Jesus had never promised such a kingdom. In fact, Jesus had repeatedly denied it, and his instruction about the kingdom was consistent: his kingdom was a spiritual kingdom in which the chief blessing was not earthly power or wealth, but the forgiveness of sins. Moreover, Jesus had never hidden from his disciples the painful truth about his death and resurrection. That teaching was uncomfortable, but Jesus had clearly warned them that he would be arrested, tried, condemned, and crucified in Jerusalem. And to that warning he had always added the comforting promise of the resurrection, which the disciples consistently failed to grasp.

The reason, therefore, that Thomas claims not to know is his lack of attention to the teachings of Jesus. Jesus asserts rightly and in truth: "And whither I go ye know" (you know that I am going to heaven) "and the way ye know" (you know that I am going to heaven by my death and resurrection). Of course, after the resurrection, things would be much clearer to Thomas and to the other disciples. Especially after the day of Pentecost, Thomas would know and understand.

We know that Jesus is the way, the truth, and the life only through faith. That Jesus is the way is of great comfort to the church, but it is terribly offensive to the world. The world sees the Christian claim that our Savior is the way, the only way, as intolerant. The world has little problem with the idea that Jesus is one possible way among many other legitimate ways, but the world opposes the exclusivity of Christianity. That was true in the early church, where the Romans and Greeks would have welcomed Jesus into their pantheon of gods if the Christians had recognized the validity of other religions and gods. When the Christians said, "Jesus is the only Savior and the gods of the heathen are no gods," they faced the ire of the civil and religious authorities. In our increasingly pluralistic society, we offend unbelievers when we insist, as Jesus did, that Jesus Christ is the way, the truth, and the life: no man cometh to the Father, but by him.

We are on the way. God has placed us on the way. Therefore, we know the way. We have the truth. God has given us the truth. Therefore, we know the truth. We have everlasting life. God has given us life. Therefore, we know life. Thomas did too, for he and the others were on the way to the Father's house, even if they did not yet fully understand that wonderful reality. If you are on the way, there is only one explanation: God has worked faith in your heart to know, recognize, and perceive the way.

Look to Jesus, for he is the way. Seek him, for he is the truth. Live out of him, for he is the life. And reject every false way, for all other ways are the ways of death. He is the way, the truth, and the life, by grace alone through faith alone, and no one comes unto the Father except by him.

Chapter 3

Seeing the Father in the Son

(John 14:7–11)

7. If ye had known me, ye should have known my Father also: and from henceforth ye know him, and have seen him.
8. Philip saith unto him, Lord, shew us the Father, and it sufficeth us.
9. Jesus saith unto him, Have I been so long time with you, and yet hast thou not known me, Philip? he that hath seen me hath seen the Father; and how sayest thou then, Shew us the Father?
10. Believest thou not that I am in the Father, and the Father in me? the words that I speak unto you I speak not of myself: but the Father that dwelleth in me, he doeth the works.
11. Believe me that I am in the Father, and the Father in me: or else believe me for the very works' sake.

It is our soul's greatest desire to have fellowship with God. Jesus awakens that desire in his disciples in his farewell discourse in the upper room. He does so in verse 2, where he speaks of the Father's house with its many mansions. When we hear about the Father's house, it makes us homesick especially as we compare that glorious place with the valley of tears in which we presently reside, and we long to be in that house of many mansions or dwelling places. Jesus awakens that desire again in verse 6, where he speaks of our coming to the Father through him, who is the way, the truth, and the life.

On hearing that wonderful truth, we desire to draw nigh to our Father through Jesus, the only mediator between God and us; we desire a deeper knowledge of the truth found alone in Jesus; and we desire to be quickened more and more, so that we increasingly enjoy that life, which is to know the only true God through Jesus Christ whom he has sent (John 17:3).

Jesus continues to awaken that desire in verse 7 when he says, "From henceforth ye know him [the Father], and have seen him." When we hear those words, our longing to know and see him intensifies. What a wonderful thing it is to know the Father and to be known of him! What a privilege it is to see the Father, to see him in his house in heaven and to see him already in this life with the eyes of faith in the holy Scriptures!

Philip, another one of Jesus' disciples, interrupts the Master. "Lord, shew us the Father, and it sufficeth us" (v. 8), he pleads. Philip is the second, after Thomas, to interrupt Jesus. The disciples usually interrupt Jesus when they fail to understand, which happens often in the New Testament. Jesus does not resent the interruption, for he is such a patient teacher. Instead, he uses it as a moment to teach his confused, baffled, and perturbed followers.

Philip's confusion is not limited to him: he speaks for the other men. Philip fails to understand because he struggles to comprehend abstract ideas. Thus far Jesus has spoken in metaphors and figures (the Father's house and the way, the truth, and the life), but Philip does not understand. He wants and he needs something solid, something more concrete, something tangible, or something that he can see. Philip wants Jesus to show him the Father so that he can actually see him with his physical eyes. In growing impatience and exasperation, Philip says in effect, "Enough of this talk about the Father: if we could only see him, then we would be satisfied." Patiently, and with a mild rebuke to his disciples' dullness, Jesus explains, "He that hath seen me hath seen the Father." Have you seen Jesus, believing reader? Then you, too, have seen the Father.

THE PROFOUND MEANING

Jesus' words in the text raise a number of important questions. Who is the Father? Is it possible for us to see the Father? If so, how can we see the Father? We need to examine these questions before we can understand Philip's request.

In the New Testament the Father has two distinct, but related, meanings. First, the Father is the first person of the Trinity, distinct from the Son and the Holy Spirit, who are the second and third persons of the Trinity. Often the Father is simply called God. For example, we read in John 1:1, "In the beginning was the Word, and the Word was with God, and the Word was God." In that verse, God in the phrase "with God" is a reference to the first person of the Trinity, while "Word" ("the Word was with God") is a reference to the second person of the Trinity, or a reference to the Son. The second reference to God in John 1:1 ("the Word was God") is a reference to the divinity of the Son as a divine person, distinct from the Father. The Word (the Son) was with God (the Father) and yet the Word that was with God is himself also God.

The Father is also a reference to the triune God or to the Godhead without distinction of persons. This might seem very complicated, but we should remember that Christians worship the triune God. We do not worship only the Father, but we worship also the Son and the Holy Spirit. The triune God, or the Father as Jesus calls him, is the God and Father of the incarnate Mediator or the God and Father of the man Jesus. In John 8:54, for example, Jesus says, "If I honour myself, my honour is nothing: it is my Father that honoureth me; of whom ye say, that he is your God." The Father is not only Jesus' Father (the first person), but he is also *his God.* The man Jesus of Nazareth worships, serves, and reveals the Father, or the triune God.

Why, then, does Jesus call God "Father," "the Father," or "my Father"? He does so because he enjoys a very close, intimate relationship with the Father. The Jews did not often call God by the name

Father. Instead, they called God Yahweh, Jehovah, Lord, or even the Father of Israel, but no Jew would say, "My Father."

Jesus always emphasized his unique relationship to the Father. On the one hand, the Son (the second person) is uniquely related to the Father (the first person), for the Bible uses the term "only begotten," which refers to the relationship of the second person to the first person within the being of God. On the other hand, the man Jesus is the Son of the Father or the Son of the triune God. For that reason the Bible refers to "the God and Father of our Lord Jesus Christ." For that reason too, Scripture speaks of Jesus worshiping the Father, obeying the Father, and praying to the Father. As a human being, Jesus, who is the incarnate Son, was subject to the Father. However, within the divine Godhead, the Son (the second person) is equal to the Father (the first person). It is sometimes difficult to determine in which sense the terms Father and Son are used in the New Testament, therefore, especially in the writings of John. There are mysteries in the divine Trinity that defy our comprehension.

At this point it is necessary briefly to summarize the doctrine of the Trinity. The true God is one divine being, the Creator of all things, the eternal, unchangeable, spiritual, and sovereign Lord. This God is the judge of all men and angels, and he is eternally exalted or transcendent above everything that he has made. There is an absolute, unbridgeable distinction between the Creator and all the creatures that God has made.

Every creature has a beginning and is dependent on the Creator, while the Creator is eternal and self-sufficient or independent of everything that he has created. Proof of this is abundant in holy Scripture: "Before the mountains were brought forth, or ever thou hadst formed the earth and the world, even from everlasting to everlasting, thou art God" (Ps. 90:2). "I am he: before me there was no God formed, neither shall there be after me" (Isa. 43:10). "I am the first, and I am the last; and beside me there is no God" (44:6). "Is there a God beside me? yea, there is no God; I know not any" (v. 8).

The whole Bible teaches strict monotheism, the truth that there is *one God*. Yet the same Bible teaches that there are three individual persons in the Godhead that are called God. The Father is called God, the Son is called God, and the Holy Spirit is called God. These three are coeternal, coequal, and coessential, or of the same essence. Of these three persons, the Son, who is the second person, became incarnate, taking upon himself a true, complete human nature consisting of body and soul.

Thus the Father in John 14:8 is, whether Philip comprehends it or not, the triune God, the Creator of heaven and earth, and the judge of all men. Philip requests to see *him*. Philip asks Jesus to reveal *him*. Undoubtedly, the other disciples have the same desire.

The other major question is this: Is it possible to see the Father? Jesus answers in the affirmative in verses 7 and 9. In verse 7 Jesus assures the disciples, "From henceforth ye know him [the Father], and have seen him [the Father]." In verse 9 Jesus affirms, "He that hath seen me [Jesus] hath seen the Father." The disciples had seen Jesus; therefore, they had seen the Father. In what sense they had seen the Father must be explained, but for now take note that they *had seen* the Father. Therefore, it is possible to see him.

Yet the Bible also teaches that it is impossible to see God. For one thing, the divine essence is invisible, for God is spiritual. In John 4:24 Jesus declares to the Samaritan woman, "God is a Spirit: and they that worship him must worship him in spirit and in truth." In addition, the Bible explicitly denies that a mere creature can see God: "No man hath seen God at any time; the only begotten Son, which is in the bosom of the Father, he hath declared him" (1:18). "Now unto the King eternal, immortal, invisible, the only wise God, be honour and glory forever and ever. Amen" (1 Tim. 1:17). Paul declares in 1 Timothy 6:13–16:

> 13. I give thee charge in the sight of God, who quickeneth all things, and before Christ Jesus, who before Pontius Pilate witnessed a good confession;
> 14. That thou keep this commandment without spot, unrebukeable, until the appearing of our Lord Jesus Christ:

15. Which in his times he shall shew, who is the blessed and only Potentate, the King of kings, and Lord of lords;
16. Who only hath immortality, dwelling in the light which no man can approach unto; whom no man hath seen, nor can see: to whom be honour and power everlasting. Amen.

But what about Jesus: Can we not see him? If it is possible to see him, is his divinity not in question? The answer is simple: Jesus is visible only in his human nature, while the divine essence of Jesus is as invisible as the divine essence of the Father and the Spirit. Nevertheless, his body of flesh and bones is visible, was visible when he was on earth, and shall be visible to us when we enter glory. Neither the Father nor the Spirit have bodies of flesh and bones; therefore, they remain forever invisible.

To complete the picture, we should add that the Bible also teaches that some have seen God, but if that is so, is there not a contradiction? If some have seen God, how can Scripture claim that no one can see God? Moses, for example, saw God, but did he really see him? In Exodus 33:18 Moses asked, "I beseech thee, shew me thy glory." God granted his request, but with this qualification: "Thou canst not see my face: for there shall no man see me, and live" (v. 20). God then explains: "Thou shalt see my back parts: but my face shall not be seen" (v. 23). Others who saw God saw him in a dream, or in a vision, or indirectly; yet no man has seen, and no man can see, the divine essence. Even the angels in heaven cover their faces with their wings rather than behold God's glory (Isa. 6:2–3).

Jesus explains in verse 9 how we are able to see the Father: "He that hath seen me hath seen the Father." If you have seen Jesus, and the disciples had, you have already seen the Father. This fits with what Jesus has already taught in the preceding verses. "I am the way, the truth, and the life" (v. 6). Therefore, Jesus Christ is the perfect, complete, and final revelation of the Father or of God. "No man cometh unto the Father, but by me" (v. 6). Therefore, he is the only Mediator through whom we enjoy knowledge of the Father or enjoy fellowship or communion with God. "In my Father's house are many mansions...I go to prepare a place for you" (v. 2). Jesus has intimate, personal knowledge of the Father's house: he has come from there, for it is his true home, and he returns there. Therefore, Jesus alone knows the Father's house and can bring us to that place. Only Jesus can show us the Father.

Other New Testament passages harmonize perfectly with Jesus' words here. For example, certain passages speak of Jesus as the Father's image. As the image of God, Jesus perfectly reflects the Father. What the Father is, Jesus is; what the Father does, Jesus does; and what the Father says, Jesus says. The Son is identical, therefore, to the Father in every way, except that he is not the same person as the Father. The devil blinds the hearts of the reprobate "lest the light of the glorious gospel of Christ, who is the image of God, should shine unto them" (2 Cor. 4:4). Paul writes about Jesus that he is "the image of the invisible God, the firstborn of every creature" (Col. 1:15) and that "in him dwelleth all the fulness of the Godhead bodily" (2:9). The writer to the Hebrews declares about the Son that he is "the brightness of [God's] glory, and the express image of his person" (Heb. 1:3).

In other words, Jesus makes the invisible God visible. He does that not as the prophets did, who also declared God and gave instruction concerning him. Jesus *is* the invisible God, for he is God in the flesh. Moses did not say, "He that hath seen me hath seen the Father." Moses did not say, "If ye had known me, ye had known my Father also." Only Jesus did make such authoritative utterances about himself, which means that he has a unique relationship to the Father as his only begotten Son.

But what about us: If he that hath seen Jesus hath seen the Father, and we have not seen Jesus with our eyes, as Philip, Thomas, and the others had, have we really seen the Father? The answer is that we also have seen the Father, for we also have seen Jesus. We have not seen Jesus in his visible, physical, human nature, but we have seen him by faith. Paul speaks of "the eyes of your understanding being enlightened" (Eph. 1:18). We do not need to see Jesus with our physical eyes. Indeed, many saw Jesus with their physical eyes but did not perceive who he truly was and is. They saw him, but they perished in their unbelief. Our vision of Jesus is much clearer, therefore, than many who saw him in the flesh. Instead, we believe what Jesus declares in the Scriptures, and we believe what his apostles have recorded about him: "Whom having not seen, ye love; in whom, though now ye see him not, yet believing, ye rejoice with joy unspeakable and full of glory" (1 Pet. 1:8).

The reason why we see the Father by seeing Jesus is that there is the closest possible union between the Father and the Son. This union applies to the first person and the second person in the Trinity, and this union is also true of the relationship between the triune God and the man Christ Jesus. In whatever sense you understand it, the relationship is expressed with the little word "in." Jesus repeatedly asserts that he is "in" the Father and that the Father is "in" him. "Believest thou not that I am *in* the Father, and the Father *in* me?" (v. 10). "The Father that dwelleth *in* me, he doeth the works" (v. 10). "Believe me that I am *in* the Father, and the Father *in* me" (v. 11). Later, he will make the astounding assertion that we also are in him: "At that day ye shall know that I am in my Father, and ye in me, and I in you" (v. 20).

Of course, our union with the Father depends upon Christ's union with the Father and Christ's union with us. If Christ is not in the Father, we have no fellowship with God. Only if Christ is in the Father is he the way, the truth, and the life for us too. Only if Christ is in the Father can we come to him and dwell in his Father's house.

We must understand how, or in what sense, the Son is in the Father and the Father is in the Son. What is the nature of this union? First, it is not a physical, material, or carnal union, but a purely spiritual union.

Second, the theological term for this union is *perichoresis* or circumincession, which words refer to the dwelling of the three persons of the Trinity within one another in the one being or essence of God. The theological term is not as important as the idea, but it is a useful term with which to be familiar. The Father dwells in the Son in the

Holy Spirit, and the Son dwells in the Father in the Holy Spirit.

Third, this union exists by virtue of the Incarnation: the divine person of the Son of God is personally united to the human nature of the man Christ Jesus (Col. 2:9). This is called the hypostatic union, where the word *hypostasis* simply means "person," a personal union, therefore.

Fourth, this is a union of deep, intimate love and affection, which is described in terms of a father-son relationship. The Father and the Son delight in one another in the Holy Spirit, enjoying the closest possible fellowship. This relationship includes free and open communication, as well as the sharing of life. Jesus describes this relationship in John 5:19–23:

> 19. Then answered Jesus and said unto them, Verily, verily, I say unto you, The Son can do nothing of himself, but what he seeth the Father do: for what things soever he doeth, these also doeth the Son likewise.
> 20. For the Father loveth the Son, and sheweth him all things that himself doeth: and he will shew him greater works than these, that ye may marvel.
> 21. For as the Father raiseth up the dead, and quickeneth them; even so the Son quickeneth whom he will.
> 22. For the Father judgeth no man, but hath committed all judgment unto the Son:
> 23. That all men should honour the Son, even as they honour the Father. He that honoureth not the Son honoureth not the Father which hath sent him.

Finally, although there is personal distinction, for the Father is not the same person as the Son, yet there is never independence. The Son never acts independently of, and certainly never contrary to, the Father. The Father and the Son act in perfect harmony because they are "in" one another. Jesus explains, "The words that I speak unto you I speak not of myself: but the Father that dwelleth in me, he doeth the works" (v. 10). This union is necessary for our salvation, for only one who is fully divine and yet also fully human can accomplish the work of suffering and dying for us on the cross, only he can lay down his life for us, only he can take his life up again, only he can work righteousness of infinite value for us in the sight of God, and only he can endure the weight of the holy wrath of Almighty God in order to deliver us from it.

THE NECESSARY KNOWLEDGE

In verse 7 Jesus asserts, "From henceforth ye know him [the Father], and have seen him." Philip is not convinced: "Lord, shew us the Father, and it sufficeth us" (v. 8). Philip finds this talk of knowing and seeing too abstract. In verse 2 Jesus spoke of the Father's house—show us the Father! In verse 6, in response to Thomas, Jesus asserted that no man comes to the Father except through him—show us the Father! Philip is impatient: he wants a display of the Father. Show us the Father, and it will be enough for us. Show us the Father, and we will be satisfied.

Who was Philip? We have already met Thomas, and we noted of Thomas that he was gloomy or melancholy: "Lord, we know not whither thou goest; and how can we know the way?" (v. 5). Now Philip asks, "Show us the Father." Philip was one of Jesus' first disciples. Jesus called him to discipleship in John 1:43: "Follow me." Philip became a disciple only one day after Peter became a disciple. That explains Jesus' question in verse 9: "Have I been so long time with you, and yet hast thou not known me, Philip? he that hath seen me hath seen the Father; and how sayest thou then, Shew us the Father?" Philip was not a new disciple: he had closely observed Jesus for three and a half years.

The gospels mention Philip on other occasions. In John 6:5 Jesus tests Philip: "Whence shall we buy bread, that these may eat?" Philip responds by stating the problem, but without offering any solution (v. 7). In John 12:21 Greeks approach Philip, whose name is Greek (meaning "horse lover"): "Sir, we would see Jesus," whereupon Philip tells Andrew, and Andrew and Philip tell Jesus. From these instances we conclude that Philip seems to have been a practical fellow. You can sense his exasperation: "Enough of this theorizing! Just show us the Father; that will be enough for us!"

Philip's question betrays not so much unbelief as a fundamental misunderstanding, a misunderstanding or lack of knowledge that is not unique to Philip, and a misunderstanding that Jesus laments and rebukes. Jesus expects Philip to have learned better than to ask such a question. "Have I been so long time with you, and yet hast thou not known me, Philip?" That question must have pierced Philip's soul.

Philip had been with Jesus and Jesus had been with Philip. Philip therefore must have observed Jesus: he saw how Jesus lived, he heard what Jesus said, he witnessed Jesus' miracles, and he was privy to the specific, private teachings of Jesus that the multitudes did not have the privilege of hearing. Philip understood that Jesus was very close to God, and he understood that Jesus' relationship to God was closer than his own. Philip longed for a deeper relationship with God, and he thought that Jesus could show him the Father. But Philip had not really understood the true identity of Jesus Christ.

We are tempted to request what Philip sought, a vision of God. We think that if we could only see God with our eyes, then our doubts and fears would be dispelled. We imagine that if we might behold the glory of God, just once, then our struggles, fears, and trials would be over. But like Philip, we do not know what we are asking. If we could see God, we would be absolutely terrified, and if we saw him, we would perish. His absolute majesty, holiness, and righteousness would consume us in a moment. Like Philip, we do not understand our privileges: we have seen the Father (and we therefore do not need another display) because we have seen Jesus.

It is God's great mercy to reveal himself in his Son rather than in some terrifying theophany. Moses and Isaiah would love to have seen what we now see: "He that hath seen me hath seen the Father; and how sayest thou then, Shew us the Father"? Jesus might well say to us, "Have you had the holy Scriptures for such a long time, and yet you do not understand?"

Jesus teaches Philip—and us—the proper knowledge and vision of the Father. We know the Father in the words and works of Jesus. Although Jesus speaks here about "words" and "works," they are really one idea. Jesus never speaks empty words, for his words are the words of power and life. When Jesus speaks, his will, which is the will of his Father, is done. And Jesus never speaks anything independent of, or contrary to, his Father: "The words that I speak unto you I speak not of myself" (v. 10). Having stated the truth, Jesus asks Philip whether he believes that: "Believest thou not that I am in the Father, and the Father in me?" In verse 11 he addresses all the disciples again: "Believe me that I am in the Father, and the Father in me." We could render Jesus' words this way: "Keep believing that I am in the Father. Your faith in that truth is beginning to waver, but hold fast to that truth, even though things will soon happen that will trouble your heart. Believe in God; believe also in me."

Philip and the other disciples ought to have concluded from Jesus' words that he was in the Father and that there was perfect, intimate union between him and God, but if they did not, they should at least be convinced through a careful consideration of his works: "Or else believe me for the very works' sake" (v. 11). Multiple times Jesus had asserted his unity with the Father, and clearly the disciples had failed to pay attention, but surely his works should convince them.

The works here are certainly a reference to his miracles, but not only his miracles. Everything Jesus did should be carefully considered and will prove that Jesus is the Son of God and that he is in perfect union with the Father. Someone who heals the lame, the blind, the lepers, and the paralyzed, someone who raises the dead, or someone who calms the sea is surely the Son of God. Someone who lives in perfect holiness, never sinning, and enjoys such intimate fellowship with the Father must be the Son of God. If he is the Son of God, he is in the Father. Philip had witnessed all those miracles and many more miracles besides. Although we have not witnessed those miracles, we have read the records of them and we receive these things by faith in God's word. Believe Jesus for the very works' sake!

Yet there was more for Philip and the other disciples to know, learn, and see. By faith we know more than Philip did, for we know the cross and resurrection. We are one step ahead of Philip, but he would know soon enough. That explains the somewhat confusing statement in verse 7: "If ye had known me, ye should have known my Father also: and from henceforth ye know him, and have seen him." There is a mild rebuke in those words: "If ye had known me, ye should have known my Father also." The implication is that they did not adequately know Jesus, and therefore they did not adequately know the Father.

There is also this important truth: the knowledge of God is inseparable from the knowledge of Jesus Christ. If you have the wrong view of Christ, you will also have the wrong view of God. You will grow in grace and knowledge of God only insofar as you grow in your knowledge of Christ (2 Pet. 3:18). That is why a proper theology of Christ is so important: it matters who Christ is and what he has done.

There is also this promise, which comes out in the word "henceforth" or "from now on." That little word "henceforth" points forward to the cross and resurrection. The disciples do not yet understand as fully as they should or as fully as they might, but after the cross and resurrection they will both know and see. (Jesus uses the perfect tense—"ye know him and have seen him"—to emphasize the certainty of it.)

That is the great wonder, for the cross that seems so confusing and contradictory (even nonsensical) to the natural mind is the greatest revelation of God that the world has ever seen. When Jesus died on the cross, hanging on the accursed tree between heaven and earth, bearing God's wrath, we see the Father in the Son. We see him in his terrible wrath, in his inflexible righteousness or justice, and in his spotless holiness, as he satisfies his law by punishing his Son. There are many displays of God's wrath and curse upon sin, but this is the greatest and clearest. So fierce is God's wrath against sin that he punishes his Son for our sins on the cross.

But we see more: when we see Jesus willingly suffering, not cursing God and not seeking vengeance upon his enemies, we see the Father in the Son, for we see him in his boundless grace, his unquenchable love, and his tender mercy. There are many displays of God's mercy, but this is the greatest and clearest. So great is God's mercy that he spares us punishment and inflicts it on a willing substitute.

We see even more: when we see Jesus endure the wrath of God and when we see him conquer sin and death in the resurrection, we see the Father in the Son. We see in the Son someone who in one person is true God and true man, and we see someone who had the power to endure death and even to rise from the dead. Without Jesus we cannot know the Father at all, and if we seek God without Jesus Christ, we will find a consuming fire, one who will destroy us for our sins. But in Christ we find our merciful Father with his house of many mansions, in which house Jesus prepares a place for all who believe in him. "For God, who commanded the light to shine out of darkness, hath shined in our hearts, to give the light of the knowledge of the glory of God in the face of Jesus Christ" (2 Cor. 4:6).

He that hath seen Jesus hath seen the Father. Have you seen him? If you are a believer, you have and you do.

Chapter 4

Believers Doing Greater Works Than Jesus

(John 14:12–15)

12. Verily, verily, I say unto you, He that believeth on me, the works that I do shall he do also; and greater works than these shall he do; because I go unto my Father.
13. And whatsoever ye shall ask in my name, that will I do, that the Father may be glorified in the Son.
14. If ye shall ask any thing in my name, I will do it.
15. If ye love me, keep my commandments.

Jesus' primary purpose in these chapters is to comfort his disciples. Their hearts are troubled in verse 1 because of Jesus' imminent departure. They fear greatly for the future, for their own immediate future, and for the future of Jesus' ministry and mission. Jesus has comforted them already and he will do so throughout the discourse. He consoles them by revealing to them the purpose of his departure: it is not, as they imagine, the end of their hopes and dreams (except that it is the end of their foolish dreams of an earthly kingdom in Jerusalem), but it is for their advantage and salvation.

This is also a theme to which he will return repeatedly: the departure of Jesus in his death, burial, and resurrection is necessary. Without it there is no possibility of salvation for the disciples from sin and death. The great pain they shall experience when Jesus is taken from them in a few hours is necessary: by his atoning sufferings and death on the cross Jesus shall make full satisfaction for all their sins, something that they in the upper room cannot yet comprehend. Jesus' departure is also the means by which he shall be glorified in his resurrection, ascension, and sitting at God's right hand. Jesus' glorification is also necessary for our salvation, for only the resurrected and exalted Savior is able to apply the benefits that he has purchased for us on the cross. The shortsighted disciples therefore must look beyond the immediate pain to the advantages that shall accrue to Jesus and to them.

In verse 11 Jesus had urged Philip to believe that he is in the Father, if not because of his words, then "for the very works' sake." These works, especially the miracles that Jesus performed, should be proof enough of Jesus' vital, spiritual union with the Father. Jesus is in the Father and the Father is in him. How else could the mighty wonders of Jesus be explained? If Philip has seen the works that prove that Jesus is in the Father, and if we have seen in the Scriptures those same works, the conclusion is inevitable: "He that hath seen [Jesus] hath seen the Father" (v. 9) and "[Jesus is] in the Father, and the Father in [Jesus]" (v. 11).

A question arises in the pious mind, however, a question that Jesus anticipates. If Jesus, the wonder worker, is going to depart, what will happen to those works when he returns to the Father? Shall they cease? How, then, shall the disciples continue the ministry of the gospel in the absence of their Lord and Savior and his mighty works? Jesus reassures his disciples: the works of Jesus shall continue, even greater works than these.

THE WORKS

Jesus' purpose in verse 12 is to address one of the disciples' fears. They feared that with the imminent departure of Jesus his work would cease and come to an end. When Jesus was with his disciples, he performed wonderful works: he preached the gospel of the kingdom and he did many miracles. Now that Jesus was departing, what would happen to his great works? How could the kingdom of God be established without the king? How could salvation be accomplished without the Savior? How could men believe in Jesus Christ if he went away? Besides this, Jesus was committing his work to his disciples, and they felt utterly inadequate for the task. Already in his ministry he had given his disciples the commission to preach. With that commission he had even enabled them to cast out devils and to perform other miracles. Read, for example, Matthew 10:5–8:

5. These twelve Jesus sent forth, and commanded them, saying, Go not into the way of the Gentiles, and into any city of the Samaritans enter ye not:
6. But go rather to the lost sheep of the house of Israel.
7. And as ye go, preach, saying, The kingdom of heaven is at hand.
8. Heal the sick, cleanse the lepers, raise the dead, cast out devils: freely ye have received, freely give.

The disciples had performed that work of preaching and performing miracles when Jesus was with them. How could they continue to do those things if Jesus departed from them? Therefore, Jesus reassures his disciples with wonderful words in verse 12: "Verily, verily, I say unto you, He that believeth on me, the works that I do shall he do also; and greater works than these shall he do; because I go unto my Father." In the context Jesus spoke of works: "Believe me for the very works' sake" (v. 11). On the basis of what I do, says Jesus, believe that I am in the Father. If you cannot take my word for it, and you must, be convinced when you see what I do. The disciples were convinced, and they did believe Jesus. They believed on the basis of his words and works that he is the Son of God.

Now Jesus promises that believers will do the same works as Jesus, and even greater works than Jesus. He prefaces his promise with "Verily, verily," indicating the seriousness of his words. Does Jesus mean that believers will be able to cleanse lepers, heal all diseases, restore sight to the blind, multiply bread, change water into wine, raise the dead, walk on water, and calm storms? Although it is true that the apostles did perform some miracles—yet they did so not in their own power, but only in Jesus' name—they did not perform more numerous, more varied, or more spectacular miracles than Jesus did. In addition, for much of the two thousand years of New Testament history no miracles were performed in the church. After the death of the apostles, miracles of the nature recorded in the New Testament ceased.

Some have tried to restrict the application of this promise to the apostles. That is not a solution, for it is not true that the apostles performed greater miracles than Jesus: they did not even perform the same miracles. Read the book of Acts and you will discover the miracles that they did: they performed some healings and a few resurrections. Besides, Jesus does not say, "*You* will do these works" (pointing to the apostles), but "*He that believeth* on me." That expression refers to all believers, for all Christians trust in Jesus, which is the meaning of the term. Do you believe in Jesus? Then this promise is for you: "The works that I do shall you do also, and greater works than these shall you do." Are you an unbeliever? Then you will not be able to do any such works as Jesus did. Instead, Jesus commands you to repent of your sins and believe in him. Only by joining the company of believers does a person join those who do these works.

Others have tried to make the promise of Jesus conditional. Then the meaning would be, "If you have strong enough faith, or if you are faithful enough, then you could do the works of Jesus, or you could do greater works than Jesus." Most people in the church, and for most of church history, have supposedly lacked this faith. Therefore, so the argument goes, the works that could have been done have not been accomplished. That is a favorite tactic among charismatics: either the so-called healer has insufficient faith or more often the sick person does not believe. Therefore, so goes the explanation, the works fail to materialize. But that is not the meaning either. Jesus says "shall": "The works that I do *shall* he do also; and greater works than these *shall* he do" (v. 12). Jesus refers to the future, the certain future. There is nothing hypothetical about this, there is nothing conditional, but Jesus makes a promise.

To understand these greater works, we must compare and contrast the public, earthly ministry of Jesus Christ with the mission of the church post-Pentecost. After Jesus ascended into heaven and poured out the Holy Spirit, the church did greater works than Jesus had ever done during his earthly ministry. Ponder the fruit that Jesus reaped in his public, earthly ministry and the state of the church at the point of his death. In some three and a half years Jesus made three public tours of Galilee, but few believed. Between those three public tours of Galilee, he visited Judea a number of times, but the opposition to him there only intensified. Finally, Jesus ended his ministry condemned and crucified with only a handful of followers, for very few, relatively speaking, were converted during the earthly lifetime of Jesus Christ.

That does not mean that Jesus' ministry was a failure, for it was not Christ's will or the will of the Father who sent him to save many souls at that time. Instead, it was the will of Christ and the Father that Jesus be rejected, for Jesus came to expose the wickedness, hypocrisy, and hatred of unbelieving Israel. Jesus did not come to be welcomed and loved by the crowds, but he came to be maligned, rejected, and ultimately crucified. Jesus came to walk a painful, lonely path of suffering because God planned greater fruit for Christ's ministry after his death, resurrection, and ascension. In fact, the fruit came through his death on the cross. Jesus explains in John 12:23–32:

> 23. And Jesus answered them, saying, The hour is come, that the Son of man should be glorified.
> 24. Verily, verily, I say unto you, Except a corn of wheat fall into the ground and die, it abideth alone: but if it die, it bringeth forth much fruit.
> 25. He that loveth his life shall lose it; and he that hateth his life in this world shall keep it unto life eternal.
> 26. If any man serve me, let him follow me; and where I am, there shall also my servant be: if any man serve me, him will my Father honour.

27. Now is my soul troubled; and what shall I say? Father, save me from this hour: but for this cause came I unto this hour.
28. Father, glorify thy name. Then came there a voice from heaven, saying, I have both glorified it, and will glorify it again.
29. The people therefore, that stood by, and heard it, said that it thundered: others said, An angel spake to him.
30. Jesus answered and said, This voice came not because of me, but for your sakes.
31. Now is the judgment of this world: now shall the prince of this world be cast out.
32. And I, if I be lifted up from the earth, will draw all men unto me.

That is exactly what we observe not only in the book of Acts, but also throughout the history of Christ's church: greater works. After Christ's death and before the resurrection, ascension, and Pentecost, the disciples performed no works: they huddled in secret for fear of the Jews. After the resurrection Jesus appeared to the disciples over the space of forty days, during which time Jesus proved to his disciples that he had risen from the dead and instructed them about the future, especially that they must tarry in Jerusalem until the Holy Spirit would be given to them. During those forty days the disciples performed no works.

The time for works came when the Spirit was poured out on Pentecost. The works after Pentecost were not miracles—at least not mainly miracles, for there were relatively few miracles—but the greater works of the spread of the truth and the conversion of souls. On the day of Pentecost three thousand people were converted and baptized: these were people who had been guilty of crucifying the Lord Jesus (Acts 2:41). Within a short time that number had increased to over five thousand men (4:4). In Acts 6:7 we read, "And the word of God increased; and the number of the disciples multiplied in Jerusalem greatly; and a great company of the priests were obedient to the faith." Nothing like that had happened when Jesus was on earth, so no wonder that Jesus promises "greater works than these." Besides, when the apostles did perform miracles, these always served to authenticate the word preached, and it was through the word preached that the people came to saving faith in Jesus Christ.

Moreover, within a few centuries Christianity became the dominant faith of the Roman Empire and survived all attempts by tyrants to extinguish it. The gospel spread by the work of the apostles, the churches, and the members so that it traversed geographical, ethnic, and social borders. Jews, Samaritans, and Gentiles were won to the faith of Jesus Christ. The unbelieving Jews attempted to stop the spread of the faith, but Paul, the chief persecutor among the Jews, was converted on the Damascus road and became an apostle. Emperors perished trying to destroy Christianity, while heretics attempted to corrupt the faith. The churches grew, the truth was defended and developed, and throughout history the church has done "greater works than these." If anyone had suggested that from a handful of cowardly disciples Jesus would build his church and the gates of hell would not prevail against it, men might have laughed, but so it proved to be: "greater works than these."

We, too, by the grace of Christ are promised "greater works than these." Believing mothers who instruct their children in the fear of the Lord do "greater works than these." The humble believer who witnesses to the truth does "greater works than these." One true church in any location in the world does "greater works than these." Collectively, as a congregation, as the word of God is preached and God is worshiped, "greater works than these" are done.

While the New Testament, post-apostolic church does not perform miracles, the conversion of souls is a greater work than any miracle. God is pleased to use his people as instruments to bring conversion to lost souls, to as many as he has ordained to eternal life (Acts 13:48). In fact, Paul writes about the Thessalonians, "For from you sounded out the word of the Lord not only in Macedonia and Achaia, but also in every place your faith to God-ward is spread abroad; so that we need not to speak any thing" (1 Thess. 1:8).

Only one who does not understand sin and the cross would deny that salvation is a greater work than the multiplying of bread, the healing of diseases, the calming of a storm, or the walking of a man on the Sea of Galilee. Indeed, we must understand that the miracles of Jesus were never an end in themselves but served to illustrate the spiritual salvation that Jesus came to bring. God uses the church today as an instrument in his hand to bring salvation and life to dead sinners: "greater works than these." While others are distracted with showy signs and wonders, which are spurious signs and wonders, we rejoice in God's greater works of salvation and conversion.

THE POSSIBILITY

There are two reasons why these greater works will be possible: Jesus' future position of glory (v. 12) and Jesus' answers to our prayers (vv. 13–14). The first reason is "because I go unto my Father" (v. 12). First, this is a reference to the ascension of Jesus to glory in heaven. When Jesus spoke these words, he was in a lowly, humble, suffering position. As the incarnate Son of God Jesus was subject to a life of misery. He suffered in his body and soul, and his suffering was about to intensify. From the upper room Jesus was looking to the future, to a time when his sufferings would be finished. He refers to that as his going to his Father (v. 12), which is something that he has mentioned several times already in John 14:1–6.

When Jesus goes to the Father, he will ascend in great power and glory into the Father's nearer presence in heaven, and he will be seated on his throne. From that position of glory Jesus will bless his church on the earth. Paul describes that glory:

> 20. [God] raised him from the dead, and set him at his own right hand in the heavenly places,
> 21. Far above all principality, and power, and might, and dominion, and every name that is named, not only in this world, but also in that which is to come:

22. And hath put all things under his feet, and gave him to be the head over all things to the church. (Eph. 1:20–22)

From that position of glory—and remember that the Son of God is glorified according to his human nature, while his divine nature is unchangeably glorious—Jesus gives gifts to his church: "Wherefore he saith, When he ascended up on high, he led captivity captive, and gave gifts unto men…and he gave some, apostles; and some, prophets; and some, evangelists; and some, pastors and teachers" (Eph. 4:8, 11). One of the first works that Jesus performed when he ascended or went to his Father was to pour out his Holy Spirit (Acts 2:33). The gift of the Holy Spirit enables the church to preach the gospel to the ends of the earth, and thus "greater works than these" are performed because Jesus goes to his Father (v. 12).

Second, the ascension presupposes and requires the death of Jesus on the cross and the resurrection, for those two events are also included in Christ's going to his Father. The cross of Christ is necessary because of the sinfulness of the disciples. They knew that they were sinners, and they would soon clearly display their sinfulness. That very evening when Jesus was arrested, they would flee from him. How, then, could such men hope to do any "greater works" in the kingdom of heaven? Jesus must suffer and die on the cross to pay the penalty for their sins and to deliver them from sin's power. Only by his death on the cross could Jesus, who is true God and perfect man, purchase a place for the disciples in the kingdom of his Father. As was explained earlier, much is implied in those words, "I go unto my Father." "I go to Gethsemane to be arrested; I go to the Sanhedrin and to Pilate's judgment hall to be condemned; I go to Golgotha to be crucified and to bear God's wrath and curse; and I go to Joseph's tomb to be buried."

The resurrection was necessary also, for Jesus must not remain dead. Jesus could clearly see the future path on which he must walk, and he walked with unshakeable confidence, for he trusted that he would rise again. The disciples' hearts were troubled at his departure, but Jesus was not troubled. He knew where he was going: "because I go to the Father." If only the disciples had shared his confidence, they could have been spared so much grief. Then they would not have reacted in despair when Jesus was taken, for they would have known that Jesus must rise from the dead. It is easy for us to see with the benefit of hindsight: we know that Jesus rose from the dead. They should have known, but they failed to grasp the truth.

The second reason why these greater works will be possible is that Jesus, from his position at the Father's right hand, will answer the disciples' prayers. Here is another advantage for the disciples in Jesus' departure to the Father. It is striking that throughout the discourse Jesus and his disciples have very different perspectives on his going away. For the disciples the departure of Jesus is an unmitigated disaster, while for Jesus his departure to the Father is joy, blessedness, and glory. The disciples' hearts are troubled: they are gloomy and filled with disquieting thoughts and questions, while Jesus urges them to see the advantages.

We have seen three advantages already. First, Jesus will prepare a place in the Father's house. Second, Jesus will enable them to do greater works than he did. Now, third, Jesus will answer their prayers. This hearing and answering of prayers is the subject of verses 13–14, where Jesus speaks of the disciples' "asking." "And whatsoever ye shall ask in my name, that will I do" (v. 13). "If ye shall ask anything in my name, I will do it" (v. 14).

That verb "ask" is always used of an inferior making a request of a superior. A beggar asks for alms. A servant asks his master. A subject asks his king. The reference is therefore to the making of humble petitions in prayer. (Incidentally, in verse 16, where Jesus is said to "ask" or "pray," the Greek word is different: Jesus never asks or begs God for anything, because he is not God's inferior but his Son, equal with the Father. We will look more at the distinctions between those two verbs in the next chapter.)

This is something new. Before this, Jesus' disciples did not pray to him or ask for things in his name because he was with them.

Soon they will begin to ask the Father, or to pray to the Father, in Jesus' name. To pray in Jesus' name is not to pray in your own name. Peter did not pray in Peter's name. John did not pray in John's name. Philip did not pray in Philip's name. They prayed and we must pray in Jesus' name because Jesus is the Mediator, who stands between God and his people and brings them back into a harmonious relationship with their Creator. Jesus can do that because he is the Son of God in our flesh and because of his work on the cross.

When we pray in Jesus' name, we come to God on the basis of the person and work of Jesus: "Accept us and hear us, we pray, for the sake of Jesus." Here, then, is the relationship: we pray to the Father (the triune God), through the Mediator Jesus Christ, by the power of the Holy Spirit, in true faith. Jesus therefore does not offer a magical formula or some mystical password by which we are guaranteed to receive whatever we want. Yes, Jesus says, "Whatsoever ye shall ask…I will do" and "If ye shall ask anything…I will do it," but do not forget the qualification: "in my name." Do not abuse this name of Jesus to ask for things so that you can consume the answers to your prayers on your lusts: "Ye ask, and receive not, because ye ask amiss, that ye may consume it upon your lusts" (James 4:3). Do not abuse this name of Jesus to ask for things that would be displeasing to him or for things that would not glorify him.

When you pray in the name of Jesus, you are praying for things for which Jesus shed his precious blood. Ask for peace and contentment. Ask for grace to bear up under trials. Ask for sanctification of life. Ask for the increase of your faith. Ask for the spread of the gospel. Ask for the gathering, defense, and preservation of the church. These kinds of petitions please God and God will give these kinds of things. In answer to her prayers Jesus gives his church the power to do "these greater works," so that souls are saved, men and women are converted, the gospel spreads, and the truth is defended, preserved, and developed. The result is verse 13: "that the Father may be glorified in the Son."

THE WORKERS

The connection between verses 14 and 15 is not altogether clear, but it seems to be this: the kind of people who do these greater works, who ask in Jesus' name, with the result that Jesus is glorified in the Father, are obedient believers. Obedient believers are those who love Christ: "If ye love me, keep my commandments" (v. 15). Many claim to love Jesus, but a life of disobedience contradicts their claims. Jesus' commandments are the same as the Father's commandments. Do you love Jesus? Avoid idolatry and blasphemy, observe the Sabbath day, honor your parents, avoid murder, adultery, theft, and deceit (and all sins connected to them), and live without covetousness, living in contentment and gratitude for the things that you have.

Jesus' chief commandment is love: "A new commandment I give unto you, That ye love one another; as I have loved you, that ye also love one another. By this shall all men know that ye are my disciples, if ye have love one to another" (John 13:34–35). It was because the disciples loved Jesus by loving one another and keeping his commandments that they turned the world upside down. It was obedient lovers of Jesus energized through prayer who preached the word to the nations. Jesus says to all would-be followers: "Do you love me?"

This, too, was instruction for the disciples: they claimed love for Jesus (and they were sincere in that claim), but their love needed direction. Do not love me, says Jesus, by crying at my departure. I have no need for that kind of love. Do not love me, says Jesus, by lamenting over my cross. Rejoice rather in my departure. Not only is it for your advantage, but it is also for my glory. Love me, rather, in this: love me by praying in my name, and love me by keeping my commandments, and you will do greater works than these to the glory of the Father.

Chapter 5

Jesus Promises Another Comforter

(John 14:16–18)

16. And I will pray the Father, and he shall give you another Comforter, that he may abide with you for ever;
17. Even the Spirit of truth; whom the world cannot receive, because it seeth him not, neither knoweth him: but ye know him; for he dwelleth with you, and shall be in you.
18. I will not leave you comfortless: I will come to you.

Have you been keeping a tally of the advantages that the believer enjoys in Jesus' departure? In his departure to the Father's house, via the cross, the tomb, the resurrection, and the ascension, Jesus prepares a place for his disciples in heaven. Given that advantage, how foolish for the disciples to try to keep Jesus indefinitely on earth with them! If Jesus had not prepared a place for the disciples in the Father's house, they could have grown old with him until they died, but they would have eventually perished in their sins. By departing, Jesus gives his disciples power to continue his work and even to accomplish greater works than the works that he had performed while on earth, as the church is gathered from the elect of all nations. By departing, Jesus occupies an exalted position at the Father's right hand where, as the mediator and advocate of his people, he now answers prayers offered in his name.

The Heidelberg Catechism directs our attention to these advantages too: "Of what advantage to us is Christ's ascension into heaven?

First, that He is our advocate in the presence of His Father in heaven; [and] secondly, that we have our flesh in heaven as a sure pledge that He, as the Head, will also take up to Himself, us, His members."[1]

The Catechism mentions also a third advantage: "that He sends us His Spirit as an earnest, by whose power we seek the things which are above, where Christ sitteth on the right hand of God, and not things on earth."[2] In this text Jesus introduces the disciples to another wonderful person, the Comforter, the Spirit of truth, who comes because of Jesus' departure to the Father. While the disciples feared being comfortless and alone, Jesus promises the Comforter, who "is also given me, to make me, by a true faith, partaker of Christ and all His benefits, that He may comfort me and abide with me for ever."[3]

WHO HE IS

The promise of Jesus is not the promise of a thing, that is, not the promise of an "it." It is the promise of a person, that is, a "he." We know this because Jesus speaks of a comforter: "I will pray the Father, and he shall give you another Comforter." The Father will not give comfort, but a comforter. He will not send help, but a helper. He will not impart strength, but give a strengthener. He will not give support, but a supporter. Therefore, we have the correct translation: "He [not it] may abide with you forever" (v. 16). The world "seeth *him* not, neither knoweth *him*: but ye know *him*; for *he* dwelleth with you, and shall be in you" (v. 17).

A personal comforter is much more blessed and much richer than impersonal comfort. A person knows the one whom he comforts, and a person is able to adapt his comfort to the personal circumstances of the one whom he comforts. The Comforter knows our sorrows, fears, anxieties, and weaknesses. The same is not true of

1 Heidelberg Catechism Q&A 49, in *The Confessions and the Church Order of the Protestant Reformed Churches* (Grandville, MI: Protestant Reformed Churches in America, 2005), 102.

2 Heidelberg Catechism A 49, in *Confessions and Church Order*, 102.

3 Heidelberg Catechism A 53, in *Confessions and Church Order*, 103.

an inanimate object. A hot water bottle can warm your feet, but it cannot comfort you. A fluffy blanket feels pleasant against the skin, but it cannot comfort you. Only a person who knows you can comfort you. A person listens to you, a person embraces you, a person wipes away your tears, and a person speaks soothing words. That is why we need a Comforter.

The word translated "Comforter" is Paraclete, which is the English transliteration of the Greek word *Parakletos*. The word *Parakletos* appears five times in the New Testament. Four times (John 14:16, 26; 15:26; 16:7) it is a reference to the Holy Spirit, while in one other place (1 John 2:1) it is a reference to Jesus Christ, the Advocate.

The technical term *Parakletos* is derived from the common Greek verb *parakaleo*, which is found just over one hundred times in the New Testament. This verb can be translated in a number of ways: encourage, console, strengthen, comfort, admonish, exhort, and even beseech. The root idea of the verb is to call alongside. A comforter or *Parakletos*, then, is one who is called to one's side to help. A comforter is someone who comes alongside another to help, strengthen, and give support.

This Comforter (Paraclete, or *Parakletos*) is closely related to Jesus, for Jesus calls him "another Comforter." This means that the disciples already had a comforter: he was Jesus. As long as Jesus walked with his disciples, and they walked with him, they had comfort in his presence, for he strengthened, supported, and consoled them. Soon, however, Jesus would be taken away from them. He would be arrested within a matter of hours, and who would comfort them when that would happen?

To answer those fears Jesus makes this promise: "I will not leave you comfortless" (v. 18). Yes, Jesus would leave them, but only for a short time. Yes, he would leave them, but he would not leave them comfortless, bereft of help, support, or assistance. The Greek word translated "comfortless" is our word *orphans*. Jesus would not leave his disciples helpless and alone like orphans in a cruel, harsh, and cold world.

Jesus calls the Comforter "another comforter" because he will be like him, where the word "another" refers to an additional comforter of the same kind, not to a different kind of comforter. The Comforter would do for the disciples in Jesus' absence what Jesus did for the disciples in his presence.

Nevertheless, this Comforter would be different from Jesus in a number of important respects. Unlike Jesus, he would be a permanent Comforter. Jesus was departing, but this Comforter would *never leave them*: "[The Father] shall give you another Comforter, that he may abide with you *for ever*" (v. 16). They would never lament the loss of this Comforter, as they would soon lament the loss of Jesus. This Comforter would not be arrested, crucified, and buried. Therefore, the disciples must not expect another human being as the Comforter. A human being can be taken away. Jesus is a human being, but the Comforter is not. Jesus is incarnate, but the Comforter is not. Instead, the Comforter is incorporeal and invisible. The Heidelberg Catechism says, "That He is also given me, to make me, by a true faith, partaker of Christ and all His benefits, that He may comfort me and abide with me for ever."[4]

Therein lies the advantage for the disciples. When Jesus was among them, he comforted the disciples, but his ability to comfort them was limited. That limitation falls away when another Comforter comes. Jesus was limited because of his human nature. His physical presence determined or limited his ability to comfort his disciples. He could not, for example, comfort one disciple in Bethany and another in Jerusalem at the same time. The Comforter whom the Father would give is omnipresent. Therefore, the Comforter could comfort John on the island of Patmos, and Paul and Silas in jail in Philippi, and certain saints in Ephesus or Corinth. The Comforter strengthens, consoles, and supports believers in all kinds of locations and situations, for he comforts us with the comfort of Jesus Christ.

---

4 Heidelberg Catechism A 53, in *Confessions and Church Order*, 103.

Jesus identifies the Comforter in a number of ways, which shows us that he expected the disciples to have some familiarity with the Comforter already: "Ye know him; for he dwelleth with you, and [he] shall be in you" (v. 17). First, the Comforter is the Spirit. In verse 26 Jesus calls him the Holy Ghost, where Ghost is another name for Spirit. The disciples were Jews; therefore, they knew something about the Spirit, for in the Old Testament the Spirit is called the Spirit of God or the Spirit of Jehovah. The Jews understood that the Spirit of God was inseparable from God: the Spirit proceeds from God, as his breath, and accomplishes God's purposes. The Spirit was present in creation: "And the Spirit of God moved upon the face of the waters" (Gen. 1:2). "By the word of the LORD were the heavens made; and all the host of them by the breath of his mouth" (Ps. 33:6). The Spirit spoke the word of God through the prophets. The Spirit anointed the Messiah for his work.

Nevertheless, despite this knowledge derived from the Old Testament, the disciples were not so familiar with the personality of the Spirit, for that aspect of the Spirit was not clearly revealed in the Old Testament. That should not overly surprise us, because God's revelation is progressive. God gives his people the truth gradually or little by little. The New Testament provides greater, richer, and fuller revelation of the truth than the Old Testament. Therefore, it is true that the disciples knew the Spirit and that he dwelt with them, but there was so much more to know about the Spirit, and that would be revealed.

We should also understand that the disciples were regenerated already. Therefore, the Spirit had worked faith in them, and the Spirit had begun to sanctify them. However, a difference was coming, which the Old Testament describes in terms of pouring. "I will pour my spirit upon thy seed, and my blessing upon thine offspring" (Isa. 44:3). "And it shall come to pass afterward, that I will pour out my spirit upon all flesh" (Joel 2:28). In the Old Testament the Holy Spirit can be likened to a trickle on certain Jews (almost exclusively prophets, priests, and kings, who were the Old Testament officebearers), while in the New Testament the Holy Spirit is poured out upon all flesh, young and old, male and female, and Jew and Gentile. The result is a richer, deeper, more blessed acquaintance with the Spirit, which Jesus indicates in verse 17: "And [he] shall be in you."

Although the experience, knowledge, and enjoyment of the Spirit by the disciples were incomplete, the disciples were not like the world. In the upper room discourse Jesus makes twenty references to the world, where the word refers to the world of the ungodly, that whole wicked system made up of wicked, unbelieving men and women. The world cannot receive this Comforter and the world does not see him, for the Comforter is a Spirit. More than that, the world cannot perceive him, and the world does not know him. The world is an utter stranger to the Comforter: "For to be carnally minded is death; but to be spiritually minded is life and peace" (Rom. 8:6). "But the natural man receiveth not the things of the Spirit of God: for they are foolishness unto him: neither can he know them, because they are spiritually discerned" (1 Cor. 2:14).

Second, the Comforter is the Spirit of truth, which identification Jesus uses for him in verse 17, as well as in John 15:26 and 16:13. We have already seen, especially from verse 6, what the truth is and that Jesus is "the way, the truth, and the life." Truth can be summarized in three words: truth is reality, truth is stability, and truth is authority. Jesus is reality, for he is the perfect revelation of the true and living God; he is stability, for he is the utterly reliable one; and he is authority, for his words have binding authority on all men.

Here, then, is the Comforter's relationship to truth: he is *the Spirit of truth*. If the Comforter is the Spirit of truth, he is the Spirit of Jesus Christ, for he is intimately connected to or related to Jesus Christ. This is true because the Spirit and the Son are, with the Father, divine persons in the being of God. The Comforter is also the perfect revelation of Jesus Christ, so that, as Jesus shall explain later, the Spirit testifies to Jesus Christ. Therefore, the Spirit always acts in service of the truth: he never lies, he hates all lies, and he delights in and loves the truth (1 John 2:21). He loves the truth that he has inspired to be written in the holy Scriptures of truth, and he works in believers to reveal the truth to them and to preserve the truth in their midst.

WHAT HE DOES

We know the Spirit's work as Comforter from his name, the Spirit of truth. The Spirit is not merely a spirit of feelings or a spirit of emotions. In the church world today many boast of the presence of the Spirit, insisting that a truly spiritual church is one with lively excitement. Some boast that the Spirit is in their church because the worship style moves them: it might even move them to tears. Others promote the idea that the Comforter whispers in Christians' ears, causing them to have ecstatic, mysterious feelings and emotions. The same Christians would condemn a Reformed worship service, where the singing is from the Psalms and the focus is on the preaching of Scripture, as boring, lifeless, and unspiritual.

Nevertheless, we must judge a church not by the feelings that the worship stirs up in the worshipers, or by the electric atmosphere that it claims to have, or because the ministry meets the felt needs of seekers, but by this: Is the worship, especially the preaching, *true*? Jesus warned the Samaritan woman, "God is a Spirit: and they that worship him must worship him in spirit and in truth" (John 4:24). Do not try to separate them, for you cannot have Spirit without truth. The Spirit of truth inspired the Psalms as a book of songs. Therefore, the Spirit of truth delights in the singing of Psalms rather than in the singing of hymns with their erroneous lyrics. The Spirit of truth inspired the Scriptures. Therefore, the Spirit of truth delights in faithful preaching rather than in the preaching of false doctrine or in the preaching of moral tales or political harangues without the pure doctrine of God's word.

Therefore, we know how the Comforter comforts: he comforts, strengthens, supports, consoles, and helps by bringing and applying the truth. When we are distressed and anxious, the only thing that we require is the truth. We need something that corresponds to reality: we need to know about the true God and his love for us, we need to know about Jesus Christ and his perfect and finished work on the cross, and we need to know about his resurrection from the dead. We need something that has stability: we need the unchanging, reliable truths about the forgiveness of sins and everlasting life by grace alone in Christ. We need something that has authority: we need something upon which we can rely for time and eternity because God has declared it.

That is exactly what the Comforter, the Spirit of truth, does. When we are sad, the Spirit, bringing the gospel, cheers our soul. When we are lonely and distressed, the Spirit, bringing the gospel, reminds us of God's promise never to leave nor forsake us. When we are suffering, the Spirit, bringing the gospel, reminds us that God's grace is always sufficient to sustain us, and that truth does sustain us. Empty, seemingly pious platitudes do not comfort us: only the truth can do that.

In other words, the Comforter, the Spirit of truth, comforts us by giving Christ to us. We must distinguish between two great works in the work of salvation. The first is the work of Jesus Christ in his earthly sufferings and death. The Son of God accomplished perfect righteousness by his life of obedience, he made perfect satisfaction for our sins on the cross, and he rose from the dead with life and immortality. But how do the benefits of that work of Christ become ours, or how do we become partakers of the righteousness, pardon of sins, and eternal life purchased by Christ?

The answer is found in the second work of salvation, the work of the Holy Spirit. That, too, is the gracious work of God, not the work of man. Christ's work does not depend for its efficacy on an act of our free will by which we accept it, so that we make ourselves to differ from unbelievers, and we do not supplement Christ's work by our own activity. Instead, the Spirit applies the work of Christ to the hearts and lives of God's elect people so that they believe in Jesus Christ. The Spirit regenerates dead, but elect, sinners by giving them life or by quickening them. The Spirit sanctifies unholy sinners by working in them true sorrow for sin, by separating them from sin, and by devoting them to God. The Spirit renews or inwardly transforms sinners, the Spirit works and strengthens faith, and the Spirit gives assurance. The Spirit does this great work of applying the work of Christ by the word.

Christ promises this in verse 17: "He dwelleth with you, and shall be in you." He further interprets this in verse 18: "I will not leave you comfortless: I will come to you." Christ promises here an internal work of the Spirit ("in you"). The Spirit was already in the hearts of the disciples, but with the outpouring of the Spirit on Pentecost that indwelling would be richer, deeper, and more blessed. The Spirit is present in our hearts too: he is present to bless us, to comfort us, and to strengthen us. He works faith, repentance, and holiness in us.

This is assuredly the greatest blessing that we possess in the Christian life. We could lose everything, but we can never lose the Spirit, because we can never lose Christ. And therefore, says Jesus, although I am leaving you physically, although I am returning to the Father's house, I will still be with you spiritually.

When Jesus promises, "I will come to you," we can interpret that coming in various ways. Christ will come back after the resurrection, he will return on the last day, but especially he will come in the Spirit to continue to be with us. Because the Comforter, the Spirit of truth, is the Spirit of Christ, the Spirit's presence is Christ's presence with and in the believer, in and with us. As the Heidelberg Catechism puts it: "With respect to His Godhead, majesty, grace, and spirit, [Jesus Christ] is at no time absent from us,"[5] and the Holy Spirit "is also given me, to make me, by a true faith, partaker of Christ and all His benefits, that He may comfort me and abide with me for ever."[6]

---

5 Heidelberg Catechism A 47, in *Confessions and Church Order*, 101.

6 Heidelberg Catechism A 53, in *Confessions and Church Order*, 103.

HOW HE COMES

The Comforter comes in answer to Jesus' prayer or as a fruit of his intercession. In verse 16 Jesus says, "And I will pray the Father, and he shall give." The prayer of Jesus is different from our prayers. In verse 13 Jesus says, "Ye shall ask in my name," while in verse 16 he promises, "And I will pray the Father." When we pray, we beg, we supplicate, or we petition the Father, and we do so not in our name, but in Jesus' name. We do so because as creatures we are utterly dependent on the Creator, and we do so because as sinners we are utterly undeserving of receiving anything from the Holy One.

The New Testament is very precise in its language, a testimony to verbal inspiration, for the apostle uses a different Greek verb. When Jesus prays, he does not beg or ask as an inferior to a superior. Instead, he makes his request as an equal, for he is equal in power, majesty, dignity, and divinity to the persons of the Father and the Spirit. Therefore, there is no begging, for the Son of God powerfully obtains his requests before the Father's throne. That is the key, of course, for when Jesus prays to the Father for us, he requests blessings for us, and he obtains blessings for us. He does so because he is the Son of God, but he also does so because he has done everything to merit the blessings of salvation for us, having made full atonement for our sins, without which the Father would not bless us.

That is the reason for the future tense: "I will pray the Father." Before the cross and resurrection, Jesus does not pray to the Father for the gift of the Comforter, but when he ascends and sits at God's right hand, he shall. That is why God waited until Pentecost to give the Holy Spirit, for Christ's work must be completed first: the order must be the cross, the resurrection, the ascension, the sitting at God's right hand, and then Pentecost.

> 30. Therefore being a prophet, and knowing that God had sworn with an oath to him, that of the fruit of his loins, according to the flesh, he would raise up Christ to sit on his throne:

31. He seeing this before spake of the resurrection of Christ, that his soul was not left in hell, neither his flesh did see corruption.
32. This Jesus hath God raised up, whereof we all are witnesses.
33. Therefore being by the right hand of God exalted, and having received of the Father the promise of the Holy Ghost, he hath shed forth this, which ye now see and hear (Acts 2:30–33).

In response to Christ's prayer, the Father gives the precious gift: "I will pray the Father, and he shall give you another Comforter" (v. 16). Notice that word "give": it speaks of grace, for when God gives, he gives in grace. He gives in love, he gives in mercy, he gives in order to bless, he gives without our merits, and he even gives despite our demerits. We do nothing to obtain the gift: we simply receive the Comforter. And we are thankful for another advantage in the departure of Jesus.

Chapter 6

God Abiding With Us in the Sphere of Love

(John 14:19–24)

19. Yet a little while, and the world seeth me no more; but ye see me: because I live, ye shall live also.
20. At that day ye shall know that I am in my Father, and ye in me, and I in you.
21. He that hath my commandments, and keepeth them, he it is that loveth me: and he that loveth me shall be loved of my Father, and I will love him, and will manifest myself to him.
22. Judas saith unto him, not Iscariot, Lord, how is it that thou wilt manifest thyself unto us, and not unto the world?
23. Jesus answered and said unto him, If a man love me, he will keep my words: and my Father will love him, and we will come unto him, and make our abode with him.
24. He that loveth me not keepeth not my sayings: and the word which ye hear is not mine, but the Father's which sent me.

Sometimes a brief departure from a loved one is necessary to guarantee richer, deeper, and more permanent communion and fellowship. When a loved one understands that, the temporary separation is more bearable. We count the temporary separation worth it if we can be together again with greater intimacy and familiarity. That is the truth Jesus seeks to impress upon his disciples. They hear,

"Jesus is going away." Jesus wants them to understand, "My going away is good." To encourage them Jesus reminds his disciples of what he will achieve for them by his departure: in short, he shall secure their everlasting salvation and blessedness in the Father's house. Even before he brings them home, they shall enjoy deeper communion with the Father in this life: "We will come unto him, and make our abode with him" (v. 23).

How different was this promise from the fears and anxieties of the disciples! They feared that Jesus' departure would leave them comfortless (v. 18, where the word is *orphans*). The disciples expected to be bereft of support, care, and love, abandoned as orphans in a cold, cruel world. What a dishonoring thought, as if Jesus or the Father would forsake his people! Jesus reassures them in verse 18, "I will not leave you comfortless: I will come to you." That coming is not yet in the flesh, which would have to wait until the last day. Instead, Jesus comes to them by the Holy Spirit, another Comforter, the Spirit of truth, whom the Father gives them.

This rich, spiritual communion with the Father in Jesus Christ is not for everyone, however. It is not for the world, but only for those who love Jesus and keep his words. The fruit of Jesus' coming by the Comforter is deeper, richer communion and fellowship of believers with the Father and Jesus Christ by the Spirit of truth in the sphere of love, a blessed fruit of Pentecost and another advantage in Jesus' departure to the Father's house.

DEEPER COMMUNION

The text describes rich, blessed, spiritual, and mysterious realities: God's abiding with us (v. 23), our dwelling in Christ (v. 20), and God's love for us in Christ (vv. 21, 23). It also includes a contrast between the blessedness of believers and the misery of the world (vv. 22–24) because the world will be excluded from this fellowship. In addition, our Savior gives the promise of seeing him and the promise of life in him (v. 19). What does this mean? It tantalizes us with its beauty, it attracts and fascinates us, our hearts and minds strain to understand and to grasp it, and it seems beyond our grasp, so close and yet so far, beyond our comprehension. Certainly, the disciples felt the same way because one of them asked in verse 22, "Lord, how is it?"

This fellowship begins with God, who is called "the Father" or "my Father" multiple times in these verses: "Ye shall know that I am in my Father" (v. 20). "He…shall be loved of my Father" (v. 21). "My Father will love him" (v. 23). "We [my Father and I] will come unto him, and make our abode with him" (v. 23). "The word which ye hear is not mine, but the Father's which sent me" (v. 24). God or the Father is the eternal Creator: he is eternal, unchangeable, spiritual, and almighty, holy, righteous, and true, the sovereign ruler and judge of all men and angels. This God is said to love, to have a certain relationship to Jesus Christ, and therefore to have a certain relationship to the disciples of Jesus Christ.

Jesus calls this God "my Father," which, as we have seen, is true in two respects. As mentioned before, the first person of the Trinity is the Father of the second person or the Son within the being of God. The Son therefore is not a creature, for he is not the product of the will of God, and he does not exist in distinction from God or independently of God or even in dependence upon God, but he is perfectly divine. The Son is God, possessing all the attributes of God, performing the works of God, and receiving the worship and glory of God. In addition, the triune God (Father, Son, and Holy Spirit) is the eternal Father of our Lord Jesus Christ. "Now the God of patience and consolation grant you to be likeminded one toward another according to Christ Jesus: that ye may with one mind and one mouth glorify God, even the Father of our Lord Jesus Christ" (Rom. 15:5–6).

The God of the man Jesus Christ is the triune God, in these verses called the Father. When Jesus lived on earth, he prayed to the triune God, and he obeyed the law of the triune God. He did not obey, serve, or pray to only the first person. This Father is also our Father: he is therefore the Father of all believers. He, the triune God, adopts his people, not all men but those whom he has chosen. They, and not the world, are the children of God. He loves them, and they render to him grateful returns of ardent love. In summary, God is Father, first, as the Father of the Son in the being of the Trinity; second, as the triune Father of the incarnate Son; and third, as the Father of adopted believers.

The Heidelberg Catechism explains this beautiful truth. "The eternal Father of our Lord Jesus Christ (who of nothing made heaven and earth, with all that is in them; who likewise upholds and governs the same by His eternal counsel and providence) is, for the sake of Christ His Son, my God and my Father."[1] "Christ alone is the eternal and natural Son of God; but we are children adopted of God, by grace, for His sake."[2] "God is become our Father in Christ, and will much less deny us what we ask of Him in true faith than our parents will refuse us earthly things."[3]

We love God because he has first loved us. The relationships in the text, whether between the Father and the Son, or between the Son and the Father, or between the Father and the Son and the disciples, are relationships of love.

Love is deep affection that exists between persons. The biblical words for love express that idea: love is a delighting in another person as precious and dear; love is a treasuring of another person; and love is a breathing after, a seeking after, or a longing for another person, so that love is a drawing of that person into one's embrace and life. In the Bible love is not so much emotional, a matter of feelings, as it is volitional, a matter of the will. We choose to love another person when we set our love upon another person.

When love becomes difficult, because the object of our love becomes unlovable or behaves in an unloving manner, we choose to continue to love that person because we promised to do so and are

1 Heidelberg Catechism A 26, in *Confessions and Church Order*, 92–93.
2 Heidelberg Catechism A 33, in *Confessions and Church Order*, 97.
3 Heidelberg Catechism A 120, in *Confessions and Church Order*, 136.

committed to our love. Married persons must continue to love and cherish their spouses because, among other things, they made vows before God to do so. When the feeling of love fades, the duty to love remains, and when love is properly exercised, the affection of love is rekindled.

Love is also a determination to do good for the person whom you love. One who loves seeks the beloved's highest good, which is his eternal salvation. When God loves, he wills, determines, and accomplishes the salvation of his beloved. God does not rest until those whom he loves are forever safely with him enjoying everlasting glory and blessedness. When we love God, we seek his glory, or as Jesus says, we keep his commandments. When we love another person, we show in thousands of little ways how much that person means to us and that we are willing to sacrifice our own happiness for the welfare of the person whom we love. In Scripture love is costly, is sacrificial, and is displayed in humble service for, and devotion to, another.

Finally, love is the establishing of a bond with another person, for to love is to cleave to your beloved and to enter into fellowship with them. If you love another person, your heart aches in their absence, and you delight in the presence of your beloved, seeking to be close to that person, as close as possible depending on the nature of your relationship with that person.

The love of the text is not primarily our love for God or for one another, but God's love for his elect children. The love of God begins within the divine being because God loves himself. Do not imagine the selfish love of a narcissist, for this love exists between the three persons of the divine Trinity. Only if God is triune can true love exist perfectly and eternally in him. Each person, a distinct, conscious, moral individual, loves. The Father loves, the Son loves, and the Spirit loves, for they love the other persons of the Trinity. So close is this love that Jesus says, "I am *in* my Father" (v. 20). The Father loves the Son in the Holy Spirit. The Son loves the Father in the Holy Spirit. The Father breathes after, delights in, and seeks the Son in the Holy Spirit. The Son breathes after, delights in, and seeks the Father in the Holy Spirit. This love is the eternal activity of the triune God. Even before God created anyone or anything, he was, and is, the God of perfect, unchangeable, blessed love.

The bond of love also exists between the triune God and the incarnate Son. The triune God delights in Jesus Christ, for he is the object of the Father's affection and care. The Son became incarnate: he took human nature, taking the name Jesus and the title Christ. About the incarnate Son Jesus Christ, the triune Father says, "This is my beloved Son, in whom I am well pleased" (Matt. 3:17).

The love of God is displayed to and bestowed upon his people. When God is said to love us, or to love believers, he loves us with the same divine love with which he loves himself and with which he loves Christ. He delights in us, he treasures us as precious and dear to him, he seeks and accomplishes our salvation, and he draws us into his fellowship. In love our God causes us to taste and to know his own blessed divine life. That is the promise of the text: "I am *in* my Father, and ye *in* me, and I *in* you" (John 14:20). Those words are words of love and intimacy. "He that loveth me shall be loved of my Father, and I will love him, and will manifest myself to him" (v. 21). "My Father will love him, and we will come unto him, and make our abode with him" (v. 23).

Yet there is a difference, for when God loves himself, perfect persons love other perfect persons. The perfect Father loves the perfect Son in the perfect bond of the perfect Holy Spirit. When God loves Christ, the perfect God loves the perfectly holy, righteous man, his own incarnate Son. But when God loves us, he loves sinners, those who are utterly unworthy of his love, those who deserve his wrath and hatred. God cannot simply shower the blessings of his love upon sinners. In order for us to know and taste the divine love, God must forgive us. Part of the display of that love is that he justifies us, and then he prepares us to dwell with him in heavenly glory by sanctifying us.

The New Testament is replete with references to this great truth. I give just one, but the reader could undoubtedly find many more:

"But God commendeth his love toward us, in that, while we were yet sinners, Christ died for us" (Rom. 5:8). In that verse the Spirit through the apostle reveals the relationship between God's love and the cross of Christ. The cause of God's love is not Christ's death for us. Christ's death does not make God love us, as if God was only persuaded to love us when he saw the shedding of his Son's precious blood. Instead, the Father sent his Son to die on the cross *because* he loves us or, to express it differently, God's love is the source of the cross, so that the fruit of the cross is that we love him who loved us.

Jesus makes reference to his death in verse 19: "Yet a little while, and the world seeth me no more." The world, which is the world of the ungodly or the world of unbelievers, represented by the Jews and Romans, saw Jesus for a time. They saw him during his public ministry, they witnessed his miracles, but they did not believe. In a matter of hours they would no longer see him, for they would arrest him, try him, falsely accuse him, condemn him, and crucify him. Jesus would be buried in a tomb, and the world will not see him again, until he returns on the last day to judge them for their sins.

The world does not see Jesus today. The world did not witness the resurrection or the ascension, for that event was revealed to a select few, to Christ's closest disciples. The Jewish leaders did not see the resurrected Jesus Christ, Pilate did not see the resurrected Jesus Christ, King Herod did not see him, and the emperor in Rome did not see him either. Peter explains, "Him God raised up the third day, and shewed him openly; not to all the people, but unto witnesses chosen before of God, even to us, who did eat and drink with him after he rose from the dead" (Acts 10:40–41). Thus says Jesus in verse 19, "But ye see me." Not only did the disciples see Jesus with their physical eyes after his resurrection, but the disciples perceived who Jesus truly is. They knew by faith that Jesus is the Son of God.

Why, then, was it necessary for Jesus to depart so that the world no longer saw him? Why was it necessary for him to die and be buried? Why did he not make a public display of glory in his resurrection, or even before his resurrection, such that everyone would see him? The answer is that a public display of glory would not serve our salvation and it was not the way in which God determined to glorify himself in his Son. Jesus must undergo the sufferings of death on the cross in order to make full payment for our sins. Jesus must fulfill the obedience of the law for us. Jesus must die to endure the death penalty for us. Jesus must suffer God's wrath in order to deliver us from his wrath and curse. "Christ hath redeemed us from the curse of the law, being made a curse for us: for it is written, Cursed is everyone that hangeth on a tree'" (Gal. 3:13). In that way, and through faith in the crucified and resurrected Jesus Christ, we come to know the love of God for us.

PARTICULAR BENEFICIARIES

One of the disciples, however, was confused. His name was Judas. John quickly distinguishes him from the traitor. He was "not Iscariot" (v. 22). Among the twelve disciples were two men called Judas. Judas Iscariot had already left to seek out the enemies of Jesus, so that he could betray the Lord for the promised reward of thirty pieces of silver (John 13:27–30). He was no longer present to hear the words of this discourse, which was for the ears of Jesus' beloved disciples only, not for the hypocrite. The second man is simply called "Judas," which is the New Testament version of Judah or Jude. This man is probably the same as Lebbaeus or Thaddaeus in Matthew 10:3. About him we know nothing more, for Scripture does not mention him again by name.

Judas Thaddaeus is the third disciple to interrupt Jesus—first, Thomas; second, Philip; and now Judas Thaddaeus. Judas had been listening carefully, trying to grasp the meaning of Jesus' words. He sensed that Jesus was describing something beautiful, but one thing confused him. Why is this self-revelation of love of which Jesus speaks only for the disciples, and not for the world? Notice verse 21: "He that hath my commandments, and keepeth them, he it is that loveth me: and he that loveth me shall be loved of my Father, and I will love him, and will manifest myself to him." Judas therefore asks in verse 22, "Lord, how is it that thou wilt manifest thyself unto us, and not unto the world?" Literally, "Lord, what has happened that you will show yourself or display yourself to us and not to the world?"

By his question Judas betrayed ignorance of Christ's mission. In Judas' heart, as in the hearts of the other disciples, the desire lingered for an earthly kingdom of splendor. Judas began to understand the need for Christ to suffer, and he began to grasp something about the resurrection. Yes, Christ would depart, and he would return in some fashion, but Judas was confused about the manner of Christ's return. Surely, thought Judas, if Jesus returns, everyone will see him. We, the disciples, will see him. The world will see him. Everyone will be amazed at his return. Everyone will worship him. Finally Christ will set up his earthly kingdom. Would that not be wonderful? Nevertheless, Judas immediately perceived something in the words of Jesus: the revelation of Jesus will not be to everyone, but only to some. The world is excluded, but why?

In response to Judas, Jesus explains a certain circle or sphere of love in which the manifestation of divine love must take place. Consider this circle of love or this sphere of love. First, there is the love of God or the love of the Father. "He that loveth me shall be loved of my Father" (v. 21). "If a man love me, he will keep my words: and my Father will love him" (v. 23). The Father's love is his setting his affection upon us, his determination to save us, and now especially in verse 23, his dwelling with us. In verse 23 Jesus promises, "My Father will love him, and we [the Father and Jesus] will come unto him, and make our abode with him." The word "abode" in verse 23 is the same as "mansion" in verse 2: "In my Father's house are many mansions... We will...make our abode with him." The idea of "abode" is not luxury and beauty (mansion), but a permanent dwelling place. We could translate the word as "home."

God will make his home with us, or God will make our hearts a home in which he will permanently dwell with us in fellowship and communion. In the Old Testament God's abode was the holy of holies in the temple. Now God's abode is the hearts of his believing people. The Father, who is the triune God and the God and Father of our Lord Jesus Christ, loves us, dwells with us, and makes his home with us in close, intimate fellowship. What a wonder of grace that is!

Second, there is the love of Jesus Christ. "And I will love him" (v. 21). Christ's love is shown in the sacrifice of his life for us on the cross. Notice, by the way, that Judas understands the implications of this: if Christ manifests himself only to those who are loved of his Father and only to those whom he loves, then the world must be excluded. The Father does not love the world of which Judas speaks. Christ does not love the world of which Judas speaks. The world of verse 19 ("the world seeth me no more") and of verse 22 ("thou wilt manifest thyself unto us, and not unto the world") is not the object of God's love. God does not delight in that world. God does not purpose the salvation of that world. God does not seek a relationship with that world. Christ does not die for that world. That world perishes.

Christ's love, therefore, is in full harmony with the Father's love, and it is particular and efficacious. "I shall love him." "My Father shall love him." "My Father shall come unto him." "I will come unto him." "My Father shall make his abode with him." "I shall make my abode with him." "We shall make our abode with him."

Third, there is the believer's love for Christ. That love is demonstrated in the keeping of God's commandments and of Christ's commandments. "He that hath my commandments, and keepeth them, he it is that loveth me" (v. 21). "If a man love me, he will keep my words" (v. 23). "He that loveth me not keepeth not my sayings" (v. 24). Jesus already stated this in verse 15: "If ye love me, keep my commandments." To "keep" in verses 21, 23, 24, and 15 is to preserve, to guard, to treasure, and to exercise watchful care over Christ's commandments.

Why do you carefully avoid idolatry? Why do you guard against having or conceiving of another god contrary to the revelation of the holy Scriptures? Why do you honor the name of God? Why are you careful to observe the Sabbath day so that you diligently frequent the church of God to hear his word and to praise him? Why do you honor your parents and all those in authority over you? Why do you guard against sins of malice, anger, envy, and hatred, which might bear the fruit of violence in your life? Why are you sexually pure and faithful in marriage and in single life? Why are you careful to avoid stealing and deception with money? Why are you meticulous in speaking the truth and careful to preserve your neighbor's good name out of love for him? Why are you careful to avoid covetousness and greed? The answer is that you keep Christ's commandments out of thankfulness and love to him. You remember that the sayings of Jesus—his words—are divine: "And the word which ye hear is not mine, but the Father's which sent me" (v. 24).

The world does not keep Christ's commandments. The world despises Christ's—and God's—word. Therefore, the world does not know and cannot know the blessedness of intimate fellowship with the triune God through Jesus Christ by the operation of the Holy Spirit. Of course Christ does not manifest himself to the world.

Jesus speaks, therefore, of three "loves" here: the love of the Father, the love of Christ, and the love of believers. What, then, is the relationship between these different examples of love? Christ does not teach that our keeping of the commandments is *the reason* that God loves us. Christ does not teach that our keeping of the commandments is *the condition* for God's love of us. Christ does not teach that God's love ebbs and flows *according to our faithfulness* in keeping God's commandments. That would be a dreadfully terrifying message: If you love Christ by keeping his commandments, then God will love you. If you keep God's commandments, then you make yourself worthy of God's love. If you keep God's commandments, then God will make his abode with you. That is not the meaning.

God's love is always first. God's love is always the source of our love. Our love is only the grateful response to his love for us.

Without God's love we could never love God. Without God's love we could only hate God and flee from him. God's love is eternal and unchangeable, expressed in the cross of Christ. John writes, "We love him, because he first loved us" (1 John 4:19). We could express it this way: "We keep his commandments because he first loved us."

This was true of the disciples. They loved Christ because he had chosen them and because he had drawn them into his fellowship. Their love for Christ was real, but it was underdeveloped. They did not yet know by experience the fullness of Christ's love for them: he had not yet died on the cross for them, and they would be initially confused when he died. Christ had not yet been resurrected from the tomb, and they would initially not understand that either. They would understand only when the Spirit would come.

That is why we have a great advantage over the disciples. We have the Spirit. We understand. We know. We experience. We taste. When the Spirit came, the disciples' love for Jesus was deepened and enriched: the Father and Jesus came to dwell with them in love. They would respond to that love with greater obedience.

That, too, is why the world is excluded. Outside the sphere or circle of keeping Christ's word, there is no knowledge of God's love in Christ. For the unbeliever there is no understanding of these things. For the impenitent person there is no experience of these things. We know this, for before we believed, we did not know this love; and when we walk in sin even as believers, our experience of this love is diminished. When we walk in obedience, we know the love of God in Christ. When we walk in sin, we do not know the love of God in Christ.

John came to understand this, for he writes, "If we say that we have fellowship with him, and walk in darkness, we lie, and do not the truth: but if we walk in the light, as he is in the light, we have fellowship one with another, and the blood of Jesus Christ his Son cleanseth us from all sin" (1 John 1:6–7). This does not mean that our fellowship with God in Christ is conditional. Nevertheless, one who walks in darkness *cannot* experience the blessing of fellowship with God, for God is holy and he does not dwell with the unholy. The holy, just God, who is pure, unsullied light, and in whom there is no darkness at all, dwells with believers who keep his commandments. Jesus is very clear on this point.

THE NECESSARY UNION

How is God's coming and making his abode with us possible? It is not because we keep his commandments, but it is made possible, indeed it actually occurs, because of Christ. First, it is possible because Christ is the living one: "Because I live, ye shall live also" (v. 19). Jesus does not say, "Because I shall live" (the future tense). The reference is not to the resurrection, but to the fact that he lives (the present tense), that is, he is the living one. In him is life and he is able to give life to others. In fact, Jesus declares in verse 6, "I am the way, the truth, and the life." Or John writes, "For the life was manifested, and we have seen it, and bear witness, and show unto you that eternal life, which was with the Father, and was manifested unto us" (1 John 1:2).

The life of which Jesus speaks here is the life of God, life with God, and life that consists of the knowledge of God and fellowship with God: "And this is life eternal, that they might know thee the only true God, and Jesus Christ, whom thou hast sent" (John 17:3). That life is described in verse 23: "We will come unto him, and make our abode with him." That is life, the only life worth living. Merely to exist in the world apart from that life is death, and to live without the blessing and favor of God is death and misery. "Because I live, ye shall live also."

Second, it is possible because of the intimate union between the Father and the Son. "At that day ye shall know that I am *in* my Father" (v. 20). The cross, the resurrection, and especially Pentecost shall make the union between the Father and the Son plain to the disciples. Jesus has a unique relationship with his Father. Without that relationship no salvation is possible for us. If Jesus is merely a creature, he cannot save us. If Jesus is an angel, he cannot save us.

Only if he is the Son of God, equal in glory to the Father and the Spirit, is his death on the cross of infinite value so that by it God is able to save us and does save us. That intimate union is expressed in verses 9–11: "He that hath seen me hath seen the Father." "I am in the Father, and the Father in me." "The Father that dwelleth in me, he doeth the works." "I am in the Father, and the Father in me."

Third, on the basis of Christ's life and on the basis of Christ's relationship with the Father, and on the basis of Christ's death on the cross, where life is purchased for us, we are joined in fellowship with him. "I am *in* my Father, and ye *in* me, and I *in* you" (v. 20). The Spirit unites us by a true faith to Jesus Christ. Therefore, we are in him, and because we are in him, the Father himself, who loves the Son, comes to us and makes his abode with us.

No wonder that Jesus urges his disciples not to be troubled in their hearts. No wonder that Jesus urges them to be comforted and to consider the great advantages in his departure to heaven for them. God will abide with us in the sphere of love, and that abiding with us is a foretaste of a greater abiding described in Revelation 21:3: "And I heard a great voice out of heaven saying, Behold, the tabernacle of God is with men, and he will dwell with them, and they shall be his people, and God himself shall be with them, and be their God."

Chapter 7

The Comforter's Teaching Ministry

(John 14:25–26)

25. These things have I spoken unto you, being yet present with you.
26. But the Comforter, which is the Holy Ghost, whom the Father will send in my name, he shall teach you all things, and bring all things to your remembrance, whatsoever I have said unto you.

In verse 25 Jesus transitions from what he taught the disciples when he was with them to what the Comforter will teach them when he departs from them. This is the second passage on the Holy Spirit in the upper room discourse, the first (vv. 16–18) being an introduction to the subject. We have learned already that the Comforter is a person who indwells the believer and who encourages, consoles, and strengthens the believer by applying the truth of Jesus Christ to his troubled soul; hence, he is called the Spirit of truth.

In this text Jesus recognizes the disciples' need for further instruction, which he will not be able to give them in person when he departs from them. The disciples were learners, which is the meaning of the word *disciple*. The disciples were also novices: they had barely begun to learn, and they were very dull students. Therefore, they would be thrown into turmoil when their teacher was taken from them. Nevertheless, they must not fear because not only does Jesus supply a Comforter, he also supplies a teacher, the very best teacher, the Holy Spirit. It is because of that teacher that the instruction of the disciples continues even after Jesus' death. Indeed, it is because of that teacher that the disciples grow by leaps and bounds in the knowledge of God, something that would not have occurred if Jesus had remained with them. This, too, is an advantage in Jesus' departure.

THE IDENTITY OF THE TEACHER

In verse 16 Jesus promised another Comforter, identifying the Comforter as the Spirit of truth in verse 17. Now in verse 26 he calls the Comforter the Holy Ghost, which is the Holy Spirit. The same Greek word (*pneuma*) underlies both translations, Spirit and Ghost. Our word *pneumatic* is derived from the Greek word *pneuma*. Pneumatic equipment, such as a pneumatic drill, operates by air under pressure. The word *pneuma* can be translated as breath or wind. Therefore, the Holy Ghost or Holy Spirit is the breath of God.

In John 3:8 Jesus says, "The wind [*pneuma*] bloweth where it listeth, and thou hearest the sound thereof, but canst not tell whence it cometh, and whither it goeth: so is every one that is born of the Spirit [*pneuma*]." In Ezekiel 37:9 the prophet is commanded, "Prophesy unto the wind, prophesy, son of man, and say to the wind, Thus saith the Lord GOD; Come from the four winds, O breath, and breathe upon these slain, that they may live." In that verse, wind and breath are translations of the same Hebrew word, the word commonly translated as spirit in the Old Testament. In John 20:22 we read, "And when he had said this, he breathed on them, and saith unto them, Receive ye the Holy Ghost." The Spirit, therefore, is the holy breath of God.

In the triune being of God, the Spirit is the breath of the Father to the Son and the breath of the Son to the Father. The Father breathes in love to the Son, while the Son breathes in love to the Father. The Spirit, therefore, is not a creature and not a mere emanation from God, but he is God. However, the Holy Spirit is unusual in this sense: the Spirit is personal, a person distinct from the Father and the Son. I maintain that this is unusual because we do not think of breath or wind as personal. Your breath is not personal. The wind that blows outside, whether a gentle breeze or a hurricane, is not personal. Yet the Bible compels us to view the Holy Spirit as a person. A person is a conscious and self-conscious individual who says "I." The Spirit is not a thing. The Spirit is not an "it." The Spirit says "I." The Spirit wills, thinks, purposes, and speaks.

We know that the Spirit is a person because of his activity. In verse 26 he performs two activities possible only of a person. First, he teaches. Impersonal breath or wind cannot teach. To teach, a person must have knowledge and understanding, which he imparts to another person. Second, the Spirit brings to remembrance or he reminds. Impersonal breath or wind cannot remind. To remind, a person must have knowledge and understanding, which he gives to another person. In addition, the Bible uses the masculine personal pronoun in verse 26: "*He* shall teach."

Therefore, do not be misled when you read the name *Spirit*. That name distinguishes the Spirit from the Father and the Son, but the Spirit is no less divine than the Father or the Son. The Spirit is not a creature but is divine. The Father is called Father because he begets the Son. The Son is called Son because he is begotten of the Father. The Spirit is called Spirit because he neither begets nor is begotten, but he proceeds, or is breathed forth, from the Father and the Son. Theologians call that the eternal procession of the Spirit, which is his personal property within the Godhead.

Moreover, Jesus calls the Comforter the Holy Ghost. That is something new: it is actually the first time that Jesus calls the Spirit the *Holy* Spirit (or Ghost) in this fourth gospel. The Spirit is holy because he is perfectly pure. There is no sin in the Holy Spirit. In fact, he hates all sin. But since the Father and the Son are also holy, there must be a reason why he is called the Holy Spirit. (Rarely is the Son called the Holy Son or the Father called the Holy Father, but the Spirit is very often called the Holy Spirit.)

Remember that holiness is consecration to God and that the

Holy Spirit is the consecration of the Father to the Son, and the Son to the Father, in the being of God. As the Father breathes the Spirit to the Son, and the Son breathes the Spirit to the Father, the three persons are eternally and unchangeably consecrated to one another in love. That is the blessed life of the Trinity, which God is pleased to reveal to us and even share with us when he loves us, comes to us, and makes his abode with us (v. 23). The Holy Spirit consecrates or devotes us to God when he breathes God's life into us through Jesus Christ, so that he separates us from sin and makes us holy, which is his work of sanctification. The holiness that we have, which is only a small, but victorious, beginning or principle, is the work of the Holy Spirit in us. When the Holy Spirit has finished his work of sanctification in us, we shall be perfectly holy in heaven.

Thus in John 14 we have already learned a number of important truths about the Holy Spirit. He is the Comforter, coming alongside us to help, to console, to encourage, and to strengthen us. He is the Spirit, for he is the breath of God, immaterial, not physical. He is personal, a conscious individual distinct from the Father and the Son, and divine. He is the Spirit of truth, bringing the truth and perfectly revealing Jesus Christ, who is the truth. He is the Holy Spirit, the one who sanctifies and consecrates us to God. Therefore, the biblical Holy Spirit is very different from the counterfeit spirit of charismaticism and Pentecostalism: he is not the jolly spirit, but the Holy Spirit. He is not the spirit of ecstatic feelings and experiences, but the Spirit of truth.

From the perspective of John 14:26 the coming of the Holy Spirit is still in the future. He will come fifty days after the resurrection of Jesus from the dead. When Jesus speaks these words, he is still with his disciples, contemplating the coming of his enemies to arrest him. Jesus is preparing for his trial before the Sanhedrin and the Roman governor. Jesus is thinking about the cross and, beyond that, of the three days in Joseph's tomb. Jesus is looking forward to his resurrection and ascension into heaven, all of which can be included under his departure. Then Pentecost shall come, when the

Holy Spirit shall finally be poured out upon the church: "The Comforter…he shall teach you all things" (v. 26).

These words are intended to encourage the disciples. Jesus was their teacher. For some three and a half years Jesus had taught them marvelous things. They had learned about the kingdom of heaven. Jesus had used parables, and he had even confirmed his teachings in miracles. Peter summed up the attitude of his disciples in John 6:68–69: "Lord, to whom shall we go? thou hast the words of eternal life. And we believe and are sure that thou art that Christ, the Son of the living God."

But if Jesus departs, who shall teach them? There was so much that they did not know. There was so much that they did not understand. Jesus had only scratched the surface of what they wanted to know and what they needed to know. Jesus says, "These things have I spoken unto you, being yet present with you" (v. 25). But soon their teacher would leave them, and then what would happen to them? Besides, Jesus expected the disciples to preach and teach after his departure. How would they do that without a teacher? How would they accomplish that without Jesus?

THE WORK OF THE TEACHER

Jesus reassures them that the teaching would continue, but the teaching would be different. Up until this point, the teaching was from the mouth of Jesus, face to face. "These things have I spoken unto you, being yet present with you" (v. 25). Later the teaching would be spiritual by the operation of the Holy Spirit within their hearts. Jesus would still teach them, but he would teach them through another teacher, an internal teacher, a spiritual teacher, and a teacher in their hearts and minds. "But the Comforter, which is the Holy Ghost… he shall teach you" (v. 26).

To teach is to impart knowledge. Usually, one who is taught or one who requires a teacher's instruction is ignorant. He needs a teacher to tell him truths that he does not yet know. He needs a teacher to explain truths that he does not yet understand.

Take a small child: He goes to school with very little knowledge. He cannot read, he cannot write, he cannot do mathematics, and he does not know about geography, history, or science. Therefore, he needs a teacher. A teacher helps him to learn. A teacher helps him to understand. Very few adults, and certainly no children, are able to learn without a teacher, for even if you learn by reading a book, someone wrote that book, and someone taught you to read so that you could benefit from such a book. A teacher is a very important influence in a child's life. Parents should be very careful about teachers: What are they teaching and how are they teaching the children? That is why Christian parents favor Christian schools or homeschooling where such Christian schools are not available. Impressionable young minds need godly instruction. Ungodly teachers corrupt the minds of the youth.

The teacher promised by Jesus is the ideal, the perfect teacher: he is the Holy Spirit, the Spirit of truth. The Holy Spirit teaches: he imparts knowledge to the mind. Jesus promises that he will do that for the disciples: "He shall teach you." The Holy Spirit begins his official teaching ministry on the day of Pentecost.

What does the Holy Spirit teach? Jesus says, "All things." Obviously, we cannot take the phrase "all things" absolutely. The Spirit does not teach chemistry, quantum physics, philosophy, and Shakespearean literature. He teaches the things of Christ, for Jesus explains that he shall "bring all things to your remembrance, *whatsoever I have said unto you*" (v. 26). There is a contrast between verse 25 ("These things have I spoken unto you") and verse 26 ("He shall teach you all things"). The contrast is between "these things" (which are some things) and "all things." But even then, we cannot expect the Spirit to teach "all things" absolutely about Jesus. He shall teach all things necessary to be known for faith and godliness. The Holy Spirit knows Jesus perfectly, and he will so teach us about Jesus that we will be comforted, strengthened, and equipped to serve him. The doctrine of the Holy Spirit concerning Jesus, when applied efficaciously through the work of the Spirit, will save our souls from sin and death. "Wherefore lay apart all filthiness and superfluity of naughtiness, and receive with meekness the engrafted word, which is able to save your souls" (James 1:21).

The Holy Spirit's teaching ministry was necessary because Jesus was preparing to depart. It was also necessary because of the disciples' ignorance. When you read through the gospels, you should be struck at the obvious ignorance of the disciples. By the end of Jesus' earthly ministry, the disciples had only a rudimentary understanding of the basics of Christianity. They had vague ideas about the identity of Jesus. They called him Christ, but they entertained wrong ideas about that important title. They viewed Christ, at least partly, as a political figure and as an earthly deliverer. They called him the Son of God, but his precise relationship to God was a mystery to them.

Three disciples in chapter 14 display their ignorance, which Jesus patiently attempts to remove. Consider his words to Philip in verse 9: "Have I been so long time with you, and yet hast thou not known me, Philip? he that hath seen me hath seen the Father; and how sayest thou then, Show us the Father?" The disciples were basically clueless about the mission and work of Jesus: they knew that he was a Savior, but they did not understand the cross or the resurrection. Even after it occurred, they could not comprehend those events, at least not until the Spirit came.

This ignorance is all the more inexcusable because Jesus had explained these things to them multiple times. In Mark 9:31–32 we read, "For he taught his disciples, and said unto them, The Son of man is delivered into the hands of men, and they shall kill him; and after that he is killed, he shall rise the third day. But they understood not that saying, and were afraid to ask him." In Matthew 16:21 we read, "From that time forth began Jesus to shew unto his disciples, how that he must go unto Jerusalem, and suffer many things of the elders and chief priests and scribes, and be killed, and be raised again the third day." What was Peter's reaction? "Then Peter took him, and began to rebuke him, saying, Be it far from thee, Lord: this shall not be unto thee" (v. 22).

Again, in Luke 18:34 we read, "And they understood none of these things: and this saying was hid from them, neither knew they the things which were spoken." Indeed, moments before the ascension of Jesus in Acts 1 the disciples were still clueless about the mission of Jesus. They ask in Acts 1:6, "Lord, wilt thou at this time restore again the kingdom to Israel?" Jesus does not even attempt to explain for the umpteenth time the spiritual nature of his kingdom, but simply instructs them to wait for the Holy Spirit to come upon them.

Now compare the ignorance of the disciples throughout the earthly ministry of Jesus with the knowledge, insight, and understanding of the same disciples in the book of Acts. Take only the example of Peter, who preached on the day of Pentecost. In that sermon he skillfully explains Joel 2, Psalm 16, and Psalm 110. In that sermon he expounds with astonishing depth the divine plan of the death of Jesus Christ. In that sermon he explains the purpose of the resurrection, ascension, and sitting at God's right hand. How can we account for that change? How can the same Peter preach in Acts 2 what he did not understand earlier?

Another example is Peter's sermon in Acts 3:18, where he declares, "But those things, which God before had shewed by the mouth of all his prophets, that Christ should suffer, he hath so fulfilled." Again Peter expertly exegetes and applies Psalm 118 to the confounding of the church's enemies in chapter 4:11: "This is the stone which was set at nought of you builders, which is become the head of the corner." Peter is also mighty in the Scriptures in the house of Cornelius the centurion: "To him give all the prophets witness, that through his name whosoever believeth in him shall receive remission of sins" (10:43). Finally, Peter defends his actions in Cornelius' house by recalling the words of Jesus, words that he had not understood earlier: "Then remembered I the word of the Lord, how that he said, John indeed baptized with water; but ye shall be baptized with the Holy Ghost" (11:16).

How did Peter understand in so short a time the truth concerning Jesus? He had not been reading books and he had not finished a course at seminary. The answer is that the Holy Spirit had taught him. The same thing is true of the other disciples, for the Holy Spirit taught them also. "But the Comforter, which is the Holy Ghost, whom the Father will send in my name, he shall teach you all things" (v. 26).

The Spirit teaches by applying the truth to the mind and especially to the memory: "He shall...bring all things to your remembrance, whatsoever I have said unto you" (v. 26). The disciples were with Jesus for three and a half years, but they did not take notes. No one had a recording device, and we all know how unreliable human memory is. Yet the disciples wrote the New Testament Scriptures. Matthew, John, and Peter, for example, were present to hear the words of Jesus in John 14–17. John records every word some years later. The other disciples, who did not write down the words of Jesus or contribute to the New Testament Scriptures, preached the gospel to many nations, and undoubtedly the Spirit brought many words to their remembrance when they preached the gospel to the ends of the earth. Others who were not present when Jesus spoke these words, men such as Paul, Luke, and Mark, came under the influence of the Holy Spirit, who brought these words to their minds, teaching them and reminding them. Thus, the Holy Spirit brought all things to their remembrance.

The result is a divinely inspired book, Old Testament and New Testament, which we call the Bible and which is the word of God. Paul explains in 2 Timothy 3:16, "All Scripture is given by inspiration of God," while Peter explains in 2 Peter 1:21, "Holy men of God spake as they were moved by the Holy Ghost." If that is true of the Old Testament Scriptures, it is equally true of the New Testament Scriptures.

Scripture includes many examples of this and testimonies to this. For instance, in John 2 Jesus spoke about "the temple of his body" (v. 21). John remarks, "When therefore he was risen from the dead, his disciples remembered that he had said this unto them; and they believed the scripture, and the word which Jesus had said" (v. 22). They remembered because the Spirit brought it to their remembrance. In chapter 12:16, when Jesus entered Jerusalem on a young donkey, John remarks, "These things understood not his disciples at the first: but when Jesus was glorified, then remembered they that these things were written of him, and that they had done these things unto him." The Holy Spirit brought the event and its significance to their remembrance.

This was comfort for the disciples. The Spirit would remind them. Not one word of Jesus would fall to the ground. Everything that must be remembered would be remembered. Everything that must be recorded would be recorded. The Bible therefore does not depend on the fallible memories of men but on the infallible, omniscient Holy Spirit for its composition.

There are also important applications for us, for although the Spirit does not work in our minds so that we infallibly know all things that Christ has taught, he does work in the hearts and minds of believers. He does not inspire us in the same way in which he inspired the apostles to write the New Testament Scriptures, but he does bring the truth to our remembrance too. That is his work as the Comforter. The Holy Spirit does not comfort us, or come alongside us to help us, by giving us nice feelings. He helps us by bringing the truth, for he is called the Spirit of truth. He helps us by teaching us the truth. He helps us by bringing the truth to our remembrance.

He does not do that in a vacuum, of course. The Christian who never reads the Scriptures and who never pays attention to the preaching of God's word should not expect the Holy Spirit to teach him or to bring Christ's words to his remembrance. Peter, John, and Matthew, for example, heard the words of Christ: the Spirit taught them and reminded them what they had heard. Mark and Luke spoke to people who had heard Christ, and the Spirit worked in their hearts to enable them to understand the words that they learned. Paul heard the words directly from Christ, for Jesus taught him and the Spirit worked in his heart. Paul writes about the Spirit's ministry in 1 Corinthians 2:12–13:

> 12. Now we have received, not the spirit of the world, but the spirit which is of God; that we might know the things that are freely given to us of God.

13. Which things also we speak, not in the words which man's wisdom teacheth, but which the Holy Ghost teacheth; comparing spiritual things with spiritual.

When we are distressed, we can ask for the Holy Spirit to bring comforting words to our remembrance. A mother stressed in the home will remember words that she read years ago or heard in a sermon months earlier: the Spirit brings truth to her remembrance. A Christian in grief will remember the comforting promises of the gospel, perhaps something she learned as a child. A Christian who is witnessing will recall the words of a text, which exactly suit the situation of his witness. A saint suffering in the hospital will remember the words of the gospel as the Holy Spirit works to comfort him. A saint in isolation, perhaps in prison, perhaps even deprived of a Bible, will experience the teaching ministry of the Holy Spirit.

Every child of God should trust God so to work by the Holy Spirit that he does not forget the precious truths of the gospel. The Holy Spirit's work is so mysterious that he works even in the hearts of saints whose minds and memories are seemingly destroyed. A Christian suffering from Alzheimer's disease, for example, is not beyond the power of the Holy Spirit, for such a believer still knows deep in his heart that he belongs to Jesus Christ. It is not a waste of time for a pastor to read the Scriptures to such a suffering saint, for the Spirit will apply them.

This promise is precious to the saints in persecution. Jesus speaks of this in Matthew 10:19–20: "But when they deliver you up, take no thought how or what ye shall speak: for it shall be given you in that same hour what ye shall speak. For it is not ye that speak, but the Spirit of your Father which speaketh in you." This does not mean, of course, that we become infallible, unthinking mouthpieces of the Holy Spirit, and that we should not, if given the opportunity to prepare a defense, prayerfully consider what we will say, but it forbids anxious fretting and commands quiet trust in God. The Spirit in those stressful times will not abandon God's children but will remind them of the words of the gospel, so that they might boldly confess the truth.

The Holy Spirit reminds us of God's love. The Holy Spirit reminds us of the cross of Jesus where our salvation is found. The Holy Spirit reminds us of the resurrection. The Holy Spirit comforts our hearts with these truths. What a wonderful gift is the Holy Spirit! In fact, the Holy Spirit teaches where Christ did not teach. Christ was not a poor teacher—do not misunderstand—but Christ did not reach the disciples' hearts. If a student is dull, even the best teacher will not reach his mind and heart. But the Spirit, unlike Christ, penetrates the recesses of the heart and mind. Or to express it more accurately, Christ, who while on earth did not penetrate the minds of his disciples, now teaches his disciples inwardly by the Holy Spirit. Never forget that the Holy Spirit does not work independently of Christ. In a very real sense, Christ continues to teach, but in a different manner by the Holy Spirit: "The former treatise have I made, O Theophilus, of all that Jesus *began* both to do and teach" (Acts 1:1).

THE COMING OF THE TEACHER

When Jesus speaks these words in John 14, the teacher has not yet come. His coming is intimately connected to the redemptive work of Jesus Christ, for the Father sends the Spirit "in [Christ's] name" (v. 26). In verse 16 we read that when Jesus prays to the Father, he shall give the Spirit. In verse 26 we read that the Father sends the Spirit, and that he does so in Christ's name.

Christ's name is the revelation of Christ, for in the Bible a name is the revelation of a person, of his person and work. The Spirit comes because of who Christ is and the Spirit comes because of what Christ has done. This explains the timing of the coming of the Holy Spirit. He did not come during Christ's earthly ministry because Christ's work was not yet complete. He did not come in the garden of Gethsemane. He did not come when Jesus was arrested. He did not come when Jesus stood before the Sanhedrin. He did not come when Jesus stood before Pilate. He did not come when Jesus hung on the cross. He did not come when Jesus gave up the ghost and died. He did not come when Jesus lay in the tomb. For three days, while Jesus lay dead in the tomb, the disciples were distraught, for Jesus was gone, and the Holy Spirit had not yet come to comfort them. Those three days constituted a terrible trial of the disciples' faith. Then came the resurrection. Jesus returned, but the Spirit did not yet come. Forty days later, Jesus ascended into heaven with the promise of the Spirit, but the Spirit did not yet come.

Finally, ten days later, Pentecost occurred and the Spirit came: "And when the day of Pentecost was fully come, they were all with one accord in one place…And they were all filled with the Holy Ghost" (Acts 2:1, 4). The Spirit came with power, he came with wisdom, and he came to teach, to remind, and to comfort. He came because salvation was accomplished. Atonement was made on the cross. Life was secured in the resurrection. The Spirit came to apply the work of Jesus Christ: he did so first in the disciples, and then he gathered many others into the church. He still works today. Where a sinner believes in Jesus Christ and turns from sin, you can be sure that the Spirit is working. He is teaching sinners about Jesus.

Chapter 8

Jesus' Bequest of Peace

(John 14:27)

> 27. Peace I leave with you, my peace I give unto you: not as the world giveth, give I unto you. Let not your heart be troubled, neither let it be afraid.

When a father is about to die, he gathers his children around his deathbed to exhort them, to express his love, and to give them a legacy. If he is a wealthy man, he may write a last will and testament in which he expresses how his property should be divided among his surviving relatives. The upper room discourse is like a deathbed exhortation except that the dying man is about to be crucified (not a comfortable deathbed by any standards) and he will rise again from the dead. Jesus, too, has a legacy to leave his "children," the disciples. He could say, as Peter later would, "Silver and gold have I none." Indeed, his last remaining possessions (his garments) will be divided among the soldiers who oversee his execution. What, then, can Jesus bequeath to his disciples?

In verse 26 Jesus promised his disciples the teaching ministry of the Holy Spirit. The Holy Spirit gives another gift too, which is really the bequest or legacy that Jesus leaves for his disciples. It is peace. "Peace I leave with you, my peace I give unto you" (v. 27). This promise of peace flows from and is based upon the promise of the previous text: the Holy Spirit, who teaches the gospel and applies it to the souls of God's people, gives peace. He gives Christ's peace, which he purchased for us on the cross, and he applies it to our souls.

What a rich legacy or bequest is this!

THE PROMISE OF PEACE

Peace is a state of the soul of one who is in a harmonious relationship with God. Peace is wholeness, completeness, safety, security, and tranquility. Peace is even blessedness and prosperity. One who has peace says, "It is well with my soul. God is not angry with me. My relationship with God is as it should be." That is peace.

In Scripture peace is a twofold blessing. First, there is objective peace. Objective peace is a fact regardless of how a person might feel. Objective peace is that harmonious relationship that exists between the believer and his God. It is the Christian's state of reconciliation and the forgiveness of his sins. Paul simply calls it peace with God: "Therefore being justified by faith, we have [objectively] peace with God through our Lord Jesus Christ" (Rom. 5:1). "But now in Christ Jesus ye who sometimes were far off are made nigh by the blood of Christ. For he [objectively] is our peace, who hath made both one, and hath broken down the middle wall of partition between us" (Eph. 2:13–14).

If God is at peace with us (if we have peace with God), we are perfectly safe for time and for eternity. God has nothing against us; instead, God is for us: "What shall we then say to these things? If God be for us, who can be against us?" (Rom. 8:31). That peace exists between God and the believer's soul regardless of the believer's circumstances. We call it objective peace.

Second, there is subjective peace. Subjective peace flows from objective peace, for it is the fruit of objective peace. Subjective peace is the conscious knowledge or experience of tranquility that the believer enjoys through faith. When a believer enjoys subjective peace, he knows that he has been reconciled to God, he knows that there is nothing between God and his soul, he knows that his sins have been forgiven, and that knowledge removes his fears and calms his soul. Paul calls it "the peace of God, which passeth all understanding, [that keeps] your hearts and minds through Christ Jesus" (Phil. 4:7).

Subjective peace ebbs and flows according to the exercise of faith, but objective peace never changes. If God is at peace with us, he will always be at peace with us, even if we sometimes experience an inner turmoil of heart.

In verse 27 Jesus promises peace to his disciples: "Peace I leave with you, my peace I give unto you." The word "my" that Jesus uses is emphatic: "*my* peace." Christ's peace is the perfectly harmonious relationship that he enjoys with his Father as the Son of God: it is both objective and subjective peace. This is true of the Son of God eternally. In Scripture, our heavenly Father is called the God of peace: "Now the God of peace be with you all. Amen" (Rom. 15:33). "And the God of peace shall bruise Satan under your feet shortly" (16:20). "And the God of peace shall be with you" (Phil. 4:9). The triune God—Father, Son, and Holy Spirit—lives a life of perfect peace, for within the being of God is not the slightest ripple of agitation, unrest, or confusion. There is no hint of disagreement, rivalry, or enmity between the persons of the Godhead. God is peace. God is at peace. Nothing disturbs his peace. The three persons of the Godhead delight in that peaceful relationship.

In addition, Christ Jesus as the incarnate Son of God in human flesh enjoyed unbroken fellowship, communion, and peace with his heavenly Father. That, too, belongs to Christ's peace in verse 27. The man Jesus of Nazareth enjoyed perfect fellowship with the triune God so that he prayed to him, delighted in him, loved him, and served him. God displayed this fellowship by declaring, "This is my beloved Son" (Matt. 3:17; 17:5). The disciples took note of the deep fellowship that Jesus enjoyed with God: they saw him praying, for example. The disciples even asked for instruction on how to pray as Jesus did (Luke 11:1). Jesus had peace with his heavenly Father.

Now Jesus promises to his disciples, "Peace I leave with you, my peace I give unto you." Jesus promises to establish a harmonious relationship between his disciples and God. He promises to establish harmony between God and all who believe in him. He promises to bring us into a relationship of perfect wholeness, completeness, safety, security, tranquility, blessedness, and spiritual prosperity. Jesus promises to establish a relationship between believers and the triune

God in which all is well with our souls, in which God is not angry with us, and in which our relationship with God is as it should be. In other words, Jesus promises that our relationship with God will be *the same as* his relationship with God, for we will taste of *Christ's own peace*. That is true both with respect to objective peace and with respect to subjective peace.

Jesus contrasts his promise of peace with the world's peace or, rather, with the world's lack of peace: "Not as the world giveth, give I unto you" (v. 27). Peace is something that the world wants and something that it needs, but something that it does not have, and therefore, although it claims to give it, peace is something that it cannot give. The world, of course, does not want peace in the true sense of the word. The world does not want Christ's peace. The world, which is the world of the ungodly, hates God and has no desire for peace with God. Instead, the world seeks peace without God.

However, the world has discovered that life without God, or life in enmity with God, has unpleasant consequences. If it could only escape those unpleasant consequences, the world would, it thinks, enjoy peace. Therefore, the world is full of people who long for peace of conscience, peace of mind, and peace in life. Nevertheless, the people of this world are plagued by fear, anxiety, and turmoil, and they do not even understand why. Scripture tells us why: "But the wicked are like the troubled sea, when it cannot rest, whose waters cast up mire and dirt. There is no peace, saith my God, to the wicked" (Isa. 57:20–21). God does not give peace to those who walk impenitently in sin.

The world lacked peace in Jesus' day. The great Roman Empire boasted of its *Pax romana*, or Roman peace. The *Pax romana* was a period of political stability from about 27 BC to AD 180, during which time commerce between nations flourished and prosperity increased. However, the *Pax romana* did not last, something that Jesus prophesied: "And ye shall hear of wars and rumours of wars: see that ye be not troubled: for all these things must come to pass, but the end is not yet" (Matt. 24:6). The source of Rome's peace was not the work of the grace of God in Jesus Christ. Instead, the *Pax romana* was an uneasy stability preserved by the edge of the sword. Roman soldiers created the *Pax romana* through the conquest of war and, since they enforced it by the threat of force, it was always in danger of fracturing.

Others in Jesus' day looked for peace not in the political stability of the Roman Empire but in religious observances. Heathen worshipers tried to please the gods and thus to obtain and to maintain peace in their souls, but their idolatry did not bring them peace, for the idolater is under the wrath of God.

In our day, too, the world seeks peace but finds peace elusive. The world labors for peace among people groups: peace between races, gender equality, peace between social classes, and peace between religions. We live in the age of the COEXIST bumper sticker and in the age of tolerance, yet people have never been more divided. Nations seek to interact peaceably: the EU, NATO, and UN attempt to secure peace. Nevertheless, the world maintains peace through the stockpiling of weapons and the ever-present threat of war.

On the individual level, people seek peace in medicine, in drugs, in recreation and entertainment, in various therapies, in special diets, in oils, and in a million other things. Yet there is an epidemic of anxiety and depression. Oh, the world offers peace and boasts of peace, but it cannot give it. The best that the world can offer is a temporary truce or an empty wish of peace. Peace or *shalom* was a common farewell greeting in Jesus' day, but no mere greeting bestows peace. "Peace I leave with you, my peace I give unto you: not as the world giveth, give I unto you" (v. 27).

The reason why the world cannot obtain, and cannot give, peace is that the world seeks peace without the forgiveness of sin. Or to put it differently, the world wants peace while it is at war with God. The world is God's enemy: the world system is his enemy, and every unbeliever in the world is at enmity with God. Therefore, God's wrath rests upon the world and upon every unbeliever in the world. Since the world is under God's wrath and condemnation, the world lacks peace. "The way of peace have they not known" (Rom. 3:17).

THE NEED FOR PEACE

The disciples needed peace and we need peace because they (and we) are sinners. In the beginning when God created the world, perfect peace reigned. The creation was in a perfectly harmonious relationship with God. This was true of all the creatures that God made: the heavenly bodies, the plants, the animals, and especially Adam and Eve, the first humans. "And God saw every thing that he had made, and, behold, it was very good" (Gen. 1:31). "The Father, by the Word, that is, by His Son, hath created of nothing the heaven, the earth, and all creatures as it seemed good unto Him, giving unto every creature its being, shape, form, and several offices to serve its Creator."[1] The world was at peace with God. This was especially true of Adam and Eve. They lived in a perfectly harmonious relationship with their Creator. They walked and talked with God in the cool of the day (Gen. 3:8). Nothing disturbed their harmony or their peace.

Then Adam rebelled against God in eating the forbidden fruit. Adam's sin was an act of war against God, and it was both wicked and foolish. It was wicked because it was an act of disobedience, for Adam violated God's law. It was foolish because only a fool shakes his fist in rebellion against the Almighty, for to make the holy, righteous God your enemy is surely the greatest folly imaginable.

When Adam committed that first sin, he drew the whole of mankind after him. Because of Adam's rebellion the whole human race became sinners: "Wherefore, as by one man sin entered into the world, and death by sin; and so death passed upon all men, for that all have sinned" (Rom. 5:12). The disciples were guilty in Adam and they were guilty of their own sins. We are in that position also: we are guilty in Adam and we are guilty of our own sins. How, then, can we have peace? On Adam's part and on our part all was lost. There was no way back to the peaceful fellowship that he had enjoyed with God, and indeed, Adam, having become God's enemy, had no desire to return.

---

1 Belgic Confession 12, in *Confessions and Church Order*, 33.

But God did not abandon his friends, Adam and Eve. God promised to restore peace by destroying Adam's pact with the devil. "And I will put enmity between thee and the woman, and between thy seed and her seed; it shall bruise thy head, and thou shalt bruise his heel" (Gen. 3:15). Throughout the Old Testament God promised peace to his chosen children. "For unto us a child is born, unto us a son is given: and the government shall be upon his shoulder: and his name shall be called Wonderful, Counsellor, The mighty God, The everlasting Father, The Prince of Peace" (Isa. 9:6). "And all thy children shall be taught of the LORD; and great shall be the peace of thy children" (54:13). Nevertheless, there can be no peace between the holy, righteous God and sinful, rebellious human beings. Therefore, God on his part promised to establish peace in his Son, and in his Son God satisfied his justice and displayed his mercy: "Peace I leave with you, my peace I give unto you: not as the world giveth, give I unto you."

The disciples also required peace because of the state of their hearts in John 14, for their hearts were troubled and afraid. Remember how the chapter began with the same exhortation, "Let not your heart be troubled" (v. 1). Now Jesus repeats it, "Let not your heart be troubled," and he adds, "Neither let it be afraid" (v. 27). The disciples' hearts were troubled. Deep in their spiritual center, the place of their thoughts, their plans, and their emotions, the disciples were in a state of confusion and turmoil. They were agitated and perplexed, and distress gripped the disciples' souls as they listened to Christ's words about his departure. They did not want their beloved Master to leave. They did not want their Lord to die. It did not make any sense to them. It seemed so counterproductive to have the Messiah suffer and die on the cross. It would not make sense to them until the Comforter, who is also the teacher, came.

In addition, the disciples were afraid. The word for "afraid" expresses their cowardice or timidity. It is fear or lack of courage in the face of danger, which brings with it the grave temptation to compromise and to sin in order to avoid suffering for the truth. Such cowardice caused them to flee when Jesus was arrested in the garden of Gethsemane (Matt. 26:56), and it caused Peter to deny Jesus three times (v. 74). Jesus had rebuked his disciples for that kind of cowardly fear in Matthew 8:26 when they had been terrified in a storm: "Why are ye fearful, O ye of little faith?" Paul writes, "God hath not given us the spirit of fear; but of power, and of love, and of a sound mind" (2 Tim. 1:7). Among those who perish in Revelation 21:8 are "the fearful, and unbelieving" (they are too cowardly to stand for the truth when persecution comes).

The cure for a troubled and fearful heart is peace: "Peace I leave with you, my peace I give unto you: not as the world giveth, give I unto you. Let not your heart be troubled, neither let it be afraid" (v. 27). Peace comes through a consideration of God's objective peace in Christ. When we lack that serenity of soul that we desire, we remember that Jesus has established peace between God in heaven and our souls. We remember that the holy, righteous God, who hates all wickedness and punishes all sin, is at peace with us, for our sins and iniquities he remembers no more. God has nothing against us, but he is for us. When we grasp that idea with our hearts and minds, the peace of God that passes all understanding keeps or guards our hearts and minds through Christ Jesus.

Peace comes also as God's subjective peace flows through us as the fruit of faith. Remember that one aspect of the fruit of the Spirit in Galatians 5:22 is peace. The knowledge of that perfectly harmonious relationship between God and our souls calms our fears, strengthens our hearts, and cheers us. Christ speaks to his anxious and frightened people in the midst of their trials. You have lost a loved one. Peace I leave with you. You are facing illness or even death. My peace I give unto you. Your family life is in turmoil. Peace I leave with you. You are worried about the future. My peace I give unto you. You are in the midst of persecution. "Peace I leave with you, my peace I give unto you: not as the world giveth, give I unto you. Let not your heart be troubled, neither let it be afraid."

Finally, notice how the upper room discourse ends: "These

things I have spoken unto you, that in me ye might have peace. In the world ye shall have tribulation: but be of good cheer; I have overcome the world" (John 16:33). The peace of Jesus continues even when the world persecutes us. The Christian in persecution can be robbed of every earthly possession, and even of life itself, but he cannot be robbed of Christ's wonderful peace.

THE OBTAINING OF PEACE

Peace is the gift that Jesus leaves for his disciples: "Peace I leave with you" (v. 27). He leaves it behind after he leaves. In other words, the very thing that the disciples feared, his departure, is the means by which he procures or obtains for them the gift of peace. To obtain peace for us, Jesus gave up the peace that he enjoyed with his Father. When Jesus procured uninterrupted peace with God for us, the peace he enjoyed with God was interrupted.

We see how the peace of Jesus was interrupted in his sufferings and death. Jesus began to have a foretaste of the interruption of his peace in John 12:27: "Now is my soul troubled; and what shall I say? Father, save me from this hour: but for this cause came I unto this hour." In Gethsemane Jesus' peace was greatly disturbed, for he "began to be sorrowful and very heavy" (Matt. 26:37), and "[his] soul [was] exceeding sorrowful, even unto death" (v. 38). "Being in an agony he prayed more earnestly: and his sweat was as it were great drops of blood falling down to the ground" (Luke 22:44). The Son of God in his human body and soul experienced great stress.

The peace of Jesus was shattered on the cross. Throughout his life Jesus had enjoyed, and been conscious of, close fellowship with his Father, but on the cross that fellowship (or at least a sense of that fellowship, for words fail us) ended. In the terrible darkness of Calvary Jesus cried out with anguish of soul, "My God, my God, why hast thou forsaken me?" (Matt. 27:46). Jesus had no sense of that harmonious relationship between God and his soul, for as he tasted God's wrath, God seemed to be against him. All was not well with his soul: the wholeness, completeness, safety, security, tranquility, blessedness, and prosperity disappeared. Who can understand what that meant for the Son of God?

God withdrew his peace from Jesus because Jesus was at that point under his wrath and curse. God viewed Jesus legally at that point as guilty of the sins of his disciples. Therefore, Jesus became the object of God's wrath, curse, and condemnation. That explains the darkness of Calvary and it explains Christ's sense of abandonment. Jesus bore our sins in his own body and soul on the cross. For one who is legally guilty of all the sins of all the elect there is no peace.

Then having made full satisfaction for our sins, Jesus regained the peace of God for himself and, crucially, for us. God's face began to shine upon Jesus again, especially when he vindicated him in the resurrection, so that God's face shines also upon us. That is why Isaiah writes, "But he was wounded for our transgressions, he was bruised for our iniquities: the chastisement of our peace was upon him; and with his stripes we are healed" (Isa. 53:5). The punishment that God inflicted on Christ, and that Christ willingly bore, is the source of our peace. Our sins make peace with God impossible. Therefore, Jesus took our sins, bore the punishment, and purchased for us peace with God for time and for eternity.

Jesus says to us, "Peace I leave with you, peace that I purchased on the cross. Peace I give unto you, peace that I wrestled from the jaws of death. Not as the world giveth, give I unto you. The world has no peace to give, and it will persecute you who have my peace. Let not your heart be troubled, neither let it be afraid."

Chapter 9

Jesus' Parting Determinations

(John 14:28–31)

28. Ye have heard how I said unto you, I go away, and come again unto you. If ye loved me, ye would rejoice, because I said, I go unto the Father: for my Father is greater than I.
29. And now I have told you before it come to pass, that, when it is come to pass, ye might believe.
30. Hereafter I will not talk much with you: for the prince of this world cometh, and hath nothing in me.
31. But that the world may know that I love the Father; and as the Father gave me commandment, even so I do. Arise, let us go hence.

The theme of John 14 is Jesus' departure and especially the advantages that come to us from that departure. The subject was already raised in chapter 13 to the consternation of the disciples. He begins chapter 14 with that theme in verse 2, "I go." In verse 3 he repeats it: "If I go." In verse 4 he restates it: "Whither I go ye know." This truth of Jesus' departure is the reason for the disciples' troubled hearts. Therefore, Jesus spends the whole chapter comforting the disciples concerning his dreaded departure. For the disciples, Jesus' departure seems to be a disaster: they cannot think of a worse thing than this. Jesus is going away. Jesus will die. Jesus will be crucified. What does this mean? Why is this necessary? How will Jesus return? These questions trouble the disciples' hearts.

To soothe their hearts, Jesus explains the advantages that they will enjoy in his departure. Have you been keeping a tally? Jesus will prepare a place for the disciples in the Father's house of many mansions. Jesus is the way to the Father because he is the way, the truth, and the life, and he who has seen him has also seen the Father. The disciples will do greater things than Jesus has done because Jesus goes to the Father and will answer prayers in his name. In response to Jesus' prayer the Father will send another Comforter, who is the Holy Spirit. By virtue of the Spirit the disciples will experience the Father's love and fellowship in a deeper, richer way, as Christ and his Father make their abode with them. The Spirit will teach them all things, and they will enjoy perfect peace.

These advantages we enjoy also, exactly because Jesus went to the Father by means of his death, resurrection, and ascension into heaven. Now as this chapter comes to a close he returns to that point: "Ye have heard how I said unto you, I go away, and come again unto you" (v. 28). Jesus is determined to go away. His mind is set on his departure, and nothing will dissuade him from it. In Luke 9:51, "He stedfastly set his face to go to Jerusalem." Now he sets his face steadfastly to go to his Father.

DETERMINED TO DEMONSTRATE HIS LOVE

It is quite astounding that Christ on the night of his betrayal and arrest and on the eve of his death did not care about himself. One word describes Christ: selfless. Two great concerns occupied his mind and heart: his disciples' welfare and his Father's glory. His own comfort, his own convenience, and his own pleasure did not concern him at all. Christ's great concern, as expressed in verse 31, is "that the world may know that I love the Father." Jesus intended his death to be a demonstration of his love for his Father. Jesus intended it to be such a demonstration that even the hostile, wicked world would be unable to deny it. When Jesus was crucified, the world would have to admit, whether they wanted to or not, that Jesus loved the Father. The cross, of course, is a demonstration of love, pure, sacrificial, selfless love.

It is a demonstration of God's love for poor sinners. "But God commendeth his love toward us, in that, while we were yet sinners,

Christ died for us" (Rom. 5:8). The triune God, the Father, Son, and Holy Spirit, gave Jesus of Nazareth to the death of the cross because he loved us. "Herein is love, not that we loved God, but that he loved us, and sent his Son to be the propitiation for our sins" (1 John 4:10). God loved us, who are poor sinners, so much that instead of punishing us for our sins, he punished a willing substitute, his own, only begotten, dearly beloved Son, Jesus, in our place.

The cross is also a demonstration of Christ's love for poor sinners. "The life which I now live in the flesh I live by the faith of the Son of God, who loved me, and gave himself for me" (Gal. 2:20). "Greater love hath no man than this, that a man lay down his life for his friends" (John 15:13). Christ loved us so much that, rather than we should perish, he willingly assumed our guilt and endured the punishment of our sins in our place.

Further, the cross is a demonstration of Christ's love for the Father. Jesus Christ loves the triune God, his Father. He loved the Father by submitting to the Father's will, and he fully understood what the Father's will was for him. He must be born in lowly circumstances, he must suffer his whole life, and at the end of his life he must be betrayed, denied, arrested, beaten, spat upon, condemned, scourged, crucified, mocked, and finally die. Because he loved the Father, he was willing to endure that: he was willing to suffer in the worst possible way to accomplish the salvation that his Father had determined for the church. God loved us so much that he gave Jesus Christ for our salvation. Jesus Christ loved us so much that he gave his life for us on the cross. Jesus Christ loved the Father so much that he willingly died in our place. "But that the world may know that I love the Father" (v. 31).

What is Jesus Christ's love for the Father? Love, we know, is a deep affection for someone, a desire for that person's good, and a desire to establish a bond with that person. Christ's love for the Father is primarily this: a determination to glorify him or a desire to display the perfections of God's character so that God is praised and honored. The world would soon see Jesus' love for the Father.

The world would see Jesus stand before the Sanhedrin without complaint, not opening his mouth in his own defense. The world would hear Jesus confess his Father before a hostile audience. The world would see Jesus submit to the authority of Pontius Pilate. The world would watch Jesus passing through the streets of Jerusalem with a cross upon his back. The world would hear him pray, "Father, forgive them; for they know not what they do" (Luke 23:34). The world would hear him say to the dying thief, "Verily I say unto thee, To day shalt thou be with me in paradise" (v. 43). The world would see him giving up the ghost.

Through these things the world would know that Jesus Christ loves the Father. In Luke 23:48 we read of the world's reaction: "And all the people that came together to that sight, beholding the things which were done, smote their breasts, and returned." The centurion who oversaw the execution of Jesus would say, "Truly this was the Son of God" (Matt. 27:54) and "Certainly this was a righteous man" (Luke 23:47). These were simply representatives of the world.

Even today the world knows that the cross of Christ is a demonstration that Christ loved the Father. Wherever the gospel is known, people know that in the cross Christ loved the Father. On the last day when the world stands in judgment, they will see Christ and they will know and confess, among other things, that Christ, in dying on the cross for his people, loved the Father.

Moreover, Christ's love for the Father is demonstrated in his obedience. In verse 31 he says, "And as the Father gave me commandment, even so I do." The whole life of Jesus can be summed up in one word: obedience. In obedience to the Father he became incarnate. In obedience to the Father he preached the gospel of the kingdom. In obedience to the Father he performed miracles. In obedience to the Father he endured the suffering of death.

Toward the end of his life Jesus is determined to complete his obedience to the Father. That obedience will be the most difficult obedience he has ever rendered. That obedience will cost him his life. In Psalm 40 we read of this obedience, "Lo, I come: in the volume of the book it is written of me, I delight to do thy will, O my God: yea, thy law is within my heart" (vv. 7–8). Paul writes of Christ's obedience in Romans 5:19: "For as by one man's disobedience many were made sinners, so by the obedience of one shall many be made righteous." In John 10:18 Christ also spoke of this obedience: "No man taketh it [my life] from me, but I lay it down of myself. I have power to lay it down, and I have power to take it again. This commandment have I received of my Father."

This commandment I have received of my Father! The sufferings and death of Christ are not tragic. They are not accidental. The death of Christ is not a defeat. The death of Christ is deliberate, planned, purposed, purposeful, necessary, and victorious. The death of Christ is obedience. The death of Christ as obedience is pleasing to God. The death of Christ is an acceptable offering to the Father. Christ offered the sacrifice of his life in love to the Father: "And walk in love, as Christ also hath loved us, and hath given himself for us an offering and a sacrifice to God for a sweetsmelling savour" (Eph. 5:2).

It is one thing to love God with the whole heart, soul, mind, and strength by keeping his commandments. Jesus did that throughout his life. It is quite another and altogether greater expression of obedience to continue to love God with the whole heart, soul, mind, and strength when one is under God's wrath and curse. Jesus was determined to do that also. When God poured his wrath upon Jesus, Jesus still loved his Father. When Jesus sank deeper and deeper under the billows of God's wrath, Jesus still loved the Father. When Jesus was so deeply under God's curse that he had no consciousness of God's love for him, he loved the Father still. When the Father pressed the cup of his wrath to Jesus' lips and made him drink every last drop, Jesus still loved his Father.

Jesus tells the disciples this. He forewarns them, lest they should be confused: "And now I have told you before it come to pass, that, when it is come to pass, ye might believe" (v. 29). When Judas comes to betray Jesus with a kiss, they must not fear. When the soldiers arrest Jesus, they must not lose heart. When Jesus refuses to defend himself, they must not misunderstand. It is not that Jesus lacks power, but that he is determined to obey the Father. Jesus could have prevented his arrest in the garden. Jesus could have escaped at any time. Jesus could even have come down from the cross, but he loved his Father, and the world must know that he loves the Father.

We must love the Father too, and we must demonstrate our love for the Father. Our love for the Father must be obvious, so obvious that the world sees it. What does the world see in your life? Does obedience characterize your life? Does devotion to God characterize your life? Does selfless devotion to your fellow saints characterize your life? In John 13:35 Jesus said, "By this shall all men know that ye are my disciples, if ye have love one to another." How do you treat your wife? Is it in selfless love? How do you treat your husband? Is it in selfless love? How do you treat your children, parents, and siblings? Is it in selfless love? How do you live in fellowship with God's people in the church? Is it in selfless love? How do you live with suffering? Is it by humbling yourself under God's mighty hand, by exercising patience, and by loving the God who brings you through such afflictions?

If Jesus was determined to demonstrate his love to the Father in his suffering and death, we must be determined to demonstrate our love too. Love is not only about flowers and chocolates, although there is an important place, especially in marriage, for such displays of affection. Love is displayed in selfless, sacrificial service. Love is a wife wiping her husband's brow while he suffers a raging fever, or spoon-feeding him after he has lost his faculties because of a stroke. Love is a husband visiting his wife who has Alzheimer's disease, even though she no longer recognizes him, because he desires to be with her. Supreme love, infinitely greater love than we have ever been able to display, is our Savior shedding his precious blood for our salvation.

DETERMINED TO ENGAGE THE ENEMY

As Christ contemplates demonstrating his love for the Father, his thoughts turn to a very different person, the devil, Satan, or as verse 30 calls him, "the prince of this world." "Hereafter I will not talk much with you: for the prince of this world cometh, and hath nothing in me" (v. 30). The prince of this world is the devil or Satan. In John 12:31 Jesus says, "Now is the judgment of this world: now shall the prince of this world be cast out." In Matthew 12:24 Satan is named "Beelzebub the prince of the devils." Jesus also calls him a "strong man," although Jesus is stronger than he (v. 29). In Ephesians 2:2 Paul calls Satan "the prince of the power of the air," while in 2 Corinthians 4:4 the designation is "the god of this world" who has blinded the minds of unbelievers. Finally, in the book of Revelation Satan is called "a great red dragon" (12:3), "that old serpent" (v. 9), and "the Devil" (v. 9).

Satan is the prince of this world because of his great power. We should not underestimate his power. The whole world has been sold into his power because of sin. John writes, "The whole world lieth in wickedness" (1 John 5:19). It is not for nothing that Jesus commands us to pray, "And lead us not into temptation, but deliver us from evil [or from the evil one]" (Matt. 6:13). That the world is the principality of Satan does not deny the sovereignty of God, however, for God is the one who has judged or punished men by delivering them into the power of Satan. That is man's great misery: because of sin he is, in the judgment of God, under the power of the evil one, and he is bound with the chains of corruption to sin. We, too, by nature suffer the same misery: slaves of sin, slaves of Satan, and bound over to death. Thankfully, we have been regenerated so that sin has no more dominion over us.

Nevertheless, Satan's principality is temporary, for Jesus by his death on the cross delivers us from the principality of Satan. Jesus wrests the world from Satan's grasp, for while Satan is prince only of this world, Jesus is the eternal king of God's kingdom. Satan's principality crashes and burns. "For this purpose the Son of God was manifested, that he might destroy the works of the devil" (1 John 3:8).

As Jesus speaks these words, Satan is marshaling his forces. Jesus demonstrates knowledge of Satan's movements: "The prince of this world cometh" (v. 30). Jesus uses the present tense. He sees Satan amassing his pieces: on Satan's side are Judas Iscariot, the chief priests, Annas and Caiaphas, a multitude of soldiers from the chief priests, Pontius Pilate, and the Roman soldiers. On Jesus' side is no one, for he must face Satan alone. Judas will betray him. Peter will deny him. The disciples will abandon him. The people will turn against him crying, "Crucify him." Later Jesus says, "Behold, the hour cometh, yea, is now come, that ye shall be scattered, every man to his own, and shall leave me alone: and yet I am not alone, because the Father is with me" (John 16:32). The time will come when not even the Father shall be with him, when he shall cry out in the agony of his soul, "My God, my God, why hast thou forsaken me?"

Jesus recognizes the Satanic influence in his enemies. In John 13:26–27 we learn, "And when he had dipped the sop, he gave it to Judas Iscariot, the son of Simon. And after the sop Satan entered into him. Then said Jesus unto him, That thou doest, do quickly." In Luke 22:52–53 he asks those who came to arrest him, "Be ye come out, as against a thief, with swords and staves? When I was daily with you in the temple, ye stretched forth no hands against me: but this is your hour, and the power of darkness."

What does Jesus say to this? Does he cower in fear? Does he attempt to avoid a confrontation with Satan? Not at all, but he willingly engages the enemy, and he is confident of victory. Satan comes with intense hatred against the Son of God, with the enmity of the serpent, with great cunning, and with great power. Satan had engaged Jesus in battle before, especially in the wilderness, where three times Satan had attempted to lure him into sin against the Father. Three times Jesus had declared, "It is written" (Matt. 4:4, 7, 10). Satan had left Jesus, but he returned on different occasions to tempt Jesus again.

Now Satan was coming with reinforcements. Now he would bring Jesus before the Sanhedrin and Pilate. Surely the threat of the cross, the awful cup of God's wrath, would deter Jesus from the path of obedience! Jesus reassures his disciples: "The prince of this world cometh, and hath nothing in me" (v. 30). This is a reference to Christ's innocence, righteousness, and perfect holiness. Satan has nothing in him. Satan cannot lodge an accusation against Jesus. Satan cannot find a weak point in Jesus. Jesus has no sinful nature that would be attracted to sin. Jesus is impervious to Satan's temptation. Cunning will not overcome him. Threats will not frighten him. Violence will not move him. Satan has nothing in him.

Satan had met his match in Jesus. He was able to tempt Eve to eat the forbidden fruit, but Jesus would not yield to temptation. He was able to tempt Noah to become drunk, but Jesus retained his sobriety. He was able to tempt Abraham to lie, David to commit adultery, Solomon to worship idols, and Peter to deny Jesus, but Jesus remained faithful. Even when Jesus lay under the wrath of God on the cross, Satan could not convince him to come down from the cross, he could not convince him to save himself, and he could not convince him to curse God. The full fury of hell could not turn Jesus from the path of obedience.

What comfort for the disciples! Jesus will be victorious where the disciples fail. Jesus is victorious where we fail. Jesus will not shrink back, he will not refuse to go to the cross, and he will not try to escape from the cross, because he loves the Father, he loves us, and he opposes Satan. Jesus says in John 12:27–28, "Now is my soul troubled; and what shall I say? Father, save me from this hour: but for this cause came I unto this hour. Father, glorify thy name." Jesus prays in chapter 17:1: "Father, the hour is come; glorify thy Son, that thy Son also may glorify thee."

We, too, can face Satan with confidence. While it is not true that Satan has nothing in us—he finds all kinds of sin in us, and he finds the propensity to sin in us, for we have a totally depraved flesh—yet because of Christ's atonement and because of Christ's justifying righteousness, he cannot accuse us.

"Who shall lay any thing to the charge of God's elect? It is God that justifieth. Who is he that condemneth? It is Christ that died, yea rather, that is risen again, who is even at the right hand of God, who also maketh intercession for us" (Rom. 8:33–34).

The devil can tempt us, he can even make us yield, but we can stand against him in the power of Christ. We have the armor of God (Eph. 6:10–18). Peter describes the devil as a roaring lion, but he also says, "Whom resist stedfast in the faith" (1 Pet. 5:9). And James writes, "Resist the devil, and he will flee from you" (James 4:7). Oh yes, as the footsteps of Judas and his companions approached, the devil was coming for Jesus, but Jesus was willing to engage him, and the devil had nothing in him. Jesus would soon prove to be victorious over the devil, the prince of this world.

DETERMINED TO GO TO THE FATHER

As the chapter comes to a close, you can almost sense the impatience in Jesus' words. It is not a sinful impatience, of course, but an expression of his eagerness to go home. "Ye have heard," he says in verse 28, "how I said unto you, I go away, and come again unto you." Jesus is determined, even keen, to go to the Father, and he rebukes the disciples for not sharing his enthusiasm. In verse 28 he says, "If ye loved me, ye would rejoice." Jesus does not deny their love for him. Clearly, they do love him. They love him dearly. Their love for him is the reason why their hearts are breaking. Yet their love for him is mixed with sin. Love is selfless, but their love is tainted with selfishness. They are concerned about how Jesus' departure will affect them, but they are not so concerned about how Jesus' departure will benefit him. How different is his attitude! He is concerned with showing them how his departure will benefit them and less concerned about how his departure will benefit him.

Therefore, Jesus rebukes his disciples (I paraphrase): "If ye truly loved me with a selfless love unmixed with selfish, self-seeking motives, you would rejoice. If you truly cared about my glory, you would rejoice. If you were truly concerned about my exaltation, instead of obsessing merely about my sufferings and death, you would be thrilled for me."

Jesus saw beyond the cross to his resurrection, ascension, and sitting at God's right hand. He prays in John 17:5, "And now, O

Father, glorify thou me with thine own self with the glory which I had with thee before the world was." Or consider Hebrews 12:2: "Looking unto Jesus the author and finisher of our faith; who for the joy that was set before him endured the cross, despising the shame, and is set down at the right hand of the throne of God." Jesus had an eye on the prize: glory with the Father, and not only that, but also glorification in the Father's presence for us. Therefore, the disciples should have rejoiced, but they did not. They would rejoice later when they would understand, but at this point they did not yet understand. Their hearts were troubled. They were afraid. They did not rejoice.

Jesus gives a reason why they should rejoice. "Ye would rejoice, because I said, I go unto the Father: for my Father is greater than I" (v. 28). Jesus' departure was not ultimately into the hands of Judas Iscariot, or the Sanhedrin, or Pontius Pilate, or the Romans, or even into the clutches of Satan. Jesus' departure was *to the Father,* and "My Father," says Jesus, "is greater than I."

Much ink has been spilled on these words. Is Jesus denying his equality with God? Is he saying, "The Father is God, but I am a mere creature, an angel or an archangel, but not truly divine"? He has already declared in the same chapter, "I am in the Father, and the Father in me" (v. 10), and "He that hath seen me hath seen the Father" (v. 9). Why would he then deny his equality with the Father? Why throw such a statement into his farewell address? What purpose would it serve?

No, the meaning is simply this: the disciples should rejoice that Jesus is going to the Father because his Father is in a greater position than he was. The Father, says Jesus, is greatly exalted in heavenly splendor, but I am in a state of humiliation. The Father is beyond all suffering and death as the perfectly blessed God, but I am about to enter the depths of death and hell on the cross. The Father sits on his throne above, but I suffer on the earth below. Therefore, Jesus looked forward to returning to him, for when he returned, he would enjoy great glory, perfect bliss, and heavenly splendor. The disciples should also have been joyful because when Jesus returned to the Father to enjoy that glory, splendor, and bliss, he would prepare a place for them.

Does it not give you joy to know that Jesus is now in heaven? Does it not give you delight to contemplate him in his glory? Does it not thrill your soul to consider his work as finished? It should, for you should rejoice in him and for him. Jesus is now in the presence of his Father. The Son of God is in the Father's bosom. The incarnate Mediator is on the Father's throne.

When all things are ready, he will call you home. Then you will see him. Then you will rejoice. Then you will enter into his joy. That joy is yours because Jesus was determined to demonstrate his love for his Father by his death on the cross. That joy is yours because Jesus was determined to engage with Satan and to defeat him. That joy is yours because Jesus was determined to return to the Father by the sufferings and death of the cross. O glorious departure of Jesus!

PART TWO

Spiritual Fellowship with Jesus Christ

Chapter 10

The True Vine and Its Branches

(John 15:1–3)

1. I am the true vine, and my Father is the husbandman.
2. Every branch in me that beareth not fruit he taketh away: and every branch that beareth fruit, he purgeth it, that it may bring forth more fruit.
3. Now ye are clean through the word which I have spoken unto you.

If the theme of John 14 was "The Disciples' Advantage in Jesus' Departure," the theme of John 15 is "Spiritual Fellowship with Jesus Christ." Jesus describes that fellowship by using a figure, an extended metaphor or a parable. The figure is of a vine and its branches. In verse 1 Jesus declares, "I am the true vine, and my Father is the husbandman," and in verse 5 he explains, "I am the vine, ye are the branches." The meaning is clear: as a branch derives its physical life by drawing the sap from the vine, so the disciples derive spiritual life from Jesus Christ through faith in him.

In verse 9 Christ drops the figure and speaks more plainly about the calling of his disciples to bear fruit, that is, good works, in union with him. While it is impossible for the unbeliever to bear fruit, since the unbeliever is not united to Jesus Christ by faith, it is not only possible but required that believers bear the fruit of good works by the power of God's grace in them. In fact, the fruit of good works performed in obedience to God's commandments out of thankfulness to him is the outstanding evidence that a person is, in fact, united to Jesus Christ. Fruitless men and women, that is, people devoid of good works, are not, and may not consider themselves to be, true believers. This fruit of good works done out of love for Jesus Christ also distinguishes true disciples from the world, which hates believers because they have been chosen out of the world to bear fruit to the glory of God. Therefore, Jesus warns the disciples, especially toward the end of this chapter, about the world's cruel and inexcusable hatred.

Many scholars have tried to guess why Jesus chooses this figure at this time. Some point to the words of John 14:31, "Arise, let us go hence." Perhaps Jesus and the disciples left the upper room at that point and walked through a vineyard, but it is also possible that Jesus remained in the upper room: his words do not necessarily mean that he left the room. Others suggest that the sacrament of the Lord's supper, not mentioned in John's account but described in the synoptic gospels of Matthew, Mark, and Luke, with its fruit of the vine, is the occasion for the figure being used.

Our Lord is speaking figuratively in a kind of parable, and a parable has one or two main ideas, while the rest of the figure is incidental to the main point. Therefore, we would be mistaken if we pushed the figure too far. We must also bear in mind Jesus' purpose in these words: it is to comfort and encourage his disciples. Too many sincere Christians have found themselves discouraged and even terrified by these words, as if they constituted a threat to them. That, too, is a grave error: while fruitless professors must be warned, there is rich comfort for the child of God, for in union with Jesus Christ the true believer will bring forth fruit to the Father's glory. If we find the text discouraging, so that it destroys our assurance, we have surely misinterpreted it, for Jesus designs to strengthen his disciples' assurance, not to destroy it.

Finally, Jesus does not pluck the figure of a vine from his own imagination, but he finds it in the rich heritage of the Old Testament. In the Old Testament the vine spoke of one great reality: the calling of Israel to bear fruit unto God's glory. Israel had failed to do this, and God was ready to cut Israel down. Out of the roots of a ruined vine Jesus springs forth as the true vine, and all those who are in Jesus the true vine shall bear fruit through vital union with him.

THE FATHER'S BELOVED VINE

A vine is a living organism whose one function is to bear fruit. There are three ideas to an organism, in this case a vine.

First, an organism is a living thing, a living entity, or a living system. A machine such as the engine of a car is made up of interdependent parts, but it is not an organism because it is not alive. The human body is an organism, animals are organisms, and plants are organisms, because these things are alive. They have life flowing through them. A vine is an organism: it lives, it grows, it produces fruit, it is alive.

Second, an organism is made up of interdependent parts. An organism is not one part. A finger is not an organism, a cat's tail is not an organism, and a branch is not an organism. The finger is part of an organism, while the whole body is the organism. The cat's tail is part of an organism, while the whole cat is the organism. The branch is part of an organism, while the whole vine is the organism. A vine is an organism, for it is made up of parts (the roots, the stem, the branches, and the leaves) and it is alive.

Third, an organism has one life or vital energy on which the entire organism depends and out of which the entire organism lives, is nourished, and grows. If you examine the human body and ask, "Where is the life?" the answer is that the life is in every part. If you observe a cat and ask, "Where is the life?" the answer is that the life is in every part. If you study a vine and ask, "Where is the life?" the answer is that the life is in every part. Cut off a finger or remove a non-vital organ and that body part dies, but the body, the organism, continues to live. Cut off the cat's tail and the tail dies, but the cat continues to live. Cut off a piece of the root or a leaf or even a whole branch and the root, or the leaf, or the branch dies, but the plant continues to live. You cannot say about a vine that the life is only in the roots, only in the stem, or only in the leaf. Instead, life permeates the entire organism, and every part lives out of that one life. That one principle of life nourishes the whole thing, every branch lives by the life of that vine, and no part of the organism can live independently of the vine.

The only purpose of a vine is to produce fruit for the enjoyment of the one who planted it. A vine is really useless for any other purpose. Some trees provide wood that can be used in construction, but this is not the case with a vine. In the Old Testament the prophet Ezekiel explained this truth to Israel. In Ezekiel 15:2–3 God asks the prophet, "What is the vine tree more than any tree, or than a branch which is among the trees of the forest? Shall wood be taken thereof to do any work? or will men take a pin of it to hang any vessel thereon?" The wood of a vine is not suitable even for firewood because it burns too quickly. God continues in verses 4–5: "Behold, it is cast into the fire for fuel; the fire devoureth both the ends of it, and the midst of it is burned. Is it meet for any work? Behold, when it was whole, it was meet for no work: how much less shall it be meet yet for any work, when the fire hath devoured it, and it is burned?" Therefore, the vine is only good for one thing and a good vine does it well: it produces fruit.

In the Old Testament God planted a vine—Israel—but Israel by and large failed to give God the good fruit that he required. Therefore, God judged Israel as a fruitless, faithless vine. In Psalm 80 we read of God's planting of the vine:

> 8. Thou hast brought a vine out of Egypt: thou hast cast out the heathen, and planted it.
> 9. Thou preparedst room before it, and didst cause it to take deep root, and it filled the land. (Ps. 80:8–9)

Later in the psalm the psalmist laments because of God's judgment:

> 12. Why hast thou then broken down her hedges, so that all they which pass by the way do pluck her?

> 13. The boar out of the wood doth waste it, and the wild beast of the field doth devour it. (vv. 12–13)

The prophets explain: "He looked that it should bring forth grapes, and it brought forth wild grapes" (Isa. 5:2). "Yet I had planted thee a noble vine, wholly a right seed: how then art thou turned into the degenerate plant of a strange vine unto me?" (Jer. 2:21). "Israel is an empty vine, he bringeth forth fruit unto himself: according to the multitude of his fruit he hath increased the altars; according to the goodness of his land they have made goodly images" (Hos. 10:1).

Israel failed as the vine because Israel is not the true vine. Jesus Christ is the true vine: "I am the true vine, and my Father is the husbandman" (John 15:1). Jesus Christ was always the true vine: in eternity when God conceived of and planned his vine, he conceived of and planned Jesus Christ. Old Testament believers in Israel longed for the flourishing of God's vine. Often the vine was horribly corrupted because of the reprobate seed in Israel. In addition, the sins of the elect spoiled the vine so that it did not bear fruit abundantly. Therefore, believers prayed in Psalm 80:14, "Return, we beseech thee, O God of hosts: look down from heaven, and behold, and visit this vine," and in verse 19, "Turn us again, O LORD God of hosts, cause thy face to shine; and we shall be saved."

In judgment God cut down the vine. He did that especially when he cut off ten of the twelve tribes and then sent Judah into captivity in Babylon. When God cut down his vine, only a stump remained. God's people might have despaired. Will we ever bear fruit to God's glory? Will we ever flourish under God's blessing? Are we doomed to perish?

From the stump of the vine God brought forth Christ. It was always God's purpose to bring forth Christ, which is why he is called *the true vine*. Before the true vine was revealed, God gave a type of the vine; and as with all types, Israel the vine had to fail to make way for the true vine, Jesus Christ. "And there shall come forth a rod out of the stem of Jesse, and a Branch shall grow out of his roots" (Isa. 11:1). "For he shall grow up before him as a tender plant, and as a root out of a dry ground: he hath no form nor comeliness; and when we shall see him, there is no beauty that we should desire him" (53:2).

Notice that God does not uproot the vine and plant a new vine. There is always only one vine: Jesus Christ is the vine. The root of Christ is found in the Old Testament. We learn this also in the New Testament: "I Jesus have sent mine angel to testify unto you these things in the churches. I am the root and the offspring of David, and the bright and morning star" (Rev. 22:16). And now Jesus declares in John 15:1, "I am the true vine." By this he means, "No one else is the true vine. I, alone, Jesus, I am the true vine." To have and enjoy salvation you must be in Jesus, the true vine.

We know this because of the word that Jesus uses: "the *true* vine." There are two words for true in the New Testament: one means true as opposed to false, and the other means true as opposed to typical. Jesus is the true vine in the sense that he is the real vine or the fulfillment of the shadowy, incomplete copy or type of the vine of the Old Testament. Jesus does not mean that Israel was a false vine; rather, Israel was only a picture, a shadow, a type of himself, and now Israel gives way to the true vine, Jesus. In fact, in the New Testament Jews and Gentiles are branches in the true vine. Therefore, Jesus was always the vine, and the root of the Old Testament vine (Israel) was the seed of Abraham, or the root of Jesse, Jesus Christ himself.

The word for true, *alethinos*, as it is used in other passages will illustrate this. In John 1:9 Jesus is called "the true Light." This does not imply that John the Baptist was a false light, but he was a lesser light pointing to the true light. In chapter 6:32 Jesus said, "My Father giveth you the true bread from heaven." Jesus does not suggest that the manna in the wilderness was false bread, but it was a type or picture of the real bread, which is Jesus, the bread of life. In Hebrews 8:2 heaven is called "the true tabernacle." However, we must not conclude that Moses built a false tabernacle; rather, his tabernacle was merely a picture of the true tabernacle of heaven.

What a wonderful truth that Jesus is the true vine! Jesus does not discourage or even frighten us by threatening us: bear fruit, or else. Instead, he encourages us: fruitfulness is guaranteed because we belong to Jesus Christ. Fruitfulness was not guaranteed in Israel, because not all Israelites were in Christ. Many Israelites within the nation of Israel were fruitless reprobates, but everyone in Christ is a fruitful elect. Therefore, only if Christ is fruitless and turns out to be a false, empty vine is it possible that we, who belong to Christ by faith, should be fruitless. What tremendous encouragement! As the vine, Jesus does what Israel failed to do: he bears fruit; he is fruitful, not fruitless. Surely, if anyone is fruitful, it is Jesus Christ, the Son of God. Because Jesus is the fruitful vine, the disciples are fruitful branches. We who are in Jesus cannot be fruitless but must be fruitful, because we live out of Christ.

THE TWO KINDS OF BRANCHES

Christ the true vine has branches "in him." This means that believers are not simply stuck onto the outside of the vine. We have a vital, living connection with Jesus Christ. We are branches in the vine not by nature, but by grace. Paul uses a very similar figure in Romans 11. The difference is that the figure is the olive tree, but the idea of an organic connection still applies. Paul, writing to the Gentiles, explains: "And thou, being a wild olive tree, wert graffed in among them, and with them partakest of the root and fatness of the olive tree" (v. 17). God took the wild branch of an olive tree and grafted it into the olive tree, which is Christ, or we might say, he grafted wild branches into the true vine.

Scripture speaks of a graft, which is a term from horticulture or gardening. A gardener desires to unite a branch of one plant to the stem of another plant, with the result that the branch lives out of the stem of the new plant. The gardener could glue or staple the branch to the outside of the stem, but this would not create a bond or union, for the foreign branch would soon wither and die since it would have no vital connection to the vine. Instead the gardener makes an incision and joins the branch to the stem, so that life-giving sap flows out of the stem into the branch. This is called a graft.

Spiritually, that is what the Father does: he engrafts us into Jesus Christ. The graft or the bond by which we are united to Christ the vine is faith. The Heidelberg Catechism refers to this in question and answer 20: "Are all men then, as they perished in Adam, saved by Christ? No, only those who are ingrafted into Him, and receive all His benefits, by a true faith."[1] Later, in question and answer 64, we read, "But doth not this doctrine make men careless and profane? By no means; for it is impossible that those who are implanted into Christ by a true faith should not bring forth fruits of thankfulness."[2]

But we need to delve deeper: how did this graft occur? The husbandman (the Father) created the graft by uniting a dead branch to the living and true vine. This shows us that salvation is gracious: a dead twig can no more join itself to a living tree than we can unite ourselves to Jesus Christ. The Holy Spirit creates the bond of faith without our input, help, or cooperation by a sovereign act of his own.

The Lord does not need to speak further about the graft in John 15 because the disciples to whom he speaks are already in him. Jesus' emphasis in these verses is not on that reality, but on the calling to abide in him, as we shall see.

The graft, then, is the explanation of how we come to be in him. Jesus explains it further in verse 3: "Now ye are clean through the word which I have spoken unto you." God works in us the power of faith by speaking the word to us through Jesus Christ, and by that word he cleanses us. In addition, we are in the vine only because of the work of Jesus Christ. Christ's death on the cross gives us the legal right to be part of the vine because Jesus bore our sins on the cross in order that we could be united to him. Christ's resurrection is the power by which we are united to the vine, because without the resurrection the vine and the branches would be permanently

---

1 Heidelberg Catechism Q&A 20, in *Confessions and Church Order*, 90.

2 Heidelberg Catechism Q&A 64, in *Confessions and Church Order*, 107.

dead. A dead vine cannot give life to branches: branches cannot be engrafted into a dead vine. Therefore, Christ's work of regeneration by the Spirit transforms us from dead twigs on the ground to living branches in the true vine.

The idea of the figure is a mutual indwelling of the believer in Christ so that the believer lives out of Christ, just as a branch in a vine lives out of the vine by absorbing the sap from the vine. The only source of sap is the vine and the only source of life for us is Jesus. Jesus teaches that plainly in verse 5: "Without me ye can do nothing." The words "without me" could be translated "severed from me, cut off from me, separated from me." This does not mean that we can be severed, cut off, or separated from the vine, but it underlines our utter and absolute dependence on him. The activity of the branch is simply to draw out of the vine because from the vine's sap the branch grows and bears fruit. If there were an interruption to that flow of sap the branch would not flourish, grow, and produce fruit.

We must not confuse the bond or graft of faith with the activity of faith. The activity of faith is our activity of believing in Christ (our knowing him, our trusting in him, our appropriating him and all his benefits), but we cannot thus engraft ourselves into the vine. Our activity of believing flows from the bond of faith, as the activity of seeing and looking flows from the faculty of sight. Therefore, before we can believe in Jesus Christ, we must be engrafted into him, and we are so engrafted by the power of his marvelous grace. John Calvin understood this; he begins the third book of his *Institutes*, "The Way in Which We Receive the Grace of Christ," with these words:

> We must understand that as long as Christ remains outside of us, and we are separated from him, all that he has suffered and done for the salvation of the human race remains useless and of no value to us. Therefore, to share with us what he has received from the Father, he had to become ours and to dwell within us...we obtain this by faith...the Holy Spirit is

> the bond by which Christ effectually unites us to himself… Faith is the principal work of the Holy Spirit.[3]

This shows us how dependent we are on Jesus. There is no other vine, he is the only vine, and outside of him are withering, death, and the fire. Behold the hopelessness of unbelief! The unbeliever is not in the vine, and he can do nothing that is good. He is totally depraved, "wholly incapable of doing any good, and inclined to all wickedness."[4] The unregenerate unbeliever is a dead twig lying on the ground of the vineyard. This is a reminder to us: where does the fruit come from that we bring forth? Do not boast in it as if we produced it of ourselves. Without Jesus we can do nothing. Jesus causes us to bring forth the fruit of prayer, good works, and sorrow over sin. Jesus causes us to bear the fruit of the Spirit, love, joy, peace, longsuffering, gentleness, goodness, faith, meekness, and temperance (Gal. 5:22–23), through the spiritual union that he has made.

The primary design of the words of Jesus is encouragement for his disciples. We cannot bring forth fruit of our own power, and we must not even try, but we also must not despair. We shall bring forth fruit by the power of the Spirit. There is therefore no reason for us not to bring forth fruit. In verse 5 Jesus says, "He that abideth in me, and I in him, the same bringeth forth much fruit." Quite simply, union with Christ results in fruit and it always results in fruit. In fact, the Heidelberg Catechism teaches, "It is impossible that those who are implanted into Christ by a true faith should not bring forth fruits of thankfulness."[5] So instead of fretting over your fruit, maintain close communion with Jesus, as close as a branch in the vine, and you will bear fruit.

---

3 John Calvin, *Institutes of the Christian Religion*, ed. John T. McNeill, trans. Ford Lewis Battles, 2 vols., Library of Christian Classics 20–21 (Philadelphia: Westminster Press, 1960), 3.1.1-4, 1:537–38, 541.

4 Heidelberg Catechism Q 8, in *Confessions and Church Order*, 86.

5 Heidelberg Catechism A 64, in *Confessions and Church Order*, 107.

There is another branch, a fruitless branch that the Father takes away: "Every branch in me that beareth not fruit he taketh away" (v. 2). This branch is not a believer who falls away and perishes, for the Bible is clear that no true believer can perish (see John 10:28). Whatever the "in me" language means, it cannot mean that. Remember we have a figure, and we cannot push the details of a figure too far. This branch, a fruitless branch, has a certain relationship to the vine, an external, formal relationship to Christ, but it is not one in which it bears fruit. The "in me" language of verse 2 is therefore only appearance: the hypocrite looks like a branch, he claims to be a branch, but his lack of fruit proves that he is not a branch in the vine. There is no real, vital, living union between this branch and the vine.

Nevertheless, this branch is different from the rank unbeliever, who is a dead twig on the ground. This branch appears to be in the vine, and it exists in the closest possible proximity to the vine. This branch is a hypocrite, a reprobate who grows up in the church and belongs for a while, but whose lack of fruit betrays him. You will find such fruitless branches in the church: they are baptized members and they seem to believe, but they have no true faith in Jesus Christ.

Do not fear that you are a fruitless branch, believing reader: the very fact that you are anxious about your fruit, that you desire to be more fruitful, that you love Jesus from the heart, and that you are sorry for your sin proves that you are in the vine. Jesus does not despise the weakest branch in him. If you are truly in him, you will bear fruit.

THE FATHER'S CARE OF HIS VINE

The Father, the divine husbandman, cares for his vine by dealing with the two types of branches in two different ways: removing the unfruitful branches and pruning the fruitful branches.

He removes the unfruitful branches: "Every branch in me that beareth not fruit he taketh away" (v. 2). The unfruitful branches, as we have noticed, are hypocrites in the visible church. They are only "in Christ" in an external sense: they are church members, they are baptized and catechized, and they even profess faith for a time, but they are not united to Jesus Christ by a true and living faith. They show this by not bearing fruit. God removes them from the vine, just as a farmer removes deadwood. It is necessary for the heavenly husbandman to do this for the sake of the overall health of the vine and for the benefit of the fruitful branches. Sometimes God removes hypocrites from the church through death, but usually hypocrites are unmasked in this life. Then such hypocrites are removed through church discipline, or they depart from the church because they cannot keep up the pretense: godly living and faithfulness in the truth, even externally, are impossible for them.

Judas Iscariot was an example of a fruitless branch. As Jesus spoke, Judas was preparing to betray Jesus, the one whom he professed to follow and love. John writes, "They went out from us, but they were not of us; for if they had been of us, they would no doubt have continued with us: but they went out, that they might be made manifest that they were not all of us" (1 John 2:19).

The Father's main work, however, is his care of the fruitful branches: "And every branch that beareth fruit, he purgeth it, that it may bring forth more fruit" (v. 2). We call this purging by the divine husbandman pruning. A gardener prunes the fruitful branches. The pruning sometimes seems severe, but it is for the benefit of the branches. Perhaps you have seen this: a gardener prunes a vine, and to the untrained eye he seems to be hacking it to pieces. You might wonder if the vine will ever survive such brutal treatment, but you are mistaken: the gardener is skilled and he knows how to prune his vine for maximum fruitfulness, to produce a good yield. God is the perfect husbandman; and he is more concerned about our fruitfulness than our happiness.

The Father prunes us by the word: "Ye are clean through the word which I have spoken unto you" (v. 3). The gospel prunes us, for the preaching prunes us, and the admonitions of the word prune us. The pruning process is not pleasant, for we have much sin in our life, which God is determined to address and remove. Therefore,

God calls us to repentance through the preaching of his word, and he brings us through unpleasant experiences because he determines in those ways to make us more fruitful. Suffering, affliction, and trials are the evidence of his pruning in our lives.

We must not fear the pruning shears of the husbandman: although he seems to be hacking us to pieces, he knows exactly what he is doing, and he acts in perfect wisdom and mercy toward his beloved vine. He knows which parts of our lives hinder our fruitfulness and he knows how best to make us fruitful to his glory. Therefore, urges the writer to the Hebrews, "Let us lay aside every weight, and the sin which doth so easily beset us, and let us run with patience the race that is set before us" (Heb. 12:1). Remember, too, the words of the apostle Paul: "And they that are Christ's have crucified the flesh with the affections and lusts" (Gal. 5:24). That, too, is part of pruning and purging: God causes us to put away our sins, which hinder our fruitfulness, in repentance. Unlike a branch, which is passive in the pruning process, we (who are living, conscious children of God) become active: we actively put away sin and actively put on virtue (Eph. 4:22–32; Col. 3:1–14).

The result of God's pruning or his care of his vine is that the deadwood is removed, the vine and its branches flourish, and the husbandman is glorified. The true vine Jesus Christ, unlike the shadowy Old Testament vine, shall bear fruit. Because we are in the vine, we will bear fruit through the power of Christ's Spirit, who is always working in us both to will and to do of God's good pleasure (Phil. 2:12–13). Let us be encouraged, then. Look to Christ, for he is your life, your sustenance, and your nutrition. Feed on him, draw out of him, and you shall bear fruit.

Chapter 11

Abiding In Christ the Vine

(John 15:4–6)

4. Abide in me, and I in you. As the branch cannot bear fruit of itself, except it abide in the vine; no more can ye, except ye abide in me.
5. I am the vine, ye are the branches: He that abideth in me, and I in him, the same bringeth forth much fruit: for without me ye can do nothing.
6. If a man abide not in me, he is cast forth as a branch, and is withered; and men gather them, and cast them into the fire, and they are burned.

At the beginning of chapter 15, drawing from the imagery of the Old Testament, Jesus asserts, "I am the true vine" (v. 1). The disciples were familiar with such figurative speech because in the Old Testament Israel was often presented as a vine that God had planted. Israel, however, failed to be the vine that God commanded her to be because, for all God's care of her, she did not bring forth fruit. John the Baptist warned Israel that the axe was at the root of the trees and that every fruitless tree would be cut down and cast into the fire. Israel was on the brink of failure and destruction: What would happen to the vine?

Jesus answers that by applying the figure of a vine to himself: he is the true vine, that is, he is what Israel should have been, but was not. A vine is a living organism of interdependent parts with one life whose one function is to bear fruit. Jesus is the vine, or the main trunk or stem of the plant, while believers are individual branches in him. Jesus is the true vine because he, unlike the Old Testament vine of Israel, is fruitful. The Father is the husbandman: the triune God planted the vine, he cares for the vine, he nurtures the vine, and he loves the vine, which is Jesus Christ. In the true vine, Jesus Christ, there are two kinds of branches, with which God deals in different ways according to his eternal purpose: he removes fruitless branches (these refer to reprobate hypocrites without faith) and he cleanses (or prunes) fruitful branches (these refer to elect, true believers) to encourage the bringing forth of more fruit.

Having explained the figure, Jesus applies it with the admonition, "Abide in me." The calling of the text, therefore, is very clear: abide in Jesus Christ. Abiding has the emphasis in chapter 15. In verses 1–16 the same verb appears twelve times, where it is translated "abide," "continue," and "remain." The preposition "in" ("in me," "in you," etc.) appears fourteen times. The idea of union dominates.

The question that faces the reader is very simple: What does it mean for a branch to abide in the vine? Is that something that the branch does, and if so, how does a branch do that? Is that something that the vine does or is that something that depends on the vine? Perhaps it is the work of the husbandman to keep the branch in the vine, and if so, how does the husbandman make sure that branches remain in the vine?

The reader will discover very quickly that it is necessary to drop the figure and to acknowledge the limitations in the imagery that Christ uses. If Christ is the vine, how do we, the branches, abide in him? Is abiding in Christ an activity of the believer, and if so, what kind of activity? Is abiding in Christ something that we do consciously and deliberately, or is it something that happens without our conscious activity? And perhaps most crucially of all, what is the relationship between abiding in Christ and bringing forth fruit, that is, doing good works? Why does a fruitless branch not abide in the vine, and why does a fruitless professing Christian, devoid of good works, perish? These questions must be faced in our study of these verses.

THE MEANING

I start with the illustration in John 15 and apply it to the idea of abiding. For the branch to abide in the vine is for the branch to remain connected to the vine. A branch abides by not being cut off or severed from the trunk of the vine: "Without me ye can do nothing" (v. 5). A branch abides in the vine by seeking its sustenance only from the vine. The abiding branch bears fruit by drawing sap out of the vine into itself: "The branch cannot bear fruit of itself, except it abide in the vine" (v. 4). That is the figure of the vine and the branches in John 15. Jesus applies the figure of the vine and branches to his relationship with his disciples: "I am the vine, ye are the branches" (v. 5); and "no more can ye [bear fruit], except ye abide in me" (v. 4).

The reality, then, is like the figure or the illustration. To abide in Christ is to stay in union with Christ; it is to remain in communion with him; it is to maintain conscious fellowship with the Savior. To abide in Christ is not to be cut off or severed from him. To abide in Christ is to seek spiritual life only in him and to draw out of him so that we bear fruit to the glory of God. That is the clear meaning: "He that abideth in me, and I in him, the same bringeth forth much fruit: for without me [or severed from me or cut off from me] ye can do nothing" (v. 5).

What exactly is involved in this abiding? What exactly is meant by staying in union with Christ, by remaining in communion with him, or by maintaining conscious fellowship with him? In a word, the answer is faith. Our text is another example in the fourth gospel of a metaphor of faith. Often the New Testament speaks of faith in Christ; frequently the Bible simply uses the word *faith* or the verb *believe*, but there are many times where metaphors and figures are used.

In John 4:14 Jesus declares to the woman at the well in Samaria, "But whosoever drinketh of the water that I shall give him shall never thirst; but the water that I shall give him shall be in him a well of water springing up into everlasting life." Drinking therefore is a metaphor to describe the activity of faith. In chapter 6:35 Jesus says, "I am the bread of life: he that cometh to me shall never hunger; and he that believeth on me shall never thirst." The meaning is faith: coming is parallel to believing. In verse 56 Jesus says, "He that eateth my flesh, and drinketh my blood, dwelleth in me, and I in him." To eat Christ's flesh and to drink Christ's blood in John 6 is not a reference to the Lord's supper, but to faith: to eat and to drink is to believe in Jesus Christ.

In John 7:37 Jesus likens faith in him to coming and drinking: "If any man thirst, let him come unto me, and drink." In chapter 8:12 Jesus likens faith in him to following him as the light of the world: "I am the light of the world: he that followeth me shall not walk in darkness, but shall have the light of life." In chapter 10:27 Jesus likens faith in him to sheep hearing the voice of the shepherd: "My sheep hear my voice, and I know them, and they follow me." And now in chapter 15:4 Jesus likens faith in him to a branch abiding in the vine. These are beautiful—and highly instructive—metaphors of faith.

Abiding in the vine, therefore, is not the same as doing good works. There is some confusion here. A branch does not abide in the vine by bringing forth fruit, and we do not maintain communion with Christ by performing good works. That is to turn the figure or the illustration upside down. The branch does not abide in the vine by bringing forth grapes, as if the presence of grapes were the prerequisite for the branch's abiding in the vine. We must not view the husbandman as standing over the branch waiting to chop it off as soon as it fails to bring forth good fruit. That is not the idea. Our Father is not scrutinizing us from heaven so that, as soon as we fail to bring forth good works or as soon as we bring forth evil works, he cuts us off, he severs us from Christ, and he casts us away. That is not the idea either. Instead, fruit is the consequence of abiding in the vine. Fruit in the branch is the result of union with the vine. Fruit depends on union with the vine. Union with the vine does not depend on fruit.

Consider a number of creedal references in connection with this. "Faith is an instrument that keeps us in communion with [Christ] in all His benefits, which, when become ours, are more than sufficient to acquit us of our sins."[1] "It is impossible that this holy faith can be unfruitful in man."[2] "It is impossible that those who are implanted into Christ by a true faith should not bring forth fruits of thankfulness."[3]

Having identified the means of our abiding in Christ the vine as faith, we need further to examine what faith is, and the role of faith in our abiding in Christ. Bear in mind that there are two aspects of faith. First, faith is a spiritual power, which we call the faculty of faith. Before a person can see, he must have the faculty of sight. Similarly, before a person can believe, he must have the faculty of faith. Before regeneration, an unbeliever is spiritually blind, but when the Spirit regenerates him and gives him life, he sees, which is to say that he begins to exercise his faculty of spiritual sight *by believing*.

The truth that faith is a spiritual power explains how we became branches united to the vine in the first place. We did not become united to Jesus Christ by choosing to connect ourselves to Jesus, or by opening our hearts to Jesus, as the Arminians teach. Instead, the Holy Spirit united us to Jesus Christ by a sovereign act of his grace. We were not active in forming the bond, for faith is the gift of God (Eph. 2:8; Phil. 1:29). I explained that union in the previous chapter in terms of a graft: we were engrafted into Christ. The Heidelberg Catechism teaches that we "are ingrafted into [Christ], and receive all His benefits, by a true faith" and adds that this true faith is "a certain knowledge" and "an assured confidence, which the Holy Ghost works [in our hearts]."[4] When asked, "Whence doth this faith proceed?" the Catechism answers, "From the Holy Ghost, who works faith in our hearts by the preaching of the gospel."[5]

1 Belgic Confession 22, in *Confessions and Church Order*, 50.
2 Belgic Confession 24, in *Confessions and Church Order*, 53.
3 Heidelberg Catechism A 64, in *Confessions and Church Order*, 107.
4 Heidelberg Catechism A 20 and A 21, in *Confessions and Church Order*, 90.
5 Heidelberg Catechism Q&A 65, in *Confessions and Church Order*, 108.

Second, faith is an activity, which can be further subdivided into two distinct activities, knowledge and confidence. Faith does not lie dormant in our hearts, for faith is active: it is a living, spiritual power in the child of God. By faith we believe, and this believing (the activity of faith) is a daily, continuous, ongoing, moment-by-moment activity. Listen to the Heidelberg Catechism on faith: "True faith is...a certain knowledge, whereby I hold for truth all that God has revealed to us in His Word." When we are active in faith, we believe everything in the Bible, and especially in this connection everything that the Bible teaches about Jesus Christ. The Catechism explains, "[It is] also an assured confidence, which the Holy Ghost works by the gospel in my heart; that not only to others, but to me also, remission of sin, everlasting righteousness, and salvation, are freely given by God, merely of grace, only for the sake of Christ's merits."[6] When we are active in faith, we have confidence and assurance in God's salvation in Christ.

Apply that to the figure of the vine and its branches of John 15. How does the branch abide in the vine? It does not do this by bearing fruit, which is the result of the abiding and not the abiding itself, but by drawing nourishment from the vine. How does the Christian abide in Christ? It is not by doing good works, which are the result of the abiding and not the abiding itself, but by drawing grace from Christ. Or to put it another way, the Christian abides by or through believing in Christ, or as the Belgic Confession explains it, "Faith...embraces Jesus Christ with all His merits, appropriates Him, and seeks nothing more besides Him...Faith is an instrument that *keeps us in communion with Him in all his benefits.*"[7] Faith is not our work, a work on which salvation depends (which is the Arminian conception of faith), but faith is God's gracious gift to us, worked in us by the Spirit: "He who works in man both to will and to do,

6 Heidelberg Catechism A 21, in *Confessions and Church Order*, 90.

7 Belgic Confession 22, in *Confessions and Church Order*, 49–50, emphasis added.

and indeed all things in all, produces both the will to believe and the act of believing also."[8]

But what does that look like exactly? First, to abide in Christ is to know him and to trust in his perfect work. That is clearly the meaning of John 6:56, "He that eateth [the present tense indicates continuous activity] my flesh, and drinketh [present tense] my blood, dwelleth [or abideth] in me, and I in him." Almost the same language is used in chapter 15:5: "He that abideth in me, and I in him." Similarly, Jesus could have said, "He that believes in the efficacy of my work on the cross abides in me, and I in him."

Every Christian trusts in Christ's perfect sacrifice as the source of his salvation, but we are tempted in the weakness of our faith to look to other objects of trust in very subtle ways. We are tempted to imagine that, if only we were more fruitful, God would accept us more or bless us more. We are tempted to imagine that God's love for us depends in some way on our performance, and although we might never express it in those words, we find ourselves thinking it. When we think along those lines, we become discouraged, for we look at our fruit or at our lack of fruit instead of looking to Christ. We must never forget that Christ makes us acceptable to God, Christ's blood washes away our sins, and Christ's wounds heal us: "We know nothing but Jesus Christ, and Him crucified; we count all things but loss and dung for the excellency of the knowledge of Christ Jesus our Lord, in whose wounds we find all manner of consolation."[9]

Christ declares to us through this figure of the vine and the branches, "Do not look at your fruit. Do not seek fruitfulness in your own efforts. Do not obsess over your fruit. Do not fret over the amount or the quality of your fruit. Instead, look to me, for I am the source of your fruit. You are not the source of your fruit. When you abide in me, you will bring forth good fruit and much fruit."

---

8 Canons 3–4.14, in Confessions and Church Order, 169.

9 Belgic Confession 21, in *Confessions and Church Order*, 48–49.

Second, to abide in Christ is to know him and to depend on him for all things. Ponder again the figure of the vine with its branches: a vine (the trunk or stem) is strong and sturdy, but the branches are weak. The vine can survive without the branches: it does not need them. But the branches need the vine: they rely upon it. The vine supports the branches or the husbandman props them up, but the branches cannot support themselves.

Sometimes Christians try to live the Christian life in their own strength. We expect to bear fruit without prayer and without the word. Sheer willpower and strenuous effort, we think, will make us fruitful. But that is a serious mistake, which leads to discouragement, fear, or pride. Instead we must remember that, as we are engrafted into Christ, now we live out of him. Therefore, we look to Christ to maintain us and support us, we look to Christ to produce fruit in us or to cause us to bear fruit, we look to Christ to make us holy, we look to Christ to give us grace and the Spirit and to give us peace, and we look to Christ for help in temptation. In short, we look to Christ for everything. A branch has no other source of sap than the vine and the Christian has no other source of life than Christ. "I am crucified with Christ: nevertheless I live; yet not I, but Christ liveth in me: and the life which I now live in the flesh I live by the faith of the Son of God, who loved me, and gave himself for me" (Gal. 2:20).

Third, to abide in Christ is to draw from him the graces and gifts that are present in abundant fullness in him, and thus to grow in our communion with him. This begins with knowledge, of course, for unless you know what is stored up in Christ, you will not draw from him the fullness of his gifts and graces. If you are ignorant of Christ, you will be tempted to seek your salvation and welfare elsewhere.

14. For this cause I bow my knees unto the Father of our Lord Jesus Christ,
15. Of whom the whole family in heaven and earth is named,
16. That he would grant you, according to the riches of his glory, to be strengthened with might by his Spirit in the inner man;

17. That Christ may dwell in your hearts by faith; that ye, being rooted and grounded in love,
18. May be able to comprehend with all saints what is the breadth, and length, and depth, and height;
19. And to know the love of Christ, which passeth knowledge, that ye might be filled with all the fulness of God. (Eph. 3:14–19)

But my God shall supply all your need according to his riches in glory by Christ Jesus. (Phil. 4:19)

9. For in him dwelleth all the fullness of the Godhead bodily.
10. And ye are complete in him, which is the head of all principality and power. (Col. 2:9–10)

These gifts, graces, and riches are not found in anyone else; therefore, do not seek them in anyone else. Are you powerless? Jesus has sufficient power to save you and to preserve you. Are you weak and defenseless? Jesus has might to defend you. Are you guilty or tormented with an evil conscience? Jesus has righteousness to cover you and grace to forgive you. Are you unclean? Jesus has sufficient holiness to purify and cleanse you. Are you oppressed and burdened? Jesus has grace to comfort you. Are you perplexed? Jesus has wisdom to guide you. Are you afraid of death? Jesus gives you eternal life and grace to conquer death.

You never need to worry that perhaps Christ will run out of patience, grace, mercy, wisdom, or anything else. The vine planted by the heavenly husbandman is an inexhaustible source of sap, from which you draw by faith alone. And do not forget that our union with Christ is not static, but a vital, living, organic union, which is capable of growth and development. We never stay still or are stagnant in the Christian life, but we grow up into Jesus Christ, or to use the figure here, we grow out of Jesus Christ. "But speaking the truth in love, [ye] may grow up into him in all things, which is the head, even Christ" (Eph. 4:15). What is fruit, then? It is not the means by which we abide in the vine, but it is the evidence that we are in the vine, and the result of our abiding.

THE WARNING

To underline the importance of abiding in the vine, Jesus describes the miserable end of those branches that do not abide in the vine. In verse 6 the destruction of the non-abiding, fruitless branch is described in five distinct steps, one after the other, in order to etch them deeply on our minds. First, "he is cast forth as a branch." He is cut off, removed from the vine, and thrown away, so that he no longer has any relationship to the vine. Second, he "is withered." The branch shrivels up and dies because it has no connection to the vine. It lies on the ground of the vineyard dry and lifeless. Third, "men gather them." Literally, Jesus says, "They gather them," without identifying the gatherers. Fourth, "they cast them into the fire." Fifth and finally, "they are burned," or "they burn" (present tense).

It does not take too much imagination to understand Christ's meaning. The unbelieving, non-abiding, fruitless, false professor of Christianity perishes. The hypocrite is cast out and the angels gather him and cast him and other hypocrites into hell, where they burn in everlasting fire forever. Certainly, that is a stark warning, a very serious warning indeed. The end of the fruitless branch, fruitless because it does not abide in Christ, is destruction.

But what does this mean and to whom does Christ refer in this warning? Certainly, Jesus refers to Judas Iscariot, for in John 13:11 Jesus warns, "Ye are not all clean." In chapter 15:3 Jesus explains, "Now ye are clean through the word which I have spoken unto you." Judas Iscariot was not clean—he was a fruitless branch that did not abide in Christ—and was cast off, withered, gathered, cast into the fire, and burned. Judas Iscariot had already departed from Christ and was not present in the upper room to hear these words: he had left during the meal; he had departed into the darkness in order to betray his Lord. In light of that, Jesus urges his true disciples, "Abide in me."

The question is, however, as we noted in verse 2, in what sense is the fruitless branch in Christ, and in what sense does the fruitless branch not abide in Christ? We cannot push the figure too far to make it teach that there are true believers who, because they fail to abide in Christ, can and do perish everlastingly. That is the view of Arminianism, which makes salvation conditional. It is also the view of certain heretical theologians in Reformed churches, advocates of the federal vision, who teach that all baptized members of the church are in Christ but could be lost.

Rejecting Arminianism and the federal vision, we remember that the Bible speaks of a category of people who are only externally, formally, or by appearance in Christ. We call such people hypocrites. For example, Romans 9:6 teaches, "They are not all Israel, which are of Israel." In the Old Testament certain people belonged outwardly to the nation of Israel without truly belonging to Israel. Similarly, in the church are some who are only externally in the congregation of God's people: they belong for a time, but they have no living connection to Christ. In other words, they have no real, saving faith. In the parable of the sower Jesus speaks of people who seem to be converts: the seed of the word of God falls on stony places or among thorns, with the result that the little seedling that sprouts up lacks a true root or is choked and perishes (Matt. 13:18–23). Such rootless, fruitless hypocrites are not true believers, which becomes obvious when they fail to show godliness or to bring forth good works.

The Bible is clear that true believers cannot fall away and perish. If there is a true, living connection between a soul and Jesus Christ, that soul cannot be lost. Jesus says, "All that the Father giveth me shall come to me; and him that cometh to me I will in no wise cast out" (John 6:37). The fruitless branch that does not abide in Christ is cast out, but the believer is never cast out.

> 27. My sheep hear my voice, and I know them, and they follow me:
> 28. And I give unto them eternal life; and they shall never perish, neither shall any man pluck them out of my hand.

29. My Father, which gave them me, is greater than all; and no man is able to pluck them out of my Father's hand.
30. I and my Father are one. (John 10:27–30)

The fruitless branch that does not abide in Christ is taken away, but the believer cannot be plucked out of Christ's hand or out of the Father's hand. Because the Spirit has united us to Christ by a true faith, we will abide in the vine forever, we will draw sap from the vine, and we will bear fruit through our union with the vine. Moreover, the Lord uses this warning to drive us closer to him. When the wind blows, a tree digs its roots deeper into the earth. When this warning comes, we trust even more firmly in Jesus Christ for salvation. Warnings do not drive us from Christ. Warnings, such as this one in John 15:6, drive us to Christ, and the closer our union with Christ is, the more fruit we will bear to his glory. This is how the Reformed fathers at Dordt explain it: "And as it hath pleased God, by the preaching of the gospel, to begin this work of grace in us, so He preserves, continues, and perfects it by the hearing and reading of His Word, by meditation thereon, and by the exhortations, threatenings, and promises thereof, as well as by the use of the sacraments."[10]

THE PROMISE

The promise of the text is simply this: Christ abides in us. Notice the promise in verses 4 and 5: "Abide in me, and I in you" (v. 4) and "He that abideth in me, and I in him, the same bringeth forth much fruit" (v. 5). With that we could include John 6:56: "He that eateth my flesh, and drinketh my blood, dwelleth [abideth] in me, and I in him." What is Christ saying here, or what is the precise relationship between the two things, between our abiding in him and his abiding in us? It is not that Christ's abiding in us depends upon our abiding in him. It is not that Christ will abide in us if we first abide in him.

10 Canons 5.14, in Confessions and Church Order, 176.

Similarly, the vine does not abide in the branch if the branch abides in the vine, for the vine is first.

Perhaps we can understand if we revert to the figure: the branch draws out of the vine, but the vine never draws out of the branch, or the flow of sap is always only one way. When we abide in Christ, we actively, consciously, continuously believe in him. But when Christ abides in us, he does not believe in us, he does not draw anything out of us, we do not supply him with anything, and he supplies us with everything. And yet there is a mutual indwelling and a close, mysterious, invisible union. The relationship is this: Christ's abiding in us is the power by which we abide in him; or Christ's abiding in us is first and therefore the source of our abiding in him. To express it theologically, the source of our faith is Christ, the object of our faith is Christ, and the source of our continuous, ongoing activity of believing is also Christ. We never believe independently of Christ. We never say after we have believed, "Now I am beyond Christ; now I no longer need Christ."

The fruit of this is, quite obviously, fruit, even "much fruit" (v. 5). Jesus promises the bringing forth of fruit. "Every branch that beareth fruit, he purgeth it, that it may bring forth more fruit" (v. 2). "Ye [cannot bear fruit of yourselves] except ye abide in me" (v. 4). "He that abideth in me, and I in him, the same bringeth forth much fruit" (v. 5). "Herein is my Father glorified, that ye bear much fruit" (v. 8).

The fruit that the branches in the vine bring forth is not grapes. Certainly, in botany a vine brings forth grapes, but at this point I must drop the figure. The fruit is good works. There is confusion in the minds of many Christians about the place of good works. Some say, "We do not need to do any good works because they automatically spring forth from our hearts without any effort on our part." Others say, "Good works are not our works: they are God's works in us, so that we do not actually do them. God does." Others say, "We cannot do good works because our best works are defiled with sin." Those three opinions about good works are incorrect.

It is absolutely true that the source of our good works is God, specifically the Holy Spirit. Jesus says, "The branch cannot bear fruit of itself, except it abide in the vine; no more can ye, except ye abide in me" (John 15:4). Jesus continues, "I am the vine, ye are the branches: He that abideth in me, and I in him, the same bringeth forth much fruit: for without me ye can do nothing" (v. 5). In other words, we do good works only because of our union with Christ; however, we do actually do them. God creates the opportunity for the work, he gives us the will or desire for the work, he provides the power for the work, he causes the activity of the work, and he receives the praise for the work. And we *do* the work.

But are our works not sins and therefore in no sense of the word "good"? If they were sins, only sins, why would Jesus call them fruit? Consider another important passage on this subject, Ephesians 2:10. Paul does not write, "For we are his workmanship, created in Christ Jesus *unto sins*, which God hath before ordained that we should walk in them." Paul writes, "unto good works." If it is not possible for a believer to do genuinely (which is not the same as perfect) good works, and if a believer's works are only sins, then Paul was mistaken in Ephesians 2:10. In fact, if after we have been engrafted into Christ we still cannot do any good works at all, Christ is but half a Savior, which is too gross a blasphemy. Then we differ nothing from the fruitless branch, which the Father takes away (v. 2), which is cast forth, withers, and is burned (v. 6). If we bring forth no fruit, then we are not his disciples (v. 8).

If God cannot so sanctify us to make us bring forth good fruit, then our case is utterly hopeless. Then Christ has failed in his redemptive work, for listen to Paul in Titus 2:14: "[Christ] gave himself for us, that he might redeem us from all iniquity, and purify unto himself a peculiar people, zealous of good works." How can a fruitless Christian who brings forth no good works (an oxymoron, by the way, a "fruitless Christian") be called "zealous of good works"? Is he zealous of good works without actually doing them? The Heidelberg Catechism explains the necessity of good works in these words: "Christ, having redeemed and delivered us by His blood, also renews us by His Holy Spirit after His own image; that so we may testify by the whole of our conduct our gratitude to God for His blessings."[11] A Christian who has been redeemed but not renewed is surely an impossibility.

It is true that our good works are imperfect, but God forgives the imperfections in our good works, and he even cleanses and purifies them so that they are good. This is the testimony of the Belgic Confession: "It is impossible that this holy faith can be unfruitful in man...[We speak of a faith] that worketh by love, which excites man to the practice of those works which God has commanded in His Word." The same article continues: "These works, as they proceed from the good root of faith, are good and acceptable in the sight of God, forasmuch as they are all sanctified by His grace." And the same article teaches, "Therefore we do good works...we are beholden to God for the good works we do...We do not deny that God rewards our good works...Though we do good works, we do not found our salvation upon them." The Belgic Confession carefully qualifies, lest we ascribe too much to our good works: "They are of no account towards our justification...Not to merit by them...We do not found our salvation upon them; for we can do no work but what is polluted by our flesh, and also punishable."[12] That our good works merit punishment because of their imperfection does not negate the fact that they are good: God for Christ's sake purifies them. They do not justify us because only perfect righteousness avails before the tribunal of God. Our good works are marred with blemishes and imperfections, but they are not thoroughly and completely rotten. If they were, they would not be fruit.

In summary, we do good works, which are the genuine fruit of our sanctification and never part of the ground of our justification before God. Despite their many imperfections, they are actually good works. They are. The Bible insists upon it. The Bible insists that there is fruit.

---

11 Heidelberg Catechism A 86, in *Confessions and Church Order*, 120.

12 Belgic Confession 24, in *Confessions and Church Order*, 53–55.

"Herein is my Father glorified, that ye bear much fruit; so shall ye be my disciples" (John 15:8). Jesus does not say, "He that abideth in me, and I in him, the same bringeth forth crabapples or thorns." He says, "much fruit." It is a perverse kind of false humility, and a denial of the promises of God, to teach that the Christian cannot and does not bring forth fruit, good fruit, even much fruit, to the glory of God.

Neither is this an excuse for laziness, for we do not say in response to God's word, "Well, if God wants me to bring forth fruit, I shall simply sit here waiting for God to work fruit in me." In some charismatic circles this is called "Let go and let God theology." It is a grievous misapplication of the truth that God works in us by his grace.

The Bible often calls good works "fruit," but we must understand the limitation of the metaphor that Jesus uses (which is true of every metaphor), for a tree produces fruit without any conscious effort on its part. That is true, *but we are not trees!* A tree produces fruit without conscious effort because a tree is not a conscious, sentient being. We are conscious, sentient beings: we are living, active, moral, rational, willing creatures. When we do good works, we do so willingly, consciously, and deliberately. Paul, for example, taught that the source of our good works is God's grace, and yet there was no more energetic worker of good works than Paul. The apostle writes, "It is God which worketh in you both to will and to do of his good pleasure" (Phil. 2:13). God works, but notice what God commands immediately before that verse: "Work out your own salvation with fear and trembling, for [because] it is God which worketh in you" (v. 12–13). Scripture does not say, "Be inactive and lazy because it is God which worketh in you." Scripture does not say, "Make no effort to do good works because it is God which worketh in you." God says, "*Work diligently and energetically,* for I work in you."

God has prepared works for his children, declares the apostle in Ephesians 2:10, for this purpose: "that we should walk in them." God prepared works in which we must walk. And we do not have to cross over land and sea to try to discover the works that God has prepared for us. They are right in front of us. You know the commandments:

keep them! Has God given you a spouse—love him or her and be faithful in marriage! Has he given you children—love them and instruct them in the fear of God! Are you a child or young person—honor your parents and your teachers! Has God placed hardships in your life—be patient and endure suffering for Christ's sake! Has God given you prosperity—be thankful to him! In summary, "Whatsoever thy hand findeth to do, do it with thy might" (Eccl. 9:10). You will never lack opportunity to do good works. You do not need to ask, when faced with an opportunity to serve your neighbor, "Is this a good work that God has prepared for me to do?" You do not pry into the secret things of God: you simply do your duty. That is enough.

Good works are not only our duty and calling: they are our privilege. God has delivered us from spiritual death so that we will perform good works of thankfulness. God has quickened us so that we will perform good works. God has created us in Christ Jesus so that we will perform good works. God has saved us in his marvelous grace so that we will walk in good works. Do good works, then, not to earn salvation, but as the expression of your gratitude for Christ's salvation.

The fruit that we bring forth is sweet to the Father's taste, and it glorifies God and benefits the neighbor. The fruit is love, joy, peace, longsuffering, gentleness, goodness, faith, meekness, and temperance (Gal. 5:22–23). We bring forth such fruit as the fruit of believing in Jesus Christ. The unbeliever, who is not in Christ, cannot bring forth any fruit pleasing to God, because without Christ he can do nothing. However, the believer, who is united to Christ by a true Spirit-worked faith, and who abides in Christ by the same faith, cannot but bring forth fruit. "It is impossible that those who are implanted into Christ by a true faith should not bring forth fruits of thankfulness."[13] Therefore, do not fret over your fruit, but look to Christ, have confidence in his finished work, trust him in all things, and draw out of his fullness, and you will bring forth fruit.

---

13 Heidelberg Catechism A 64, in *Confessions and Church Order*, 107.

Chapter 12

Christ's Words Abiding In Us

(John 15:7–8)

7. If ye abide in me, and my words abide in you, ye shall ask what ye will, and it shall be done unto you.
8. Herein is my Father glorified, that ye bear much fruit; so shall ye be my disciples. (John 15:7–8)

In the first six verses of chapter 15 Christ has laid the foundation in a beautiful and intriguing figure: the vine and its branches. The disciples must derive comfort from the truth that their beloved Lord is the true vine, not an empty, fruitless vine such as Israel proved to be, but a true, flourishing, fruitful vine. While the wicked enemies of Jesus appeared to be readying themselves to cut down the vine, in reality God, who cares for his vine, would never cut it down. In fact, the crucifixion and resurrection of Jesus Christ in a few hours, while horrifying for the disciples, would simply make the vine even more fruitful. Therefore, these verses echo the theme of chapter 14: Jesus' departure would be advantageous for the disciples.

The calling of the disciples, who were branches in the true vine, was to abide in Christ. The disciples were in Jesus Christ the true vine not because they had chosen to unite themselves to him, but because God had graciously engrafted them into him. United to Jesus Christ in true faith, the disciples enjoyed a constant supply of life from the Holy Spirit, who dwells both in Christ and in believers. Just as the branch derives sap from the vine and gives nothing to it, so the believer receives every blessing necessary for life and fruitfulness from Jesus Christ and gives nothing to him. The fruit that the branch brings forth is due to the life-giving sap, not to something that the branch itself supplies; so the good works that the believer brings forth are the fruit of the grace of Jesus Christ flowing by the power of the Holy Spirit into the believer's heart.

Therefore, Jesus does not say, "Bear fruit, and you will abide in the vine," but "Abide in me, and you will bring forth good fruit." To make good works the reason or even the condition or prerequisite for abiding in Jesus Christ is to turn everything upside down. We abide in Jesus Christ by faith alone: we cling to him, we rely upon him, we draw out of him everything that we need, and we bring forth good fruit or we do good works.

But there is more to say about this abiding. In verse 7 Jesus connects abiding in him to his words: "If ye abide in me, and my words abide in you." It is the relationship between abiding in Jesus Christ and abiding in his words that we study in this chapter.

THE MEANING

Jesus gives two examples of abiding in verse 7. The first abiding is the believer's abiding in Christ: "If ye abide in me" (v. 7). I explained that abiding in the previous chapter, so I can be brief here. To abide in Christ is for the believer to stay or remain in Christ. It is for the believer to maintain union with Christ. It is for the believer to continue in conscious fellowship or communion with Christ. We abide in Christ through faith in his finished work on the cross as the only ground of our salvation. We abide in Christ through continual dependence on him for all things, not seeking any of our salvation elsewhere. We abide in Christ by drawing out of him the fullness of the riches of his grace, finding our sufficiency in him, and never departing from him.

In verse 6 Christ warned about the consequences of unbelief: the hypocrite, who for a time boasts some kind of connection to Christ, does not abide in Christ and perishes. Judas Iscariot is the prime example of a non-abiding, fruitless branch, the end of which is hellfire.

Furthermore, we must remember that union with Christ, and therefore abiding in him, is an organic idea. By organic, I mean living. The illustration that Jesus uses is that of a living vine with living branches. A living connection is different from a static connection. A living connection is capable of growth, but it is also capable of regression. A believer can make progress, but he can also backslide or go backward. The Canons of Dordt address that point: "Although the weakness of the flesh cannot prevail against the power of God, who confirms and preserves true believers in a state of grace, yet converts are not always so influenced and actuated by the Spirit of God, as not in some particular instances sinfully to deviate from the guidance of divine grace, so as to be seduced by and comply with the lusts of the flesh."[1]

The same creed goes on to explain that one of the consequences of such a deviation from grace is a "lamentable fall," and one of the consequences of such "enormous sins" is that they "interrupt the exercise of faith."[2] When the exercise of faith is interrupted, the branch at that instance is not properly drawing out of Christ and therefore is not properly abiding in Christ.

Peter is an example of this. Peter is not Judas Iscariot. Judas Iscariot fell because he was not truly in Christ, and he fell finally and irrevocably. Peter was truly in Christ, but in a moment of weakness and in a moment of prideful and presumptuous self-sufficiency he fell. He fell publicly, he fell lamentably, and he fell into an enormous transgression. Peter fell because he did not abide in the vine. Be careful: he did not depart from the vine so that he was severed from the vine. Nevertheless, the flow of sap to Peter was not as it should have been, so that he did not bear fruit at that point in his life in the way that he ought to have. And that was Peter's fault. Peter did not watch and pray. Peter imagined at that moment that he could stand without Christ. To seek to stand without Christ is

---

1 Canons 5.4, in Confessions and Church Order, 174.

2 Canons 5.4–5, in Confessions and Church Order, 174.

not to abide in Christ. By seeking to stand without Christ, Peter fell (1 Cor. 10:12).

Remember, too, the mercy of the Father, the husbandman, and the mercy of Christ, the vine. Peter was pruned with a painful, humiliating pruning. God pruned him of his pride and self-sufficiency. Peter's pride and self-sufficiency hindered Peter's fruitfulness. Peter learned through that bitter experience the important lesson, "He that abideth in me, and I in him, the same bringeth forth much fruit: for without me ye can do nothing" (v. 5). Our flesh brings forth no fruit. Our flesh hinders fruitfulness. Therefore, God deals with our flesh, often harshly. He calls us to deal harshly with our flesh. We must crucify it. We must welcome the pruning of our flesh, for it serves our salvation. Resist the temptation, therefore, to look away from Christ. Abide in Christ, trust in Christ, seek your life only in Christ, seek your fruit only from Christ, and you will bear fruit. That is Christ's beautiful promise here.

The second abiding is the abiding of Christ's words in the believer: "And my words abide in you" (v. 7). Christ's words cannot be separated from Christ himself because Christ is the Word. To say it another way, Christ abides in us by his words. Or the abiding of Christ's words in us is the abiding of Christ in us. Or to express it differently again: we commune with Christ—and he with us—by or through his words.

Christ's words are the utterances of his mouth. During his ministry with his disciples Christ spoke many words, words about many things. He spoke the "word" (singular) and "words" (plural), and when he spoke, he spoke the word of God. Remember John 14:10: "The words that I speak unto you I speak not of myself: but the Father that dwelleth in me, he doeth the works." Or remember verses 23–24: "If a man love me, he will keep my words: and my Father will love him, and we will come unto him, and make our abode with him. He that loveth me not keepeth not my sayings: and the word which ye hear is not mine, but the Father's which sent me."

Christ's words are profitable, living, life-giving words, and the disciples recognized as much. In John 6:60 after the Jews hear Christ's words they exclaim, "This is an hard saying; who can hear it?" Jesus does not retract or even modify his words but insists, "It is the spirit that quickeneth; the flesh profiteth nothing: the words that I speak unto you, they are spirit, and they are life" (v. 63). When the crowd departs, Jesus asks the twelve disciples in verse 67, "Will ye also go away?" Peter, answering for the twelve, declares, "Lord, to whom shall we go? thou hast the words of eternal life. And we believe and are sure that thou art that Christ, the Son of the living God" (vv. 68–69).

The words of Christ, then, are Christ's teachings, promises, and precepts. The words of Christ are not only those words printed in red in some Bibles, but they also include the whole of the Bible—the Old Testament and the New Testament—because the whole Bible is the word of Christ, which is the word of God. When Jesus says, "My words abide in you" (v. 7), he presupposes that his words were already in them. Christ's words had taken root in the hearts and minds of the disciples. They had embraced the words of Christ by faith because they had embraced Christ by faith.

The same applies to every true believer because it is not possible to be a Christian and for the words of Christ not to abide in you. A Christian meditates on Scripture. A Christian thinks biblically. Remember the elements of saving faith: there is the spiritual power or faculty of faith by which we are united to Jesus Christ as a husbandman unites a branch to his vine by a graft, and there is also the activity of faith. "Faith is...a certain knowledge, whereby I hold for truth all that God has revealed to us in His Word,"[3] or to put it another way, faith is to have the words of Christ abide in us.

What, then, is it for Christ's words to abide in us? Christ's words abide in us when they take root in our hearts, when they influence our thoughts, when they determine our decisions, and when they regulate our emotions. If Christ's words abide in us, we do not ask,

---

3 Heidelberg Catechism A 21, in *Confessions and Church Order*, 90.

"What do I want?" but "Lord, what does thy word require of me?" If Christ's words abide in us, our thinking is biblical. Every thought is brought captive to the obedience of Christ (2 Cor. 10:5). If Christ's words abide in us, we respond biblically to afflictions in our life: in brief, the mind of Christ is in us.

A Christian in whose heart the words of Christ abide lives according to the will of Christ. But how do Christ's words abide in us? Or by what power do they abide in us? The answer is, of course, by the power of Christ. We do not have the power to cause the words of Christ to abide in us: we would let them slip, and we often do! As Christ abides in us, he supplies to us the life-giving sap of the Spirit, and we draw strength from him as we exercise faith. The deeper our union with Christ—and his with us—the deeper the words of Christ dwell in us.

Remember, too, that Christ is the Lord of means. The words of Christ abide in us as we read and meditate on the Scriptures. If you are willfully ignorant of the Bible, do not expect the words of Christ to abide in you. If you are inattentive or irregular in your attendance at the faithful preaching of God's word, do not expect the words of Christ to abide in you. If you fill your mind with TV, movies, YouTube videos, social media, and worldly music, but not Scripture, do not expect the words of Christ to abide in you. If you imbibe worldly philosophy or turn to the world to teach you to live in your marriage or to be a parent or to be successful in life, do not expect the words of Christ to dwell in you.

Read good books, but drink deeply from the Scriptures. Listen to James: "Wherefore lay apart all filthiness and superfluity of naughtiness, and receive with meekness the engrafted word, which is able to save your souls" (James 1:21). The word is "engrafted" or rooted in our hearts by faith. Listen to Peter: "Wherefore laying aside all malice, and all guile, and hypocrisies, and envies, and all evil speakings, as newborn babes, desire the sincere milk of the word, that ye may grow thereby: if so be ye have tasted that the Lord is gracious" (1 Pet. 2:1–3). Listen to Paul: "As ye have therefore received Christ Jesus the

Lord, so walk ye in him: rooted and built up in him, and stablished in the faith, as ye have been taught, abounding therein with thanksgiving" (Col. 2:6–7). "Let the word of Christ dwell in you richly in all wisdom; teaching and admonishing one another in psalms and hymns and spiritual songs, singing with grace in your hearts to the Lord" (3:16). Thus Christ's words abide in us.

THE PROMISE

To that twofold abiding Jesus attaches a promise in verse 7: "If ye abide in me, and my words abide in you, ye shall ask what ye will, and it shall be done unto you." In a word, the promise is prayer. This is one of a number of places in the upper room discourse where Christ gives instruction to his disciples in prayer. The instruction is designed to encourage them to pray and to give them incentives to pray. Prayer is very important, and therefore Jesus urges prayer upon the disciples.

Prayer is one of the ways in which we have communion or fellowship with God: we pray to the triune God, through the mediator Jesus Christ, and by the power of the Holy Spirit. Prayer is a way in which we consciously seek the sap that flows from the vine to the branches in order that we might bring forth fruit. "God will give His grace and Holy Spirit to those only who with sincere desires continually ask them of Him, and are thankful for them."[4]

We should not view this promise of prayer in isolation from the rest of the Bible's teaching, but we should interpret this in light of other passages. In many Christian circles prayer is a matter of technique. Books are published to promote various secrets of prayer. Such books come and go like ever-changing fads. But Jesus does not give us a secret or a technique. Jesus explains the relationship between abiding in him, his words abiding in us, and prayer. Jesus gets to the heart of the issue: prayer is answered only as we abide in Christ and only as Christ's words abide in us. In other words, prayer

4 Heidelberg Catechism A 116, in *Confessions and Church Order*, 134.

is the fruit of faith and of a sense of constant dependence on Christ. One who does not consciously depend on Christ does not pray. One who does not abide in Christ cannot pray. Such a person certainly will not receive favorable answers to his petitions before the throne of grace because he does not truly come.

Christians would be better served through studying the Heidelberg Catechism, which is based on God's word, rather than seeking a new technique to guarantee success in prayer. The Catechism on prayer teaches two main truths: the necessity of prayer and the requisites of prayer. Prayer is necessary because "it is the chief part of thankfulness which God requires of us." We do not pray first of all in order to receive certain benefits from God, but to express our gratitude to our heavenly Father. God requires that we are thankful, and he requires that we show our gratitude by praying and by obeying his commandments. Moreover, "God will give His grace and Holy Spirit to those only who with sincere desires continually ask them of Him, and are thankful for them."[5]

True prayer comes from a sense of need: "We rightly and thoroughly know our need and misery." True prayer springs from faith: we are "fully persuaded that He, notwithstanding that we are unworthy of it, will, for the sake of Christ our Lord, certainly hear our prayer, as He has promised us in His Word."[6] We pray because God has promised to give. We do not pray because we are worthy of an answer, however, for we must underline these words: "for the sake of Christ our Lord." God does not hear our prayers because we perform sufficient good works to obtain an audience, but because of Christ and only because of Christ. A self-sufficient, proud, presumptuous person does not pray, for he sees no need to pray. A believer prays. One abiding in Christ prays. One in whom Christ's words abide prays.

What, briefly, does Christ teach in the upper room discourse about prayer? Jesus addresses the subject of prayer in John 14:13–14:

---

5 Heidelberg Catechism A 116, in *Confessions and Church Order*, 134.

6 Heidelberg Catechism A 117, in *Confessions and Church Order*, 135.

"And whatsoever ye shall ask in my name, that will I do, that the Father may be glorified in the Son. If ye shall ask any thing in my name, I will do it." The lesson is that prayer must be made in harmony with the name of Jesus, that is, in harmony with the self-revelation of Jesus. We ask only on the basis of the person and work of Jesus. We ask because Jesus is the Son of God and because he has made perfect satisfaction for our sins on the cross. We ask on his authority, using his name for access into the Father's presence. We do not come in our name, we do not come in the name of any creature, whether in the name of a saint or an angel, but we come in the precious name of Jesus. When we do so, our prayers will certainly be answered. In 1 John 5:14 the apostle writes, "And this is the confidence that we have in him, that, if we ask any thing according to his will, he heareth us." In Mark 11:24 Jesus promises, "What things soever ye desire, when ye pray, believe that ye receive them, and ye shall have them."

Put those three things together. Acceptable prayer is in Jesus' name. Acceptable prayer is according to God's will. Acceptable prayer is by faith. The emphasis in verse 7, however, is on our will: the disciples' will and our will. "Ye shall ask what ye will, and it shall be done unto you." In fact, in the Greek text our will is underlined. Literally, Jesus says, "Whatsoever ye will, ye shall ask." The will is placed at the forefront. Whatever we will is whatever our heart desires. Whatever we will is that on which our affection is set. Whatever you will, says Jesus, ask for it, and it shall be done.

Some Christians have misunderstood this, and some false teachers have sought to exploit these words. They have turned Jesus' words into a *carte blanche* or a blank check. Advocates of the prosperity gospel thrive on texts like these. Do you want a pony? Ask God and you shall have it! Do you want a cottage by the lake or a mansion? Ask God and you shall have it! Do you want perfect health, a beautiful body, lots of money, or a new car? Ask God and you shall have it!

That is not Christ's meaning, and the Christian knows that Christ does not mean that! Notice the relationship in the text: "If ye abide in me, and my words abide in you, ye shall ask." Christ's words will mold and shape your desires. If Christ's words abide in you, his words will determine your desires, change your priorities, temper your affections, and direct your thoughts. If Christ's words are in you, you will not ask for a pony, a cottage, a mansion, perfect health, a beautiful body, lots of money, or a new car. You will have better, more spiritual, holier desires, which you will express in prayer. Your chief desire will be for the glory of God, and all other desires (even lawful desires) will be made subject to your chief desire. Remember Psalm 37:4: "Delight thyself also in the LORD; and he shall give thee the desires of thine heart." Of course! If you delight in the Lord, the Lord *is* the desire of your heart. Earthly things are not the desires of the heart of one who delights in the Lord.

Jesus therefore is not giving a guarantee by which we obtain our carnal, worldly desires. Jesus instead promises that as our desires are changed through the indwelling word, when we express these sanctified desires in prayer, these desires will be fulfilled. Apply this to the disciples after Jesus' departure into heaven. When opposition and persecution increased against them, they did not pray for earthly prosperity, but they prayed for boldness to preach the truth. God answered that prayer because it was in accordance with Christ's words, which abode in them.

The desires of a Christian are not the desires of a carnal man. Yes, the Christian has carnal desires in his flesh, but the Christian crucifies the lusts of the carnal flesh (Gal. 5:24); he does not pray for their gratification. The Christian minds the things of the Spirit (Rom. 8:5). We desire to be holy and the Lord grants us holiness by sanctifying us by his Spirit. He even uses the sufferings of this present life to prepare us for the glory of heaven. We desire to glorify God and the Lord grants that desire. We desire strength to fulfill our calling in the world and the Lord grants that desire. We desire grace to endure hardship and the Lord grants that desire. We desire the comforting sense of God's presence and the Lord grants that desire. We desire to be fruitful and the Lord grants that desire.

What the Lord does not grant are those foolish requests inspired by the flesh. To such foolish Christians James writes, "Ye lust, and have not: ye kill, and desire to have, and cannot obtain: ye fight and war, yet ye have not, because ye ask not. Ye ask, and receive not, because ye ask amiss, that ye may consume it upon your lusts" (James 4:2–3). If your motivation is self-aggrandizement, earthly ambition, or some other carnal motive, the words of Christ are not abiding in you, and God will not grant you the desires of your flesh. In mercy he does not grant them because he knows that they would not be for your benefit.

Think, too, how the indwelling words of Christ keep us from many foolish petitions. We think of asking for earthly riches, but we remember Christ's words, "Take heed, and beware of covetousness: for a man's life consisteth not in the abundance of the things which he possesseth" (Luke 12:15). We think of asking for the removal of some affliction, but we remember Christ's words, "My grace is sufficient for thee: for my strength is made perfect in weakness" (2 Cor. 12:9), and we pray for grace instead. We think of praying only for ourselves, but then we remember that Christ is gathering a church, and we offer petitions for our fellow saints and seek the coming of the Father's kingdom. You see how Christ's abiding words in us determine our desires, and therefore our prayers. They change a bad petition into a good petition or a good petition into a better one.

THE ENCOURAGEMENT

The encouragement for the believer who abides in Christ and in whose heart the words of Christ abide is threefold. First, he bears much fruit; second, he glorifies the Father; and third, he is Christ's disciple, or he demonstrates himself to be Christ's genuine disciple. Think of the negative. Judas Iscariot, who did not abide in Christ and in whose heart the words of Christ did not abide, did not bear fruit, did not glorify the Father, and demonstrated himself to be a hypocrite and not a genuine disciple. The hypocrite in the church who does not abide in Christ, and in whose heart the words of Christ do not abide, does not bear fruit, does not glorify the Father, and demonstrates himself to be a false professor and not a genuine disciple. That is because the hypocrite never had true faith, as we have seen.

The issue, as it always is in John 15, is fruit. The Father planted the vine with a view to fruit. The Father engrafted us into Christ with a view to our bringing forth fruit. The Father prunes the fruitful branches—he prunes us—so that we become more fruitful. The key to bringing forth fruit is not the performance of good works (that *is* the fruit) but abiding in Christ the vine. The key to fruitfulness is union with Christ: outside of Christ, fruit is impossible. In union with Christ, not only is fruit possible, but fruitlessness is impossible.

It is true, of course, that we do not bring forth the fruit of good works unconsciously, with no effort on our part. Paul exhorts Titus to "affirm constantly, that they which have believed in God might be careful to maintain good works" (Titus 3:8). In that sense, the metaphor of a branch and its fruit has its limitations. A branch brings forth fruit without conscious effort, but we strive to bring forth good works as we fight against our sins, the world, and the devil.

Nevertheless, we must never forget that the source and the power behind our good works is the grace of God in Jesus Christ. Without God's grace operating in us we have neither the will, the desire, nor the ability to bring forth good works. Jesus is speaking here to disciples who are in him, and in whom are his words. He promises them the fruit of good works and a ripened Christlike character as the fruit of the grace of God: "He that abideth in me, and I in him, the same bringeth forth much fruit...Herein is my Father glorified, that ye bear much fruit; so shall ye be my disciples" (John 15:5, 8). As the sap from the vine flows into the branch, the branch bears grapes. As the grace of God, which flows to us from Christ, operates in us, we bear fruit. The result is the cultivation of Christlike character in many good works, as described in Scripture.

These fruits of Christ are not merely external deeds of morality and common decency. You can stick plastic grapes on a branch, but that is not fruit. An unbeliever's morality and decency are like plastic grapes or, as the Bible puts it, "dead works" (Heb. 9:14) or "fruit unto death" (Rom. 7:5). A believer has fruit, which genuinely comes forth from him by the grace of God. The fruit of the believer is true, genuine, sweet, and pleasant to the taste. The fruit of the Spirit cannot be mimicked: love, joy, peace, longsuffering, gentleness, goodness, faith, meekness, and temperance (Gal. 5:22–23).

To glorify the Father is to make him appear glorious to others. We glorify the Father by bearing much fruit. Such fruit glorifies the Father because the fruit is the reflection in the believer of the perfections of God, for the believer has the mind of Christ and is remade in the image of Christ, which is the image of God.

"So," says Jesus, "shall ye be my disciples" (v. 8). The eleven were already his disciples, but their discipleship would be proved genuine and true. Not by a loud profession, but by fruit! And that fruit is ours in only one way, by abiding in Christ so that his words abide in us.

Chapter 13

Abiding In Christ's Love

(John 15:9–11)

9. As the Father hath loved me, so have I loved you: continue ye in my love.
10. If ye keep my commandments, ye shall abide in my love; even as I have kept my Father's commandments, and abide in his love.
11. These things have I spoken unto you, that my joy might remain in you, and that your joy might be full.

One of the main themes of John 15, especially verses 1–11, is abiding in Jesus Christ. The idea itself is simple: we abide in Christ by staying connected to him, by remaining in him, or by continuing in him. This presupposes a union, for you cannot abide in Jesus Christ unless you are already in him. To use the figure, a dead stick on the floor of the vineyard does not abide in the vine, for it was never in the vine; or to speak without the figure, a pagan on the mission field does not abide in Jesus Christ, for he was never united to him by true faith.

Jesus does speak of two kinds of branches in him: the abiding kind and the non-abiding kind. The non-abiding kind is the person who had some kind of superficial connection with Jesus Christ and his church: he is the hypocrite, often a child of believing parents, who seems to be a true believer for a time, but who is eventually revealed to be a fruitless professor and is cut off. Judas Iscariot was such a fruitless branch: he did not abide in Jesus Christ. Of course, such non-abiding branches were never truly in Jesus Christ; they only seemed to be in him for a time. The abiding kind is the true, elect, redeemed, regenerated believer: he is in Jesus Christ by a true faith, and by virtue of his union with Christ he brings forth the fruit of good works.

Thus far Christ has spoken of three kinds of abiding. The first and fundamental abiding is Christ's abiding in us: "And I in you" (v. 4); "and I in him" (v. 5). Christ does that by the second kind of abiding, which is the abiding of his words in us: "And my words abide in you" (v. 7). Christ's abiding in us by his word is the fundamental abiding, for without that abiding there is no other abiding. The vine is always first and then the branches, for the branches need the vine, but the vine does not need the branches. The vine supplies life-giving, nourishing sap to the branches, so that they bear fruit, but the branches supply nothing to the vine. The third kind of abiding is our abiding in him. The branch abides in the vine, and the believer abides in Christ: "abide in me" (v. 4); "except ye abide in me" (v. 4); "he that abideth in me" (v. 5); "if ye abide in me" (v. 7).

This abiding of the believer in Jesus Christ is by faith alone, for we do not abide in Jesus by works, by acts of obedience. That would reverse the relationship, for works are the fruit of abiding in Christ, not the reason for such abiding or the condition for such abiding. Having been united to Christ or engrafted into Christ by a true faith, we become active in that abiding, so that by faith we remain in union with Christ and maintain conscious fellowship with him. We exercise faith by trusting in the perfect work of Christ as the only ground of our salvation, by depending upon him alone for all things, and by drawing out of his fullness the gifts and graces necessary for the Christian life. These things are important aspects of the activity of faith. The result of such abiding is fruit, the fruit of a ripened Christian character bearing the fruit of the Spirit, fruit that is the evidence of genuine discipleship, and fruit by which the Father is glorified.

But Christ has yet more instruction on this abiding, which is a vitally important subject for his disciples to understand, especially as he prepares to depart from them. In these verses Jesus speaks of a fourth kind of abiding, which is abiding in Christ's love: "If ye keep my commandments, ye shall abide in my love." Crucially, he establishes a relationship between abiding in his love and the keeping of his commandments. It is that relationship that we must seek to understand and apply in this chapter.

THE LOVE IN WHICH WE ABIDE

In these verses, Jesus drops the figure: he no longer speaks of the vine and its branches. Now he is more direct, for he speaks of love. Christ begins with the Father's love: "As the Father hath loved me" (v. 9). The meaning here is not the love of the first person for the second person within the triune being of God: the Father's love for the Son in the Holy Spirit. Instead, the meaning is the love of the triune God (the Father) for the incarnate Son, the Mediator, who is Jesus Christ. We know this because of verse 10: "I have kept my Father's commandments." The second person of the Trinity does not keep the commandments of the first person until he becomes incarnate and is "made under the law" (Gal. 4:4). Only the incarnate Son of God in his human nature keeps the Father's commandments.

The triune God (the God and Father of our Lord Jesus Christ), therefore, loves Jesus Christ. What a wonderful truth that is, about which we seldom think! He loved Jesus Christ when he was as yet unborn in his mother's womb. He loved Jesus Christ when he lay in Bethlehem's stable in a manger. He loved Jesus Christ as he grew up in Nazareth "and the grace of God was upon him" (Luke 2:40). He loved Jesus Christ in his baptism, he loved him when Satan tempted him in the wilderness, he loved him throughout his public ministry, and he still loved him when he was preparing to take his leave of his disciples in the upper room. "And lo a voice from heaven, saying, This is my beloved Son, in whom I am well pleased" (Matt. 3:17). "While he yet spake, behold, a bright cloud overshadowed them: and behold a voice out of the cloud, which said, This is my beloved Son, in whom I am well pleased; hear ye him" (17:5). "For thou lovedst me before the foundation of the world" (John 17:24).

Do not think of that abstractly, for in loving Christ, the Mediator, the incarnate Son, the triune God also loves all those who are "in Christ." The Father views the Son as the head of the elect church and as the husband of the elect church. He never views him as separate from the church. God's love is never abstract or unconnected to you, believing reader: you are loved *in Christ*. When you think of God's love, never look at yourself, for because of your sins you are unlovely and unlovable. Look to Christ, for only in him do you know the love of God.

But what is that love with which the triune Father loves the incarnate Son? We can say three things about that love, three aspects of a definition of love. First, the triune God delights in the Son as his most precious possession, highly prizing his Son as precious and dear to himself. "He hath made us accepted in the beloved" (Eph. 1:6). "And hath translated us into the kingdom of his dear Son" (Col. 1:13). He is the beloved, the dear, Son of God.

Second, the triune God seeks in all things the welfare of his Son and the eternal blessedness of his Son. The Father has prepared a kingdom for the Son, the Father has prepared glory for the Son, the Father has planned blessedness for the Son, and the Father has made the Son heir of all things. "And I appoint unto you a kingdom, as my Father hath appointed unto me" (Luke 22:29). "Father, the hour is come; glorify thy Son, that thy Son also may glorify thee" (John 17:1). "And now, O Father, glorify thou me with thine own self with the glory which I had with thee before the world was" (v. 5).

Third, the triune God draws the Son into close fellowship and communion with himself, so close that the Father is in the Son, and the Son is in the Father. "The Father that dwelleth in me, he doeth the works" (John 14:10).

We can also draw out some important implications about that love. We share in that love, for the Father loves us with that same love. Therefore, we can confess: we are the objects of the Father's delight, we are precious and dear to the Father, the Father seeks our salvation and has planned a glorious inheritance for us in Christ, and the Father draws us into his fellowship and communion by the power of the Holy Spirit of Christ. In addition, since Christ is the object of the Father's eternal and everlasting love, we can understand something of the cost of that love. When the Father sent the Son to die on the cross for our sins, he did not send an angel or some other creature, but he sent the object of his everlasting delight. "For God so loved the world, that he gave his only begotten Son, that whosoever believeth in him should not perish, but have everlasting life" (John 3:16). Familiar words, but profound meaning! Moreover, God's love for his Son is spontaneous and natural: Jesus is forever worthy of the Father's love, for he always pleased the Father. God's love for us is voluntary and purposeful: he chose to love us despite our unworthiness.

"As the Father hath loved me" (v. 9): Jesus draws a direct comparison or correlation between the Father's love for him and his love for the disciples, and by extension, his love for us. "So have I loved you" (v. 9). Here is an exact correlation: "As…so." Apply those three points above to Christ's love for us. Jesus delights in us, highly prizes us, and views us as precious and dear to himself. Jesus has planned the highest blessedness for us, for he seeks our salvation in all things, he has prepared for us a kingdom, and he has prepared glory for us. Jesus the Mediator draws us into his holy embrace of love, he establishes a relationship of friendship with us, and he has fellowship with us.

What else is characteristic of Christ's love for us? We can name some additional things. Christ's love is selfless and sacrificial. Jesus knew our need. He knew our misery. He knew that we were lost in sin. He knew that our sin left us exposed to the wrath of God. Because he desired to save us from that wrath, he died for us out of love for us. It is for that reason that he came into the world: to suffer and die for our sins.

Christ's love is sovereignly free. Christ was not obligated to love us, but he chose to love us: he set his love on us. Because Christ's love for us is a sovereign choice of his will, his love for us does not depend upon us: it does not depend on any quality in us. What was there in Peter, John, or Philip to attract the love of Christ to them? Nothing! And if nothing in us drew him to love us in the first place, nothing in us will repel him from us so that he ceases to love us in the future.

Christ's love is everlasting and unchanging. Christ's love does not ebb and flow as the tide; it does not wax and wane as the moon. It is constant. "Having loved his own...he loved them unto the end" (John 13:1). Christ's love does not vary according to the worthiness of the objects of his love. While we always remain unworthy of his love, his love remains constant and firm.

"As the Father hath loved me, so have I loved you" (John 15:9)!

OUR ABIDING IN IT

Jesus adds the urgent exhortation "Continue ye in my love" (v. 9), where the word "continue" is the same word as "abide." Take note of the order. I have loved you; therefore continue or abide in my love (v. 9). You are branches in the vine; therefore abide in the vine (v. 4). My words are in you; therefore let my words abide in you (v. 7). This is not ultimately your activity, and it does not depend on your activity. You did not engraft yourself into the vine and you do not keep yourself in the vine. You did not unite yourself to Jesus Christ and you do not keep yourself in Christ. You did not place Christ's words in yourself and you do not keep them in yourself. Similarly, you did not bring yourself into Christ's love and you do not keep yourself in Christ's love. In other words, while you are active in this, you do not abide in his love in your own strength. Nevertheless, this is a command: "Continue ye." We are active, or we become active, in this.

The love in verse 9 is emphatically Christ's love. Therefore, the meaning is not our love for Christ. Our love is certainly important, but it is not the meaning here. That meaning would not fit the context of verse 9, for Jesus is not exhorting, "Keep on loving me" or "Continue to love me." Rather, he urges, "I have loved you. Now, continue, remain, or abide in my love for you." "Remain once and for all time in my love." "Abide permanently in my love."

Abiding in Christ's love for us includes at least four things. First, we continue to believe it. We have assurance of it. We trust in the truth and faithfulness of Christ's love. We do not abide in Christ's love when we question or doubt his love for us, for has Christ not decisively proved his love for us in his death on the cross for our salvation? Second, we remember it. We have knowledge of it. We even grow in our knowledge and appreciation of it. Abide in Christ's love. Meditate on it. Study it. Occupy your mind, your heart, and your soul with it. Third, we dwell in the consciousness and enjoyment of it. We dwell in Christ's love, as it were, under Christ's shining smile. We abide in the experience of it. We know that he loves us, and we rejoice in and delight in that love. Fourth, we abide in Christ's love when it is the motivating factor in our life. Christ's love motivates us to good works. Christ's love motivates us to avoid sin. Christ's love motivated Paul in 2 Corinthians 5:14: "For the love of Christ constraineth us." Elsewhere Paul writes, "The life which I now live in the flesh I live by the faith of the Son of God, who loved me, and gave himself for me" (Gal. 2:20). When we consider Christ's love, we are moved: we think of its depth, its faithfulness, its power, its constancy, its efficacy, its beauty, and its sweetness. Such delightful thoughts of Christ's love move us to thanksgiving, to worship, to service, to patient endurance, and to obedience. "Because thy lovingkindness is better than life, my lips shall praise thee" (Ps. 63:3).

Is that not the testimony and the experience of God's children? Why did Paul gladly suffer the loss of all things and endure persecution and opposition for the gospel? The love of Christ constrained him. By grace he abode in Christ's love and that love sustained him. This, too, is the teaching of the Reformed confessions. The third section of the Heidelberg Catechism grounds our obedience in gratitude, gratitude that is our response to God's gracious redemption of us in Jesus Christ. The Belgic Confession article 24 states, "Therefore it is so far from being true that this justifying faith makes men remiss in a pious and holy life, that on the contrary, without it they would never do anything out of love to God, but only out of self-love or fear of damnation."[1] Love for God motivates us because God loved us in Jesus Christ. Canons 1.13 explains, "The sense and certainty of this election [and therefore of Christ's love] afford to the children of God additional matter for daily humiliation before Him, for adoring the depth of His mercies, for cleansing themselves, and rendering grateful returns of ardent love to Him, who first manifested so great love towards them."[2] God has loved us; we render grateful returns to him.

But why is this exhortation—"Continue ye in my love"—necessary? Surely, we know Christ's love. If we know Christ's love, we do not need to be exhorted to continue in it, do we? Peter, John, James, and the others knew Christ's love; yet Jesus exhorted them. We know too, but we still need the exhortation and reminder. We need this reminder because we do not always live in the conscious enjoyment of that truth. Often we doubt it. Sometimes we cannot sense it. Then we are tempted to imagine, "Christ no longer loves me." When our faith is weak, we struggle to believe. Such struggles are not unusual, which is why we need this exhortation.

Two things tempt us to doubt the love of Christ. The first is suffering or affliction: when life is hard, we find it more difficult to believe in Christ's love for us. When we are sick, we are quick to jump to conclusions—Christ hates me! We are too quick to measure Christ's love by our circumstances and our feelings. The disciples would need to abide in Christ's love when persecution came. When the Sanhedrin turned against them, when they were cast into prison and beaten, then they would be tempted to doubt. They would be tempted to forget, question, lose the sense of, and even deny Christ's love.

The second thing is sin: when we walk in sin, Christ's love seems to be hidden behind a cloud, for in those times he chastises us,

---

1 Belgic Confession 24, in *Confessions and Church Order*, 53.

2 Canons 1.13, in Confessions and Church Order, 157.

sometimes with very painful chastisements. We cry out, "Lord, thou dost hate me!" But Christ disciplines us in love in order to deliver us from our sins. His love never changes: he loves us, but he hates our sin. Therefore, out of love for us he is determined to separate us from our sin, even by inflicting pain and suffering upon us. Nothing can separate us from Christ's love, but Christ's love separates us from sin.

Beloved believing reader, if you think that you can abide in the conscious enjoyment of Christ's love while you walk deliberately in sin, a whole host of biblical witnesses will rise up to testify to the folly of such a course. David will tell you, "When I kept silence, my bones waxed old through my roaring all the day long" (Ps. 32:3). Jonah will tell you how he tried to flee from the presence of the Lord, only to be swallowed up by a great fish until he cried out of hell's belly (Jonah 2). Samson will tell you about his presumptuous playing with Delilah until God broke his heart in a Philistine dungeon (Judges 16). Peter will tell you of his bitter weeping outside the courtyard of Caiaphas's palace (Matt. 26:75). But even without the testimony of those men, we have the words of Jesus Christ: "If ye keep my commandments, ye shall abide in my love."

Jesus connects our abiding in Christ's love to the keeping of his commandments in verse 10: "If ye keep my commandments, ye shall abide in my love." On the face of it, Jesus seems to be teaching conditional salvation or at the very least conditional experience of salvation. Does Christ's use of the word "if" indicate a condition that we must fulfill in order to abide in his love?

We must understand what a condition is, for there is much confusion on this point. A condition is something we must do upon which the obtaining of something else depends. If Jesus meant that our abiding in his love was conditioned on our obedience, he would have said, "Your abiding in my love depends on your obedience to my commandments." Furthermore, although the grammar of the sentence is in the form of a condition—"if"—the meaning of the sentence is not a condition. Sometimes "if" is not conditional but evidentiary, or it serves to identify those to whom the promise pertains. In other words, "if" does not express a condition but proves the evidence of something.

How are those to be identified who abide in Christ's love? They keep his commandments. They and only they abide in Christ's love. The deliberately disobedient do *not* abide in Christ's love. There are other evidentiary "if sentences" in the Bible: "Ye are my friends, *if* ye do whatsoever I command you" (v. 14). The thrust of these words is this: "You prove yourselves to be my friends by doing what I say," or "Your obedience is the proof that you are my friends, but not the condition for being, becoming, or remaining such." Therefore, an acceptable paraphrase of Christ's words, which brings out the meaning, is this: "If you keep my commandments, *you show that* you abide in my love."

We know that the meaning is not conditional but evidentiary because of how Jesus continues in verse 10b: "Even as I have kept my Father's commandments, and abide in his love." If our abiding in Christ's love depends upon our keeping of Christ's commandments, then Christ's abiding in his Father's love depended on Christ's keeping of his Father's commandments. But the Father's love for Christ is not conditional. Therefore, Christ's love for us is also not conditional. There is comfort: if you can imagine Christ not abiding in the Father's love, then you might freely imagine a situation in which you (believer) would not abide in Christ's love or in which you might be separated from Christ's love. Both ideas are absurd. And in case the reader entertains any lingering doubts, listen to Paul:

> "For I am persuaded, that neither death, nor life, nor angels, nor principalities, nor powers, nor things present, nor things to come, nor height, nor depth, nor any other creature, shall be able to separate us from the love of God, which is in Christ Jesus our Lord" (Rom. 8:38–39).

Yet there is a connection between abiding in Christ's love and keeping Christ's commandments. We must not dismiss Christ's words too quickly or lightly, but we must take them seriously and do justice to them. There is no enjoyment of Christ's love while we walk in sin. God's love is holy. Therefore, it is enjoyed only in the sphere of holiness. One who walks in disobedience will doubt and question Christ's love, for his conscience will oppress him. One who walks in disobedience will not appreciate or enjoy the consciousness of Christ's love, for God will chastise him by withdrawing the sense of his favor. One who walks in disobedience is not motivated by Christ's love, but something else, such as pride, lust, selfishness, or some other sin, motivates and blinds him. There is a sphere in which we enjoy, experience, delight in, and are confident of the love of Christ. It is the sphere of obedience or the sphere of holiness. There is also a sphere in which we are oppressed with doubts and are not conscious of the love of Christ for us. It is the sphere of darkness and disobedience.

5. This then is the message which we have heard of him, and declare unto you, that God is light, and in him is no darkness at all.
6. If we say that we have fellowship with him, and walk in darkness, we lie, and do not the truth:
7. But if we walk in the light, as he is in the light, we have fellowship one with another, and the blood of Jesus Christ his Son cleanseth us from all sin. (1 John 1:5–7)

Incidentally, John uses the word "if" in 1 John 1, but like Christ's words in John 15, the apostle does not express a condition that we must fulfill before we can have fellowship with God, as if our fellowship depended on our walking in the light. John identifies those who have fellowship with God as those, and only those, who walk in the light. One who does not walk in the light, but walks in darkness, does not have fellowship with God, no matter how orthodox he might claim to be.

When we do not walk in Christ's commandments, we do not enjoy Christ's love. Be careful: Christ does not cease to love us. Nevertheless, our enjoyment of Christ's love is diminished and even interrupted. Take a teenage boy who rebels against his father. His father disciplines him, with the result that he sulks in his room. Such a boy, as long as he remains in a sulking mood, does not enjoy his father's love. He does not believe it, he questions it, and he doubts it. He does not know it, appreciate it, or enjoy it, for he does not dwell in the consciousness of it, and he is not motivated by it. And yet what parent makes his love dependent or conditioned on the obedience of his children? The father's love has not changed: his discipline is no manifestation of hatred. The father disciplines his son in love. If the father hated his son, he would permit him to go on in his sins. But the rebellious son does not interpret his father's actions as love.

That is an illustration of a rebellious Christian: he does not keep Christ's commandments and he does not abide in Christ's love. As long as he is determined to walk in darkness, the Father withholds his approving smile. The Father's love has not changed, but the manifestation of the Father's love has changed: he shows his love in discipline. The creeds testify to this: "They…lose the sense of God's favor for a time, *until*, on their returning into the right way of serious repentance, the light of God's fatherly countenance again shines upon them."[3] Do not make any mistake, therefore: God loves us too much to allow us to walk in sin and God's love is enjoyed only in the sphere of holiness, which manifests itself in a life of obedience to God's commandments. Our Father chastises us "for our profit, that we might be partakers of his holiness" (Heb. 12:10). Although our Father aims at our holiness, not our happiness, it is in holiness that we will find our ultimate happiness.

Apply this to Jesus: "Even as I have kept my Father's commandments, and abide in his love" (v. 10). Although it was impossible that it should be otherwise, Jesus enjoyed the smile of his Father's love while he kept his Father's commandments. Yet he says in John 10:17, "Therefore doth my Father love me, *because* I lay down my life, that I might take it again." In the sphere of perfect obedience, obedience that led to the cross, Christ enjoyed the Father's love. There is

---

3 Canons 5.5, in *Confessions and Church Order*, 174, emphasis added.

something deeply mysterious here: when Jesus suffered on the cross and obeyed God to the uttermost, loving God while enduring God's wrath and curse for our sins, God still loved Jesus, although Jesus could not sense it. Jesus did not sense it because he was made an offering for sin, for our sin. Christ did not sense God's love for a time so that, having purchased salvation for us, he might cause us to enjoy God's love forever.

THE PROMISE OF ABIDING JOY

Jesus connects this abiding to joy: "These things have I spoken unto you, that my joy might remain in you, and that your joy might be full" (v. 11). Jesus does not tell the disciples these beautiful truths for the sake of mere information. God does not reveal truth to us merely to inform us, but to motivate us to action. Abide in Christ's love! Keep Christ's commandments! Have joy! Have the fullness of joy! Or to quote Paul, "Rejoice in the Lord alway: and again I say, Rejoice" (Phil. 4:4).

Joy is a deep, spiritual gladness of heart or a profound cheerfulness of the soul. Joy is not the same as happiness, for happiness depends on circumstances (it contains the word *happen*), while joy transcends circumstances; we are happy when good things happen to us, and while we find it difficult to be happy in affliction, we always rejoice in God, in Christ, and in Christ's love. Jesus commands his disciples to abide in his love as they keep his commandments because he wishes to keep them from misery and to fulfill their joy. Jesus sees miserable times ahead for the disciples, about which he warns them extensively in chapter 16. Nevertheless, Jesus knows that the real source of misery is not persecution or tribulation, but sin. Every Reformed Christian who reads the Heidelberg Catechism knows that too: "my sins and miseries."[4] Peter did not weep when he was beaten and imprisoned; in fact, he rejoiced (Acts 5:41), but he did weep bitterly when he fell into lamentable sin (Matt. 26:75).

---

4 Heidelberg Catechism A2, in *Confessions and Church Order*, 84.

There is a way to be miserable: it is to walk in disobedience, and not to abide in Christ's love. David learned that. Samson learned that. Jonah learned that. And Peter learned that. Those lessons were very bitter. Out of love Jesus warns his disciples not to walk in the way of misery but to walk in the way of joy and peace: keep my commandments. Godly parents tell their children this too: son, daughter, keep my commandments in the home. Obey me, and you will know my approval, but break the rules of my house, disobey me, and you will be miserable until you repent and walk in obedience again. Peter had to learn that the hard way: when he denied Jesus, he did not abide in the consciousness of Jesus' love. Jesus loved Peter with an eternal love rooted in election, but Peter had to weep bitterly with tears of repentance, which were the fruit of God's grace, *before* he came to the renewed assurance of Jesus' love for him.[5]

For the Christian who abides in Christ's love and keeps his commandments, there is rich, blessed, abiding joy, not because he walks obediently, as if obedience were a condition he must fulfill to obtain joy, but in the way of obedience, as he walks in the light. What greater joy than to be loved by Jesus and to know it! Here is the way of joy: abide in Christ's love; abide in his love in the sphere of holiness; and you will know, and continue to know, eternal, everlasting joy. That joy cannot be taken from you, for it transcends all circumstances of life.

That joy is in Christ. Abide in him; abide in his love, and you shall have joy, the joy of Jesus Christ, forever.

---

5 Canons 5.5–7, in Confessions and Church Order, 174.

Chapter 14

Jesus Calls Us His Friends

(John 15:12–15)

12. This is my commandment, That ye love one another, as I have loved you.
13. Greater love hath no man than this, that a man lay down his life for his friends.
14. Ye are my friends, if ye do whatsoever I command you.
15. Henceforth I call you not servants; for the servant knoweth not what his lord doeth: but I have called you friends; for all things that I have heard of my Father I have made known unto you.

There are different ways in which the Bible describes and explains the relationship between Christ and his disciples. The disciples are Christ's servants, while he is their lord. "Ye call me Master and Lord: and ye say well; for so I am," Christ affirms in John 13:13. The disciples are Christ's sheep, while he is their shepherd, a theme of chapter 10. Christ's sheep hear his voice and follow him. The disciples are fruitful branches in Christ the true vine, which is the dominant figure in chapter 15. With that figure Christ especially teaches his disciples their absolute dependence on him for all things, including the ability to bring forth fruit. "Without me," warns Christ, "ye can do nothing" (v. 5). Flip that around: united to Christ we can do many things. United to Christ we can, we do, and we must bring forth good fruit, even much good fruit, to the glory of our Father. Indeed, as Paul writes in Philippians 4:13, "I can do all things through Christ which strengtheneth me," where the immediate context is the ability to be content in every circumstance of life.

Therefore, these words do not encourage passivity in the believer. Instead, they encourage activity, the vibrant activity of faith, with the result that we bring forth many good works to the glory of our Father. That activity Christ has described as abiding: abiding in Christ by faith, abiding in Christ by abiding in his word, and abiding in Christ's love.

In these verses Christ draws our attention to another aspect of our relationship to him. We are not only servants under his lordship, sheep of his fold, and branches in the vine, but we are also his friends. The idea of friendship fits beautifully with the context, which is love: the Father's love for Christ, Christ's love for us, and our love for one another. Jesus introduces the calling to love in verse 12, "This is my commandment, That ye love one another, as I have loved you." But we can only truly love one another through abiding in Christ's love, for Christ's love is always first. Out of his love for us he calls us his friends.

WHAT THIS MEANS

What is a friend? What does Jesus mean in verse 14 when he says, "Ye are my friends"? Why does he add, "I have called you my friends"? In an age of social media the term *friend* has been devalued and cheapened: a person can claim five thousand online friends when very few—if any—of them are actual friends in the proper sense of the word. A friend is much more than pixels on a screen.

First, a friend is one for whom you have affection and even love. This goes well beyond an acquaintance, for a friend is much closer than an acquaintance. Solomon writes about friendship in the book of Proverbs. "A friend loveth at all times, and a brother is born for adversity" (Prov. 17:17). "A man that hath friends must show himself friendly: and there is a friend that sticketh closer than a brother" (18:24). "Faithful are the wounds of a friend; but the kisses of an enemy are deceitful" (27:6). "Ointment and perfume rejoice the heart: so doth the sweetness of a man's friend by hearty counsel" (v. 9). The best example of friendship in the Old Testament is David's friendship with Jonathan, which was a friendship of genuine affection and even love. The friendship begins just after David defeats Goliath: "The soul of Jonathan was knit with the soul of David, and Jonathan loved him as his own soul" (1 Sam. 18:1; 20:17). David was Jonathan's friend in that they cared for one another, they sought the welfare of one another, and they were united together in the bonds of fellowship. If there is one person whom you can call in the middle of the night in a panic because you know that he will listen and help, he is your friend. Jesus says to his disciples—and to us—"Ye are my friends" (v. 14). "I call you not servants...I have called you friends" (v. 15).

By these words Jesus means, "You are they for whom I have deep affection and love. I care deeply about you. My desire is for your welfare, even your salvation. Everything I do, I do with a view to your blessedness." If we are Jesus' friends, we must love him, we must seek his glory, and we must not be afraid to trust him, especially when we are deeply distressed. Jesus uttered these words, "I have loved you" (v. 12), "Ye are my friends" (v. 14), and "I have called you friends" (v. 15) when the disciples experienced great sorrow, fear, and trouble of heart. These words must comfort us when we take them to heart and when we receive them by faith.

Second, a friend is one with whom you enjoy familiarity and even intimacy. With a true friend there is a sharing of knowledge and close communication. This is because friendship is a relationship of trust. You tell a friend something because you trust that he will not betray your confidence. You tell a friend your secrets because you are confident in his presence. Again we think of the example of David and Jonathan: when David was in peril, he confided in Jonathan and he trusted Jonathan not to betray him to Saul. What you would not post on your social media account, even with the restricted settings so that only your online friends would see it, you would tell a close friend. If there is someone to whom you tell your intimate thoughts, your ideas, your plans, and your feelings, which you would not tell to another soul, he is your friend. If there is someone to whom you would unburden your heart, he is your friend.

There is therefore something devastating about betrayal among friends. Micah writes, "Trust ye not in a friend, put ye not confidence in a guide: keep the doors of thy mouth from her that lieth in thy bosom" (Mic. 7:5); and the psalmist writes, "Yea, mine own familiar friend, in whom I trusted, which did eat of my bread, hath lifted up his heel against me" (Ps. 41:9), a prophecy fulfilled in the betrayal of Judas Iscariot.

Since friendship includes a sharing of knowledge, friends should be open. When something bothers you, you should not hide it from your close friends. Friends should not have secrets from one another. The closer the friendship, the more communication there is and should be. We read of such communication in the Old Testament. God called Abraham his friend and in Genesis 18:17–18 God said, "Shall I hide from Abraham that thing which I do; seeing that Abraham shall surely become a great and mighty nation?" The reference is to the destruction of Sodom: God did not share that information with the Sodomites, but he told his friend Abraham. If God calls us his friends in Jesus Christ, shall we hide from him? Shall we not pour out our hearts to him in prayer? Shall we not seek to know him through the preaching of his word?

Jesus says to his disciples and to us, "Ye are my friends" (v. 14). "I call you not servants…I have called you friends" (v. 15). By these words Jesus means, "You are they with whom I share my secrets: I make known my intimate thoughts, desires, and plans only to you. I tell you things that I do not tell others. I do so because I want you to know me, so that we can enjoy sweet, intimate fellowship together." Jesus explains this in verse 15: "Henceforth I call you not servants; for the servant knoweth not what his lord doeth: but I have called you friends; for all things that I have heard of my Father I have made known unto you." A servant knows the master's will, but he does not know the master's mind. A servant receives orders that he obeys unquestioningly and unhesitatingly. Our relationship is greater than that of a master and his servant: we are Christ's friends.

You can see this in how Jesus treats his disciples differently from the common people of his day. In Mark 4:33–34 we read, "And with many such parables spake he the word unto them, as they were able to hear it. But without a parable spake he not unto them: and when they were alone, he expounded all things to his disciples." To the disciples in private Jesus said, "Behold, we go up to Jerusalem; and the Son of man shall be betrayed unto the chief priests and unto the scribes, and they shall condemn him to death, and shall deliver him to the Gentiles to mock, and to scourge, and to crucify him: and the third day he shall rise again" (Matt. 20:18–19). The entire upper room discourse is private, intimate instruction for his disciples, which was not preached openly.

The Heidelberg Catechism summarizes this beautifully: "[He is called Christ] because He is ordained of God the Father, and anointed with the Holy Ghost, to be our chief Prophet and Teacher, who has fully revealed to us the secret counsel and will of God concerning our redemption."[1] Jesus reveals all things to us, inasmuch as we are able to receive them and bear them. What Jesus did not reveal at that time, the Holy Spirit revealed later and recorded in the New Testament.

Third, a friend is one with whom you share not only knowledge, but also life. Again David and Jonathan are exemplary in this aspect of friendship. "The soul of Jonathan was knit with the soul of David" (1 Sam. 18:1). There was a close, intimate union between Jonathan and David. Because of their friendship they not only shared secrets, but they also spent time together. Friends delight in being together, for they love one another's company. They dwell closely together, they play together, and they go on adventures together.

There are different kinds of friendships, but the closest earthly friendship is marriage. Sadly, for David, his marriage was not happy

---

1 Heidelberg Catechism Q&A 31, in *Confessions and Church Order*, 95–96.

or close. This is why, for example, David eulogizes Jonathan at his death: "I am distressed for thee, my brother Jonathan: very pleasant hast thou been unto me: thy love to me was wonderful, passing the love of women" (2 Sam. 1:26). In a good marriage, husband and wife are best friends, lifelong companions, sharing a house, a table, a sofa, and a bed. They spend time together, they delight in one another's company, they look forward to being together, and they are sad when they are apart. That is what makes widowhood so lonely, for one's best, lifelong friend has passed away.

We need friends in the real world, and we must encourage our children and young people to cultivate friendships in the real world, for there is no sharing of life with online friends or with pixels on a screen.

Jesus says to his disciples—and to us—"Ye are my friends" (v. 14). "I call you not servants…I have called you friends" (v. 15). By these words Jesus means, "You are they with whom I share my life. I am determined to dwell with you. We have spent these years together, and I plan to spend the whole of eternity with you in fellowship and love." Therefore, Jesus makes preparations to share his life with us. He dies upon the cross to secure our salvation, he sends his Holy Spirit into our hearts, he writes his word on our hearts, and he prepares mansions in his Father's house. Jesus prays to his Father, "Father, I will that they also, whom thou hast given me, be with me where I am; that they may behold my glory" (John 17:24).

This friendship with Jesus, however, is unique: it is no ordinary friendship. When Jesus calls us friends, he does not invite us to call him "pal" or "buddy." Our friendship with Jesus, in which he calls us friends, is not a friendship among equals. Friendship involves familiarity, but let not familiarity breed contempt. There is a danger in this.

We are Jesus' friends, but he is still our Lord. You will notice that Jesus does not say—and the Bible never says—that he is our friend. He says, "Ye are my friends"; "I have called you friends." But Jesus does not say in so many words, "I am your friend." In fact, Jesus says in John 13:13, "Ye call me Master and Lord: and ye say well; for so I am." Jesus calls us friends, while we call him Lord. Similarly, although the Old Testament speaks of Abraham as God's friend, Scripture does not call Jehovah "Abraham's friend." Listen to Jehoshaphat's prayer in 2 Chronicles 20:6–7: "O LORD God of our fathers, art not thou God in heaven?…Art not thou our God...who gavest [the land] to the seed of Abraham thy friend forever?" Jehoshaphat did not say, "O Lord God, art thou not our Friend?"

God's saints refer to themselves as God's people, as his servants, and as his children, but they do not address God as their Friend. In the New Testament the apostles introduce themselves as apostles and servants of Christ, but never as Christ's friends; they never say, "Christ is our Friend." Perhaps the best way to designate the relationship is to call Jehovah or Christ our "Friend-Sovereign" or our "Friend-Lord" and we his "friend-servants."

Jesus makes clear in verse 15 that, although the relationship is changed by virtue of our friendship with Jesus, his lordship is by no means obliterated or canceled. Jesus differentiates between servants and friends in only one respect. "The servant," says Christ, "knoweth not what his lord doeth" (v. 15). A friend, however, is privy to his master's mind. Perhaps the designation could be "intimate, privileged friend-servants." Nevertheless, as we shall see later in this chapter, the friends of Jesus are required to obey him. We are not required to obey our ordinary friends, but we are required to obey Jesus Christ, for we are his friends, while he is our Lord: "Ye are my friends, if ye do whatsoever I command you" (v. 14).

We understand what it is to be a friend of Jesus. We are the objects of his intimate affection, for he has loved us. We are his close confidants, for he shares his intimate secrets, reveals his plans, and makes known his counsel to us. We have his mind and his heart. We are those with whom he shares his life and with whom he dwells forever. We enjoy these privileges with our Lord, whose obedient friends we are.

HOW THIS IS DEMONSTRATED

Jesus demonstrates his friendship not by going on a dinner date with us, not by sending us flowers, and not by playing ball with us, but by loving us: "So have I loved you" (v. 9). "As I have loved you" (v. 12). Love, however, is not a romantic, sentimental emotion, but love is sacrificial, costly. There are various things that friends are willing to do for one another. A person will give his friend a meal, a person will buy his friend a coffee, a person might choose to go on vacation with his friend, a person will give his friend a ride in his car, and a person will offer his friend a shoulder to cry on. Those are good things and they are to be encouraged, but Jesus has other things in mind: costlier activities, even sacrificial love.

Friendship—if it is true friendship—will gladly be inconvenienced, especially if the friendship is particularly close. If your friend calls you in a panic desperate for help, you will help him. You will take time out of your day, even your busy schedule, to meet the needs of a friend. You are more likely to do this for a friend than a stranger. A true friend understands that friendship requires time, effort, and commitment. Such activities are rarely the activities of people you befriend online.

Jesus describes the pinnacle of friendship as sacrificing one's life for a friend. Very few people ever make this ultimate sacrifice for their friends. Mothers sacrifice almost their entire lives in order to serve their children. Children do not know it until they are much older: your parents have sacrificed countless hours, sleepless nights, and a lot of money for you. They are not sorry: they did it because they love you and they would do it again. Love motivates a person to give sacrificially for the welfare of a friend. Our calling is to give our lives for the sake of our friends and especially for our fellow saints in the church: they are—and ought to be—our friends.

The test is, how much are you willing to give up to serve your friends? Are your fellow saints nuisances or are they your friends? If a friend in the church suffers, how do you respond? Do you meet their needs or are you indifferent? Paul writes, "And whether one member suffer, all the members suffer with it; or one member be honoured, all the members rejoice with it" (1 Cor. 12:26). John even writes:

> 14. We know that we have passed from death unto life, because we love the brethren. He that loveth not his brother abideth in death.
> 15. Whosoever hateth his brother is a murderer: and ye know that no murderer hath eternal life abiding in him.
> 16. Hereby perceive we the love of God, because he laid down his life for us: and we ought to lay down our lives for the brethren.
> 17. But whoso hath this world's good, and seeth his brother have need, and shutteth up his bowels of compassion from him, how dwelleth the love of God in him?
> 18. My little children, let us not love in word, neither in tongue; but in deed and in truth. (1 John 3:14–18)

Jesus demonstrated his love toward his friends in the ultimate sacrifice: "Greater love hath no man than this, that a man lay down his life for his friends" (v. 13). Jesus is not speaking merely hypothetically here. That is what he actually did. A man's life is his most precious possession; without life a man has nothing. Some people donate blood to save their friends and even to save strangers. Others donate bone marrow or a bodily organ, such as a kidney, to a family member. But ordinarily, in such a procedure the organ or blood donor lives. Even Satan understands: "Skin for skin, yea, all that a man hath he will give for his life" (Job 2:4). A man might lose many precious things, but if he has his life, he has not yet made the ultimate sacrifice.

Jesus laid down his life for his friends—for us—when he died upon the cross. Jesus had life. He had earthly life, that mysterious principle that holds the body and soul together, and he moved and breathed by virtue of his earthly life. But one day his life came to an end: "Father, into thy hands I commend my spirit: and having said thus, he gave up the ghost" (Luke 23:46). His life did not come to an end because cruel men killed him: they were merely wicked instruments in Christ's hand. Christ's life came to an end because he willingly sacrificed his life for our salvation: "that a man lay down his life for his friends" (v. 13). "Therefore doth my Father love me, because I lay down my life, that I might take it again. No man taketh it from me, but I lay it down of myself. I have power to lay it down, and I have power to take it again. This commandment have I received of my Father" (John 10:17–18).

In addition, Jesus' death was not merely physical death. Jesus experienced the horrifying reality of the wrath of God against him. Jesus endured the curse of the law against him. Jesus experienced the misery of forsakenness of God. In a word, Jesus experienced *hell* on the cross, hell for us, his friends.

But perhaps you wonder, why does Jesus say that there is no greater love than that a man lay down his life for his friends, when elsewhere in Scripture we read of God reconciling his enemies to himself by the death of the cross? Romans 5:6–11 has a different context, for Paul writes about the ungodly and sinners, while in John 15 the subject is friendship. It would hardly be fitting for Jesus to say, "Ye are my friends," and then say, "Greater love hath no man than this, that a man lay down his life for his enemies." Jesus does not deny that we are by nature his enemies. The fact is, Jesus makes us his friends. Jesus views us in John 15 from the perspective of grace, not from the perspective of nature: "Ye are my friends." Jesus died in order to make us (who were his enemies) the friends of God because he loved us. Do not be distracted from that: Jesus' death is his act of friendship.

Therefore, do not doubt Jesus' friendship. Do not doubt that you are his friend. Do not judge your status of friend from your earthly circumstances, but from the objective fact of the sacrificial death of Christ. When Peter was in prison, he did not wonder, "Am I really Christ's friend? Would Christ's friend suffer like this? Would Christ put his friend through such suffering?" Instead, Peter remembered the cross of his Savior. When the apostle James was condemned to death, before the sword fell upon his neck, he did not wonder, "Am I truly Christ's friend? Would Christ not spare me from Herod's cruel sword if I were truly his friend?" Instead, James remembered the cross of his Savior. When you are afflicted, sick, suffering, lonely, despairing, or afraid, do not linger upon your problems, and do not be tempted to deny Christ's friendship in light of your trials, but remember what Jesus did for his friends: "Greater love hath no man than this, that a man lay down his life for his friends" (John 15:13).

WHAT THIS DEMANDS

Jesus indicates that friendship with him has implications. We are still, even as friends, under Christ's lordship. We are friends, while he is the Lord. Jesus makes that clear in verse 12, "This is my commandment." We do not ordinarily issue commandments to our friends. Instead, we make requests. Jesus gives us commandments. A commandment is an order, an instruction, or a charge, something that we are required to do. A commandment is not a suggestion or a request. A commandment is not even a promise: you shall do this. A commandment is a requirement: you must do this. Jesus gives commandments because he is the Lord. He is the master: he owns us and he rules over us because we are his purchased property, redeemed by his blood. Jesus' commandment is not only that we love one another, although that is a good summary of the second table of the law, but Jesus commands us to keep the ten commandments. In fact, says Jesus in verse 14, "Ye are my friends, if ye do whatsoever I command you."

That word "if" is significant; it indicates a relationship between friendship with Jesus and obedience to Jesus' commandments. In the Christian life, friendship with Jesus and obedience are inseparable. One who does not keep Christ's commandments is not—and must not consider himself to be—a friend of Jesus. Jesus disavows such so-called friends. Nevertheless, the "if" is not conditional. Our friendship with Jesus does not depend on our faithful adherence to his commandments. Our obedience is the demonstration (an evidentiary "if" again, as in verse 10) that we are his friends. Obedience is the fruit of our friendship with Christ, for as his friends we respond in thankful obedience.

Another important consideration is this: you are not the only friend of Jesus. "I have called you friends" (v. 15). "Ye are my friends" (v. 14). In both cases, the word is plural, "friends." Therefore, you have a calling toward Jesus' other friends. That calling is very simple to state, but it is very difficult to carry out: "This is my commandment, That ye love one another, as I have loved you" (v. 12). This commandment is repeated throughout the Bible: "A new commandment I give unto you, That ye love one another; as I have loved you, that ye also love one another. By this shall all men know that ye are my disciples, if ye have love one to another" (John 13:34–35). "These things I command you, that ye love one another" (15:17). "For this is the message that ye heard from the beginning, that we should love one another" (1 John 3:11).

The world, if it has even the most rudimentary knowledge of Christianity, understands that Christians are called to love one another. The world, however, has wrong notions about the nature of love and the practice of love. In the world love is about acceptance, tolerance, and inclusivity. Worldly love is incompatible with holiness. But biblical love "rejoiceth not in iniquity, but rejoiceth in the truth" (1 Cor. 13:6).

Love does not consist of empty sentimental feelings, but it is very practical. Love selflessly gives itself for the welfare of the other. Love spends itself and is spent on the other. Love empties itself of everything in order to serve the other. That was Christ's love for us, and it must also be our love for our fellow saints. The more we abide in the love of Christ—by believing it, dwelling upon it, rejoicing in it, and being motivated by it—the more we will love one another.

This love must characterize our congregational life, our homes, the relationship between husbands and wives, the behavior of parents and children, the interactions between siblings, and the conduct of children in the Christian schools. As a society of Jesus' friends, we must display love not only for him, but also for one another. You are Jesus' friends. Keep his commandments.

Chapter 15

Chosen By Jesus Unto Fruitfulness

(John 15:16–17)

16. Ye have not chosen me, but I have chosen you, and ordained you, that ye should go and bring forth fruit, and that your fruit should remain: that whatsoever ye shall ask of the Father in my name, he may give it you.
17. These things I command you, that ye love one another.

Christ has just declared and explained his friendship to his disciples. Friendship includes three things: it is deep affection and love, it is familiarity and even intimacy, and it is the sharing of life. Without those things, or where those things are withheld, friendship cannot function properly. Our human friendships only dimly reflect the true friendship, which is, first, the communion and fellowship that exist within the triune God, and second, the communion and fellowship that exist between the triune God and the incarnate Mediator, Jesus Christ. Recall that Jesus declares in verse 9 the Father's love for him and in verse 10 he testifies that he abides in the Father's love.

Reformed believers are very familiar with the concept of divine friendship because we believe in the covenant of grace. The covenant is a relationship of friendship that God establishes in Jesus Christ, the head of the covenant, with his elect, believing people and their elect children, so that God calls his elect, believing people and their elect children his friends. That is essentially the meaning of Jesus' words to his disciples in verse 14: "Ye are my friends."

While friendship is a relationship of familiarity and even intimacy, familiarity must never be allowed to breed contempt in our souls. Jesus guards his disciples against that danger by reminding them that he is still their Lord. That is clear because in this friendship, this covenantal relationship, Jesus still requires obedience. In fact, obedience is the outstanding evidence of friendship in the covenant: one who persistently disobeys Jesus Christ cannot be considered his friend. Jesus puts it very strongly: "Ye are my friends, if ye do whatsoever I command you" (v. 14).

In addition, while we enjoy immense privileges as Jesus' friends, we also have responsibilities. We have been chosen so that we will bear fruit, the chief of which is love. Christ's friends love one another: they highly esteem one another and delight in one another, they seek one another's welfare, and they seek to establish a bond with one another. "These things I command you, that ye love one another" (v. 17).

But what is the origin of this friendship? It is not found in us, as if we decided to become Christ's friends, or as if we attracted him to us by some quality in us so that he took us to be his friends. Jesus grounds his friendship with us in divine election: "Ye have not chosen me, but I have chosen you" (v. 16). That is humbling and also very comforting: we were given to Christ by the Father before the foundation of the world.

CHOSEN: BY WHOM?

Friendship usually involves a choice. I can illustrate this with the example of children on a playground. Two children meet for the first time on a playground and become friends. When they become friends, it is usually a mutual decision. Perhaps one child approaches the other child: he has a toy in his hand. "This is my toy car," he says. "Would you like to play with it?" The second child agrees, "Yes, and you can play with my toy truck." In a few moments, the children, who before this were strangers, are playing happily together while their mothers look on, pleased that their children have found new friends. One of the children took the initiative, but the second child consented to play. As the children meet regularly—and even go to the same school—a friendship develops between them. Perhaps other friends are added to the group. The point is this: friendship is based on a mutual decision to be friendly.

That is not the case with the friendship described in John 15. Our friendship with Jesus in which he calls us his friends is not based on a mutual decision. Jesus says, "Ye have not chosen me, but I have chosen you" (v. 16). The reference is first to the eleven disciples in the upper room. Peter did not choose Jesus, but Jesus chose Peter. Thomas did not choose Jesus, but Jesus chose Thomas. Philip did not choose Jesus, but Jesus chose Philip. It is not the case that one day Peter, Thomas, or Philip approached Jesus and said, "We have seen you, Jesus. We would like to be your friends." Nor is it the case that Jesus offered the possibility of friendship to these men, and they accepted his offer: "Peter, Thomas, Philip, would you like to be my friends? I would like that very much, but you must choose me first." Jesus is very clear: "Ye did not choose me, but I have chosen you."

The same is true of all true believers in Christ, of all true Christians, and of us. Why do you believe in Jesus? Why do you love him from the heart? Why do you seek to follow him? Are you a Christian because one day you heard the gospel and you said, "You know what—I like that message. I think I will accept Jesus as my savior. He wants me to be his friend. I will accept his offer of friendship"? The answer is very simple: you are a Christian because Jesus chose you.

Jesus therefore teaches the doctrine of election, a doctrine that is cordially hated in many churches today: "Ye have not chosen me, but I have chosen you" (v. 16). The verb "chosen" in verse 15 is often rendered "elected" in the New Testament. The verb "elect" or "choose" means "to choose out for oneself." Jesus did not choose everyone, but he made a choice among various options. Before Jesus stood the whole of mankind, and out of them Jesus chose certain persons or certain individuals in distinction from those not chosen. To make it concrete: Jesus chose Peter, while he rejected Caiaphas the high priest; he chose Thomas, while he rejected Pontius Pilate the Roman governor; and he chose Philip, while he rejected many of the scribes and Pharisees.

Do not forget either that Jesus' choice (election) of some implies and requires his rejection (reprobation) of others. He chose you, but he rejected others. Jesus further elaborates on this choice (or election) of the eleven disciples in verse 19: "Ye are not of the world, but I have chosen you out of the world." The disciples—Peter, Thomas, Philip, and the rest—had belonged to the world. That world was the fallen world, a world of sinners, a world in rebellion against God and in enmity against him, but Jesus delivered them out of it. Jesus chose the disciples out of the world for himself: he chose them to be his friends; he chose them to be his peculiar treasure, to be his beloved church. The same is true of us: he chose us out of the world for himself.

This choice of Jesus is a divine choice: "I have chosen you" (v. 16). Jesus is divine, for he is the second person of the blessed Trinity. The triune God—the Father, Son, and Spirit—has one divine will. Paul writes, "[God] worketh all things after the counsel of his own will" (Eph. 1:11). According to the eternal will of the eternal God, the eleven disciples—Peter, Thomas, Philip, and the rest—were chosen unto everlasting life and glory. Paul writes, "According as he hath chosen [elected] us in him [in Christ] before the foundation of the world…having predestinated us" (vv. 4–5).

Jesus is also human: he is the incarnate Mediator, the second person made flesh, and therefore Jesus also has a human will, which operates in time. The subject of Jesus' human will caused considerable controversy in the early church: a heresy called Monothelitism (the doctrine of one will) was condemned in AD 680–81. The church confesses that Jesus has a human will, as well as the divine will. We know this from Jesus' statement in Gethsemane, where he deliberately submits his human will to the divine will: "O my Father, if it be possible, let this cup pass from me: nevertheless not as I will, but as thou wilt" (Matt. 26:39). Elsewhere Jesus says, "For I came down from heaven, not to do mine own will, but the will of him that sent me" (John 6:38). These passages indicate that there is a distinction between Jesus' human will and the divine will. Nevertheless, there is no conflict or struggle between the human and divine will in Jesus, and never did Jesus desire to sin. Jesus accomplishes in perfect obedience—even willingly—the Father's will.

The Father (the triune God) chose the whole elect church in eternity. He gave the whole elect church to Jesus Christ in his eternal decree, and Jesus Christ the Mediator also chose the eleven disciples in time. The gospel according to John speaks often of this: "And this is the Father's will which hath sent me, that of all which he hath given me I should lose nothing, but should raise it up again at the last day" (John 6:39). "As thou hast given him power over all flesh, that he should give eternal life to as many as thou hast given him" (17:2). "I have manifested thy name unto the men which thou gavest me out of the world: thine they were, and thou gavest them me; and they have kept thy word" (v. 6). "I pray for them: I pray not for the world, but for them which thou hast given me; for they are thine. And all mine are thine, and thine are mine; and I am glorified in them. And now I am no more in the world, but these are in the world, and I come to thee. Holy Father, keep through thine own name those whom thou hast given me, that they may be one, as we are" (vv. 9–11).

Many professing Christians are frightened when they hear words such as "chosen" or "elected" or even "predestination," but Jesus uses these words to comfort us. We should remember that the Bible speaks of election in terms of love. We are not frightened when we hear about God's love, are we? Then we should not be afraid of sermons or books about election or predestination.

> 7. The LORD did not set his love upon you, nor choose you, because ye were more in number than any people; for ye were the fewest of all people:
> 8. But because the LORD loved you, and because he would keep the oath which he had sworn unto your fathers. (Deut. 7:7–8)

4. According as he hath chosen us in him before the foundation of the world, that we should be holy and without blame before him in love:
5. Having predestinated us unto the adoption of children by Jesus Christ to himself, according to the good pleasure of his will. (Eph. 1:4–5)

Election is God's choice of love. Election is God choosing a bride for his Son: I love this bride and I give her to my Son. Election, then, is Christ's delight in the bride that God has chosen for his Son.

We must also remember the context of verse 16 in which these words are found: the tone of the upper room discourse is about to turn very dark. Christ will turn from the subject of God's love to the sobering subject of the world's hatred. Before he does that, however, he reminds the disciples of their election. Do not fear, my beloved disciples, for although the world hates you and will even persecute you, I have chosen you; and that is an unchangeable reality. My choice of you is steadfast and firm, my election of you guarantees your salvation, and no one—not the world and not Satan—will pluck you from my hand.

CHOSEN: WHY?

But why did Jesus choose Peter, Thomas, Philip, and the others? Why did he not choose, but reject, Judas Iscariot, Caiaphas, Pilate, and many of the scribes and Pharisees? And why did he choose you, believing reader, and not choose, but reject, others? Some theologians suggest that Jesus chose his disciples because of something in them. That is always the answer of Arminianism: conditional election.

Before Jesus stood the whole of mankind. Certain individual persons, such as Peter, Thomas, and Philip, possessed the right qualities, so he chose them. Jesus saw Peter: he perceived that Peter would be loyal to him. Therefore, he chose him. Jesus saw Thomas: he knew Thomas would have strong faith. Therefore, he chose him. Jesus saw Philip: he perceived Philip would be humble and pious. Therefore, he chose him. On the other hand, Jesus saw Judas Iscariot: he understood that Judas was treacherous and covetous. Therefore, he did not choose him. He saw the scribes and Pharisees: he perceived their self-righteousness and pride. Therefore, he rejected them.

The same principles, say advocates of conditional election, apply today. God foresaw that, if you heard the gospel, you would believe it. Therefore, he chose you. He foresaw that others would reject the gospel. Therefore, he rejected them. There was something in you—either truly in you or potentially in you—that attracted God to you, and because of that quality in you, he chose you. God foresaw wisdom, piety, humility, meekness, zeal, loyalty, or purity in you. Whatever it was, it was the reason why God chose you above others.

Clearly, such a presentation is not only nonsense, but it is blasphemous, for it robs God of the glory and gives the glory to man. We become robbers of God's glory if we believe such blasphemous doctrines as conditional election. Consider the eleven disciples for a moment: what qualities were in them? Peter was impetuous and unreliable: he even denied Jesus three times. Thomas was gloomy, pessimistic, and slow to understand: he was slow to believe in the resurrection even after his ten fellow apostles witnessed to him about it. James and John were hotheads, overly zealous, lacking in love: they desired to call down fire upon the Samaritans, which earned them a sharp rebuke from Jesus. All the disciples struggled with pride, vying for privileged positions in the kingdom, competing with one another about who should be the greatest. When Jesus was arrested, all eleven of them abandoned Jesus and fled. If Jesus had been looking for qualities, he certainly would not have chosen them!

Make the personal application: what qualities attracted Jesus to you? Did Jesus perceive some loyalty in you, when you know that you disobey him and thus betray him multiple times a day? Did Jesus see that you would be pure of heart, when you know that your heart is full of unclean thoughts? Was Jesus impressed with your strong faith, when you know that your faith is weak and that you are prone to be plagued with doubts? Did Jesus admire your humility or wisdom, when you know your struggles with pride and you cringe at the foolishness of which you are guilty? Beloved readers, if our election depended on us, Jesus would never have chosen us!

In fact, conditional election turns everything upside down: we are loyal, faithful, humble, wise, pure, and pious (to a very small degree) *because* we have been chosen. Or to put it another way, we have been chosen not because of our fruit, but we have been chosen in order to bring forth fruit. Conditional election contradicts everything Jesus has taught thus far in John 15. Then the Father, who is the husbandman, would engraft branches into Jesus, who is the vine, because they were already bearing fruit. That is not the teaching of John 15, for Jesus says, "Without me ye can do nothing" (v. 5). If the eleven disciples were already bearing fruit before they were engrafted into Christ, they did not need Christ; and if we were already bearing fruit before we were engrafted into Christ, we would not need him either. Then Jesus' calls to abide in him for fruit would be nonsensical: we could bear fruit by ourselves without Jesus, without abiding in him, which is impossible.

The truth is that the triune God chose the disciples, Jesus chose the disciples, and we were chosen so that we would bring forth fruit. That is what Jesus says in this chapter: the Father prunes us so that we bear more fruit (v. 2), we cannot bear fruit except we abide in the vine (v. 4), and those who abide in Christ the vine bring forth much fruit (v. 5). The fruit that we bring forth glorifies God and proves that we are disciples (v. 8). In this text, Jesus says, "I have chosen you, and ordained you, that ye should go and bring forth fruit, and that your fruit should remain" (v. 16). Jesus does not say, "I have chosen you because you have brought forth fruit," or even "because I see potentiality of fruit in you," but he says, "I have chosen you so that you should bring forth fruit." Paul teaches the same idea in Ephesians 1:4: "According as he hath chosen us in him before the foundation of the world, that we should be holy." Paul does not write, "He chose us because we were holy," or "because he foresaw that we would be holy," but he chose us "that we should be holy." Holiness is the fruit of election, not the cause of election.

That, of course, is what makes election such a comforting doctrine: if our election does not depend on us, then our continued salvation and final glory do not depend on us either. But if some quality in us attracted Jesus to us, then if we lose that quality or fail to develop it, we could easily repel Jesus from us. When Jesus chose his disciples, he knew exactly what kind of people they were. He knew that Peter was impetuous and unreliable, but he chose him anyway. He knew that Thomas was gloomy, pessimistic, and weak in faith, but he chose him anyway. He knew that James and John were hotheads who lacked love, but he chose them anyway. He knew that all the disciples were proud, self-seeking, sinfully ambitious, and cowardly, but he chose them anyway. He knew all your sins, character weaknesses, and foibles, but he chose you anyway. Nothing you do, even those things that shock your spouse, your parents, your children, your siblings, and other members of the church, shocks Jesus. Nothing will make Jesus "unfriend" you!

Moreover, Jesus loved his disciples too much to leave them in their sins. Peter was impetuous and unreliable, but Jesus died for his sins and purchased the Holy Spirit to make Peter holy, so that he became loyal to Jesus, not perfectly, but there was a true transformation of Peter's heart and life. Thomas was gloomy, pessimistic, and weak in faith, but Jesus suffered God's wrath against Thomas's sins, purchased the Holy Spirit to make Thomas holy, and strengthened Thomas's faith. James and John became humble and filled with love because Jesus died for their sins and purchased for them the Holy Spirit.

The same is true of all the disciples and the same truth applies to Christians in every age. Jesus died for your sins and purchased the Holy Spirit for you so that he would make you a saint, not perfectly holy in this life, but he works in you a small beginning of the new obedience. What a difference the cross makes! The cross transforms depraved sinners into holy saints. The cross makes of proud sinners humble believers. The cross makes of foolish sinners wise Christians.

The cross transforms hateful, spiteful sinners into compassionate, merciful, benevolent believers.

CHOSEN: UNTO WHAT?

We are chosen to salvation, eternal life, and glory. Before we address the question of the purpose of Christ's choice, we face an important question: What about Judas Iscariot? Was he not also chosen? Some people point to Judas Iscariot as supposed proof that Jesus is not teaching election unto salvation in this text, but merely election unto apostleship or service.

Many people dislike the teaching that God has chosen only some unconditionally unto eternal salvation and glory. However, the same people often argue that God chose the nation of Israel to certain external privileges, although not to salvation. The same people also accept the teaching that God chose certain people to temporary offices in the church and state. They will point to King Saul in the Old Testament: he was chosen temporarily to be king. They will appeal to the example of Judas Iscariot: he was chosen temporarily to be a disciple or an apostle among the twelve. Therefore, they conclude: election is not about eternal salvation, glory, and going to heaven, but about position or service in this world.

It is true, of course, that there is a sense in which Judas Iscariot was chosen, for there is a sense in which Jesus could say to Judas, "You have not chosen me, but I have chosen you." Jesus makes that explicit in John 6:70: "Have not I chosen you twelve, and one of you is a devil?" Judas was chosen, but he was a devil. Clearly, then, Judas was chosen only to a temporary position as disciple, not to eternal salvation and glory.

Nevertheless, the context of John 15:16 forbids the conclusion that Jesus is speaking merely of election to a temporary position of service as apostles. Jesus speaks of friendship: they were chosen to be friends. Judas was not a true friend of Jesus. Jesus speaks of fruitfulness: they were chosen to bring forth fruit. Judas did not bear fruit. Judas was a fruitless branch and was cut off because he only appeared for a time to be in Christ. He was never truly in Christ. Only those who enjoy salvation bring forth fruit.

Besides that, Jesus clarifies the question of Judas' election elsewhere. In John 13:11 he says, "Ye are not all clean." In verse 18 he explains, "I speak not of you all: I know whom I have chosen." The difference between being clean and not clean in the context is election. Because the eleven were elect, Jesus died for them on the cross to cleanse them, but because Judas was reprobate, Jesus did not die for him to cleanse him from his sins. Therefore, cut off from salvation, Judas Iscariot perished in his sins. In chapter 17:12 Jesus contrasts the eleven elect disciples with Judas: "While I was with them in the world, I kept them in thy name: those that thou gavest me I have kept, and none of them is lost, but the son of perdition [Judas—he is not elect but reprobate]; that the scripture might be fulfilled."

Furthermore, even if someone argues that Jesus is not speaking of election unto salvation in John 15:16, there are still many other passages that speak of that truth: "And when the Gentiles heard this, they were glad, and glorified the word of the Lord: and as many as were ordained to eternal life believed" (Acts 13:48). "But we are bound to give thanks alway to God for you, brethren beloved of the Lord, because God hath from the beginning chosen you to salvation through sanctification of the Spirit and belief of the truth" (2 Thess. 2:13).

Jesus identifies the main purpose of his choice of the disciples as their fruitfulness. The Lord ordained and sent them: "I have chosen you, and ordained you, that ye should go" (v. 16). When Jesus says, "I ordained you," he does not mean some ecclesiastical ceremony in which the disciples are installed into an office in the church. The word means "I have put" or "I have set" you in a position: Jesus set the eleven disciples in positions as, first, his friends, second, his servants, and third, his apostles. He adds that they "should go." This does not necessarily imply a journey, although many of the apostles did travel in their apostolic labors, but he sends us too. He sends us to bear fruit to his glory in our family, in the church, at school, in society, in our neighborhoods, and wherever else we live.

Jesus chose, ordained, and sent the disciples so that they would bear fruit, abiding, lasting, permanent fruit: "that ye should go and bring forth fruit, and that your fruit should remain" (v. 16). Some commentators view the fruit that the disciples should bring forth as converts in their missionary labors, but although the Bible sometimes refers to converts as fruit, it does not fit the context here. It does not fit with the illustration of the vine and the branches of John 15. A branch does not have the calling to bring new branches to the vine (that is the work of the husbandman), but the branch bears fruit, which in the case of a branch in a vine are grapes. If we narrowed the application to converts, we would exclude most Christians, for it is not the calling of most Christians to win converts to Christ, but to bear the fruit of good works. Those good works glorify God, and they are sometimes even instrumental in the winning of others to the faith: "By our godly conversation others may be gained to Christ."[1]

The primary meaning of fruit in the New Testament is good works. When we bring forth the good fruits of thankfulness, the good fruits of ripened Christian virtues, the good fruits of obedient behavior, then we fulfill the purpose of Christ's election of us. Our good works are the fruit of the Spirit's gracious work in us. Our good works are never perfect, but they are good, and God accepts our good works for Jesus' sake:

> These works, as they proceed from the good root of faith, are good and acceptable in the sight of God, forasmuch as they are all sanctified by His grace; howbeit they are of no account towards our justification. For it is by faith in Christ that we are justified, even before we do good works; otherwise they could not be good works, any more than the fruit of a tree can be good before the tree itself is good.[2]

---

1 Heidelberg Catechism A 86, in *Confessions and Church Order*, 120.

2 Belgic Confession 24, in *Confessions and Church Order*, 53–54.

Specifically, the fruit that Jesus seeks from us and for which he chose us is love. It is possible to mimic godliness and morality. An unbeliever can mimic morality and can even have a form of godliness, while he denies the power of godliness. But you cannot mimic or fake love: love is the fruit of the Spirit and love is the grateful response of every child of God. We love God and the neighbor from the heart. We love God by keeping his commandments. That is Jesus' chief commandment in verse 17: "These things I command you, that ye love one another."

Finally, there is the role of prayer. Christ urges the disciples—and us—to prayer. He urges us to pray because prayer is the chief part of thankfulness, and "God will give His grace and Holy Spirit to those only who with sincere desires continually ask them of Him, and are thankful for them."[3] How can we live as Christians without prayer? How can we bear fruit without prayer? How can we love God from the heart and our fellow saints without prayer? Thus Jesus gives us the promise, "Whatsoever ye shall ask of the Father in my name, he may give it you" (v. 16). Remember that this is not a blank check for prayer, for acceptable prayer is made in Jesus' name, according to God's will, and for God's glory. Therefore, when we ask for fruit, God will certainly give it to us. We are chosen to be Jesus' friends and not because we are worthy. We are chosen to bear fruit, lasting fruit. We are chosen to pray with the promise of a gracious answer. How gracious is our God!

3 Heidelberg Catechism A 116, in *Confessions and Church Order*, 134.

Chapter 16

Forewarned of the World's Hatred

(John 15:18–21)

18. If the world hate you, ye know that it hated me before it hated you.
19. If ye were of the world, the world would love his own: but because ye are not of the world, but I have chosen you out of the world, therefore the world hateth you.
20. Remember the word that I said unto you, The servant is not greater than his lord. If they have persecuted me, they will also persecute you; if they have kept my saying, they will keep yours also.
21. But all these things will they do unto you for my name's sake, because they know not him that sent me.

At this point in the upper room discourse Christ's message to his disciples changes in tone. Throughout chapter 14 Jesus encouraged his disciples to remember the advantages that would be theirs in his departure. This was necessary because the thought of Christ departing to the Father greatly troubled their hearts. In chapter 15:1–17, Christ describes the wonderful relationship that his disciples have with him: they are in Christ, as branches are in a vine; and by virtue of that union the life of Christ flows into them by the power of the Holy Spirit so that they bring forth fruit to the glory of God. They enjoy the love of Jesus Christ, which is the love of the Father, and they are Jesus' true disciples and his beloved friends, chosen to be fruitful. They have the promise that God answers their prayers when they pray in Jesus' name, they have the calling to abide in Christ's love, and they have the command to love one another. Within the circle of disciples, which will expand as more and more people are gathered into the church through their preaching, they enjoy love, fellowship, and peace.

However, there is another relationship about which they must be aware: not everyone loves them. In fact, the world hates them, which must not take them by surprise, for the world hated Jesus first. They had seen the world's hatred already in the opposition of the Jewish leaders to their Lord, and it would be manifested in a horrifying way that very night, when Jesus would be taken away from them, arrested, tried, beaten, and finally crucified.

The disciples' friendship with Jesus would make them the objects of the world's hatred, something for which they must be prepared. The disciples must not imagine that the world would accept them and receive their message. The opposite is the case; indeed, the more the disciples would experience the world's hatred, the more fervently they must love one another. In these verses, Jesus mercifully warns the disciples about the gathering storm of the world's hatred so that they will be ready by God's grace and through faith to face the wrath of the enemy.

THE REALITY

This is not the first time that the world is mentioned in the upper room discourse of John 14–16. In John 14:22 Judas Thaddeus interrupted Jesus to ask, "Lord, how is it that thou wilt manifest thyself unto us, and not unto the world?" Jesus explained that the world, which does not keep his word, is excluded from the fellowship of the Father and the Son: "If a man love me, he will keep my words: and my Father will love him, and we will come unto him, and make our abode with him. He that loveth me not keepeth not my sayings: and the word which ye hear is not mine, but the Father's which sent me" (vv. 23–24). In verse 30 Jesus warns of the coming of the prince of the world, who is the devil, but he assures the disciples that the prince of the world has nothing in him. In verse 31 Jesus promises that the world will be a witness of Jesus' love for the Father when he willingly goes to the cross to suffer for our salvation.

These, however, are only passing references to the world, for the focus of the upper room discourse is on comforting the disciples in preparation for Jesus' departure from them. Having assured the disciples of his love and having commanded them to love one another, Jesus now instructs them about the world. In verses 18–19 the word "world" appears six times: "If the *world* hate you…" "If ye were of the *world*, the *world* would love his own: but because ye are not of the *world*, but I have chosen you out of the *world*, therefore the *world* hateth you." In the rest of the text, the pronoun "they" appears a further six times in reference to the world: "If *they* have persecuted me, *they* will also persecute you; if *they* have kept my saying, *they* will keep yours also. But all these things will *they* do unto you for my name's sake, because *they* know not him that sent me" (John 15:20–21). In verses 22–25 the words "they," "their," and "them" appear a further nine times, again in reference to the world. Clearly, then, the focus of Christ turns from his disciples to the world.

The first question is this: What is the world? And specifically, what is the world in this text? In the New Testament the Greek word is *kosmos*. From that Greek word we derive our English words "cosmos" and "cosmetic." The main idea of the Greek word *kosmos* is an orderly arrangement. That is why, for example, our English word "cosmetics" comes from the same root. "Cosmetics" are substances applied to the body, especially the face, to enhance its appearance. A *kosmos* in Greek is a beautiful, orderly, arranged system or whole.

There are four main meanings of *kosmos* (world) in the New Testament. First, the world is the orderly, arranged, physical universe that God created. The world or the *kosmos* is the sum total of created reality, especially the creation of this world in which we live. The world is a perfectly ordered, beautiful system, which reflects the glory of God. Clearly, that is not the meaning here, for the physical creation does not hate Christ and his disciples.

Second, the world is sometimes a reference to humanity in general. The world consists of all nations, Jews and Gentiles alike, as humanity exists not as a collection of unrelated individuals, but as an organic whole or an ordered society. That is not the meaning here either, because it is not true that the whole of humanity without any exception hates Christ and his disciples.

Third, the world is the world of God's people, the world of believers, or the world of the elect and redeemed. That world, for example, is the object of God's love in John 3:16–17: "For God so loved the world, that he gave his only begotten Son, that whosoever believeth in him should not perish, but have everlasting life. For God sent not his Son into the world to condemn the world; but that the world through him might be saved." Clearly, that is also not the meaning here, because the world of God's people does not hate Christ and his disciples.

Fourth, and finally, the world is the world of the ungodly, or humanity arranged under the power of sin, subject to the power of the devil, and in hostility to God. Such a world is a whole or an entity but has lost its beauty and order, having been corrupted through sin. The apostle John speaks of the world in 1 John 5:19: "And we know that we are of God, and the whole world lieth in wickedness." That is clearly the meaning here: the wicked world hates Christ and his disciples.

The world, then, is the society of humans, whether in ancient Israel, Greece, or Rome, or in modern Europe, America, Australia, Africa, the Middle East, or the Far East. That world is united in opposition to God, to Jesus Christ, and to Christ's church. That world is fallen in Adam, arranged under the power of sin and death, allied to Satan, and hostile to the truth, to godliness, to righteousness, and to holiness. Satan is called that world's prince or ruler in John 14:30.

The world, therefore, is not a motley band of disorganized individuals who dislike Christianity. The world is a *kosmos*, an arranged society of ungodly men. The world has a unifying philosophy, unifying values, and unifying goals. There is much diversity and difference in the world: the world is divided into classes, into races, and into nationalities and nations. The world is divided socially and economically. The world is even divided religiously. Nevertheless, one thing unites all the sections of fallen humanity: hatred for God, hatred for Christ, and hatred for the church. On that one point the whole world is agreed. In addition, the world has immense power, political power, military might, legal power, and even the power of propaganda through the media. Furthermore, the world seeks for earthly unity in one great leader. That leader, when he comes, will be the final manifestation of the antichrist. The antichrist will unite the world politically, socially, and religiously against Christ and against his people.

The world of Christ's day referred to the nation of Israel and to the Roman Empire. These two entities united to oppose Christ, and they combined their efforts to oppose the church. The world today, whether the secular state or false religion, does the same thing. Politicians legislate against the church. The media relentlessly mocks and attacks true Christianity. The false church in alliance with the secular state promotes the persecution of the church.

The apostle John summarizes what the world is in essence in 1 John 2:15–17:

> 15. Love not the world, neither the things that are in the world. If any man love the world, the love of the Father is not in him.
> 16. For all that is in the world, the lust of the flesh, and the lust of the eyes, and the pride of life, is not of the Father, but is of the world.
> 17. And the world passeth away, and the lust thereof: but he that doeth the will of God abideth forever.

The world is a system of philosophy or belief that appeals to the carnal flesh of man. The ruling principle of the world, by which Satan enslaves men and women, is lust. The people of the world are concerned with lust, with satisfying their desires for earthly things without God. That in a nutshell is the world. We live in the world and we are called to interact with the people of the world. We are not called to leave or abandon the world. Nevertheless, we must not belong to the world. Jesus forewarns his disciples that when they meet the world, the reaction will be hostility.

Jesus does not command his disciples to hide from the world, because in the world there are men and women who must hear the gospel of Jesus Christ. In the world there are men and women who must be saved. Jesus will soon leave the disciples: he will die upon the cross, he will rise from the dead, and he will ascend into heaven. Ten days after his ascension Jesus shall pour out his Holy Spirit upon the church. Empowered by the Holy Spirit, the disciples must preach the gospel to the world. Some of the people in the world are the objects of God's love: they must hear of God's love. Some of them are those for whom Christ died: they must hear about the death of Christ on the cross. Some of them are those for whom Christ prepares mansions in his Father's house: they must hear about the Father's house. Through the preaching of the gospel many in the world must be delivered from the prince of the world. Moreover, a testimony of the truth must be given to the world. Only then, says Jesus in Matthew 24:14, can the end come.

But how will the world respond to the disciples when they preach Christ? How will the world respond to Christians when they live in holiness before them? How will the world respond to the presence of Christians in its neighborhoods, towns, cities, and countries? The answer is hatred. There is a striking transition in verse 18. In verses 9–17 the word "love" appears nine times. In verses 18–25 "hatred" is mentioned eight times: "If the world *hate* you, ye know that it *hated* me before it *hated* you...Therefore the world *hateth* you...He that *hateth* me *hateth* my Father also...But now have they both seen and *hated* both me and my Father...They *hated* me without a cause."

Hatred is an intense dislike for someone or something. Compare hatred to love, which is its opposite. Love is a deep affection, while hatred is intense loathing or detestation of someone or something. Love is a desire for the welfare of someone, while hatred is ill will, a desire for the destruction of someone, and a determination to harm someone. Love is the establishing of a bond of fellowship with someone, while hatred is the thrusting away of someone.

The world hates us: it dislikes us intensely, it determines to harm us, and it thrusts us away from itself. This is because it cannot—and will not—have fellowship with us. This hatred is rooted in Satan's hatred for God. Because the prince of the world hates God, the world of which Satan is the prince hates us. Since Satan detests the Son of God, the world detests the disciples who represent the Son of God. This hatred is also rooted in the covenant. God has placed hatred, enmity, and hostility between his people and Satan. God declared to Satan in the beginning: "And I will put enmity between thee and the woman, and between thy seed and her seed; it shall bruise thy head, and thou shalt bruise his heel" (Gen. 3:15).

Jesus makes the warning explicit. "If the world hate you [and it will], ye know that it hated me before it hated you" (v. 18). "Therefore the world hateth you" (v. 19). "But all these things will they do unto you" (v. 21). Do not expect, therefore, to be popular in the world. Do not expect, as a Christian, to receive the approval or even the praise of the world. Instead, expect, and be prepared to face, the world's intolerance, opposition, hostility, and hatred. That is the warning of the text, a warning that we must always heed.

THE REASONS

The reasons for the world's hatred are not social, sociological, or economic, but they are spiritual. The world does not hate Christians because we are weird, annoying, obnoxious, or deliberately offensive. We must not be weird, annoying, obnoxious, or deliberately offensive. We must not suffer as evildoers or because of needless fanaticism. Peter warns, "But let none of you suffer as a murderer, or as a thief, or as an evildoer, or as a busybody in other men's matters.

Yet if any man suffer as a Christian, let him not be ashamed; but let him glorify God on this behalf" (1 Pet. 4:15–16).

The world hates us because we do not belong to it. Jesus uses the phrase "of the world." "If ye were *of the world*"; "ye are not *of the world*" (v. 19). The preposition, the little word "of," indicates source. That word is often rendered "out of" in the New Testament. The source of something determines its nature. The source of something determines its character. And the source of something determines its possessor. Jesus makes a similar assertion about his kingdom in John 18:36: "My kingdom is not of this world." The kingdom of Jesus is heavenly and spiritual, not earthly and carnal.

The disciples were not of the world, and we are not of the world. That is not true by nature, however, for by nature we are of the world. By nature we have our source in this world and by nature we belong to this world. The source of the world is the fall of man into sin. God created a perfect world, of course. When Adam, who was the head of the world under God, rebelled against God, he brought the whole world, and especially the world of men, under the power of sin. It is because of Adam's first transgression that we are by nature totally depraved. It is because of Adam's first transgression that our children are born in sin. The present state and condition of the world can be traced back to Adam's first transgression and the development of that transgression into the ungodly humanity that is the enemy of God's people today.

The eleven disciples had belonged to that world. That was their origin or source. We also belonged to that world. As long as the eleven disciples belonged to the world, the world loved them. As long as we belong to the world, the world loves us.

But something happened. The relationship changed. Love turned into hatred. If we still belonged to the world, the world would recognize in us a kindred spirit. The world would say, "He is one of us; she is one of us." The world would be on our side and we would be on the world's side. The world would have affinity with us. The world loves sin. Insofar as we love sin, the world loves us.

Insofar as we stand against sin, oppose sin, and expose sin, the world hates us. The world loves darkness. Insofar as we love darkness, the world loves us. Insofar as we walk in the light, the world hates us. The world loves the gratification of its lusts. Insofar as we join the world in the gratification of its lusts, promote the lusts of the flesh, and approve of the lusts of the flesh, the world loves us. Insofar as we avoid and crucify the lusts of the flesh, deny the lusts of the flesh, and condemn the lusts of the flesh, the world hates us.

If we live like the world, the world will love us. If we talk like the world, the world will love us. If we join the world, holding hands with the world to help the world in its rebellion against God, the world will applaud us. The apostle John explains: "Ye are of God, little children, and have overcome them: because greater is he that is in you, than he that is in the world. They are of the world: therefore speak they of the world, and the world heareth them" (1 John 4:4–5). Or as Jesus puts it in verse 19: "If ye were of the world, the world would love his own."

The world is not capable of true love because true love is the love of God. True love is selfless, giving itself for the welfare, and even the salvation, of others. The word "love" in verse 19 refers to affection, desire, or attraction, but not to true love. If you were of the world, the world would have some affection or affinity with you. The world would be attracted to you. The world would have something in common with you. But it does not and it must not!

The reason for this lack of affinity is God's election. "Ye are not of the world, but I have chosen you out of the world" (v. 19). Election makes the difference between the world's friends and the world's enemies. Election is God's eternal decree whereby in love he chose a people for himself out of the world. Election is eternal, unconditional, and unchangeable.

Salvation, then, is not only deliverance from sin, death, and hell. Salvation is also deliverance from the world. To be saved is to be chosen out of the world. To be saved is to be chosen for God's gracious purpose. Paul writes about Jesus, "Who gave himself for our sins, that he might deliver us from this present evil world, according to the will of God and our Father" (Gal. 1:4). Because election delivers us from the world, the cross delivers us from the world too. The cross separates us from the world. On the cross Christ made satisfaction to God's justice for the sin that joins us to this evil world. Paul even writes, "But God forbid that I should glory, save in the cross of our Lord Jesus Christ, by whom the world is crucified unto me, and I unto the world" (6:14).

Therefore, the world views us with particular detestation and loathing. We used to belong to the world. We used to have an affinity with the world. We used to be devoted to sin. Our prince used to be Satan. But we have changed sides: we are now on the side of Christ. Of course, we are on that side not because we escaped by our own power, skill, or ingenuity, but because Christ delivered us: we are elected, and we are redeemed. Paul writes about God, "[He] hath delivered us from the power of darkness, and hath translated us into the kingdom of his dear Son" (Col. 1:13).

Imagine a prison where the prisoners, although they are in captivity, enjoy the prison. They love their chains and they even think that they are free. Such a prison is sin, and such a jailer is Satan. Now Jesus has delivered us from that prison. We now understand that we were not free. We now understand the misery of our captivity to sin. We can now see very clearly how the world is in the prison of sin. Jesus sends us back on a mission to talk to our former fellow prisoners. Our commission is to show them freedom in Christ. We call to them, "If the Son therefore shall make you free, ye shall be free indeed" (John 8:36). We warn them that they are on death row, and that although the prison might seem pleasant, the day of their execution draws nigh. We show them the glory of our great liberator, Jesus Christ. We show them the delightful life of holiness that we now live. We command them to repent and believe in Jesus. We promise in God's name that whoever believes in Christ crucified shall have everlasting life.

How will they react? Jesus explains, "Because ye are not of the world, but I have chosen you out of the world, therefore the world hateth you" (John 15:19). Elsewhere, Peter explains, "They think it strange that ye run not with them to the same excess of riot, speaking evil of you" (1 Pet. 4:4). They say to us, "You used to walk with us. What happened to you? We used to have fun together. Why did you leave our company? Now you pray, read the Bible, and go to church. What is wrong with you? You want us to join you? We will never join you. Come back to us." That is how the inmates of Satan's prison—the world—react to former, but now freed, prisoners. They react with hatred. The world hates the light, while the Christian walks in the light. The world cannot stand holiness, while the Christian walks in holiness. Therefore, the Christian necessarily clashes with the world.

To put it another way: the world does not hate us for what we are by nature, but the world hates us for what we have become. The world hates what God's grace has made us. The world is so perverse that it would rather have a sinner than a saint. The world enjoys the company of sinners, while saints make the world uncomfortable. Saints enrage and infuriate the world. But, says Jesus, do not be surprised at that.

The world hates us because we belong to Christ. "Ye know," he says, "that it hated me before it hated you" (v. 18). This is not true mainly from a temporal point of view, that the world hated Jesus first in time. It is mainly true from a priority point of view: the world hated Jesus above all others. In fact, the world hates us only in connection with its hatred of Jesus Christ. When Christ entered the world, the world hated him. Satan was stirred up against him. Satan used his fiercest and cruelest weapons against him. Men and women spoke against him. The religious leaders became his most inveterate enemies. Herod and Pilate united against him. Jews and Gentiles conspired against him and finally crucified him. Such was their hatred for Jesus that they hounded him to death. They detested him, they loathed him, they had no room for him, they chased him out of the world, they nailed him to a cross, and they thought that they had destroyed him. Jesus sums it up: "They have persecuted me" (v. 20).

We represent Christ or, as Christ explains in verse 21, Christ's name, which is the revelation of Christ. Because we represent Christ, the Messiah, the prophet, priest, and king, and the only Savior from sin, the world hates us. Since the world does not know God, the world also does not know the one who sent Jesus: "because they know not him that sent me" (v. 21).

Jesus warns the disciples that association with him will bring suffering. There are wonderful blessings in Jesus Christ, but there is also a serious cost. Are you prepared to become the world's enemy and to be the object of the world's hatred? Peter, Andrew, James, John, Thomas, Philip, and the others were not ready, but when the Spirit came, they were made ready. God's grace enabled them to suffer for Christ's sake.

To encourage them, Jesus reminds them of his earlier saying: "The servant is not greater than his Lord" (v. 20). Some preachers have suggested that, since Jesus is the Lord, we are little kings or princes. We should live like kings or princes, free from suffering and enjoying prosperity. But that is not how Jesus applies it. Expect, says Jesus, the same treatment from the world as the world gave to me.

Jesus says in Matthew 10:24–25, "The disciple is not above his master, nor the servant above his lord. It is enough for the disciple that he be as his master, and the servant as his lord. If they have called the master of the house Beelzebub, how much more shall they call them of his household?" In John 13:16 he says, "Verily, verily, I say unto you, The servant is not greater than his lord; neither he that is sent greater than he that sent him." The whole New Testament speaks of this. Salvation in Christ does not exempt us from suffering; rather, it makes us sharers in Christ's suffering. "And if children, then heirs; heirs of God, and joint-heirs with Christ; if so be that we suffer with him, that we may be also glorified together" (Rom. 8:17). "That I may know him, and the power of his resurrection, and the fellowship of his sufferings, being made conformable unto his death" (Phil. 3:10).

THE MANIFESTATION

Jesus describes two ways in which the world shows its hatred. The first is persecution and the second is rejection of Christ's word. "If they have persecuted me, they will also persecute you" (v. 20). To persecute is to chase after, to pursue, or to hunt down. The ungodly world persecuted Jesus: they did not rest until they had apprehended him, mocked him, mistreated him, and killed him. The ungodly world persecuted the apostles. Indeed, most of Christ's disciples died as martyrs. The ungodly world still persecutes Christians today.

Paul writes, "Yea, and all that will live godly in Christ Jesus shall suffer persecution" (2 Tim. 3:12). The issue is not whether you will be persecuted. The issue is to what degree you will be persecuted. Will the persecution take the form of ridicule, disdain, and mockery? Will it take the form of being no longer invited to family events? Will it take the form of the loss of friends? Will it take the form of difficulty in finding employment? Will it take the form of boycotts? Or will it take the form, as it does elsewhere, of fines, imprisonment, and even death?

"If they have kept my saying, they will keep yours also" (v. 20). The world did not keep Christ's word, for very few believed. Very few submitted to his doctrine. When the apostles preached, few—relatively few—believed. The message of the gospel was generally rejected, which is the case today also.

However, some do believe. They believe because God chose them in Christ before the foundation of the world. They believe because Christ redeemed them by the blood of his cross. They believe because the Holy Spirit opened their hearts to believe. Then they come to the Lord's side, the side where the world hates them, but the side where they are the Lord's friends, where they enjoy his love, and where they live in holiness of life. Do not expect love from the world. Love God. Love Christ. Love one another.

Chapter 17

The World's Inexcusable Hatred For Christ

(John 15:22–25)

22. If I had not come and spoken unto them, they had not had sin: but now they have no cloak for their sin.
23. He that hateth me hateth my Father also.
24. If I had not done among them the works which none other man did, they had not had sin: but now have they both seen and hated both me and my Father.
25. But this cometh to pass, that the word might be fulfilled that is written in their law, They hated me without a cause.

The world's hatred of Jesus and of Jesus' disciples was and is utterly irrational. Jesus is the Son of God who came from heaven to do good: he performed miracles, he spoke gracious words, and he did mighty deeds that no other man had done. Should a man who heals lepers, feeds the multitudes, gives sight to the blind, and raises the dead be so hated? Should a man who teaches wonderful truths about the kingdom of heaven be so despised? Should a man who calls people who are laboring under the burden of sin and guilt to come to him for rest and peace be so detested? None of his enemies were able to withstand him: they could not deny his miracles, nor those of his disciples; they could not contradict his authoritative teaching; and they could not stand before his awesome power. Had he desired, he could have destroyed his enemies with a single word, or he could have called down multitudes of angels to his aid.

If any man deserved not to be hated, it was surely Jesus Christ. Yet no man was more hated than Jesus Christ. No man experienced more opposition from men and devils than Jesus Christ. No man suffered more at the hands of ungodly men than Jesus Christ. "For consider him that endured such contradiction of sinners against himself, lest ye be wearied and faint in your minds" (Heb. 12:3).

In these verses Jesus explains the occasion for the world's hatred and God's purpose in the world's hatred. Especially significant is how Jesus explains how utterly inexcusable the world's hatred is. In hating Jesus, the world reveals its true character, and in hating Jesus, the world seals its own doom. This is comfort to us when the world, having hated Jesus, turns its hatred on us.

THE DREADFUL SIN

In verse 22 Jesus says, "If I had not come...they had not had sin." The issue is the world's sin or guilt. Jesus' words are curious, for surely the world would have sin and be guilty of sin whether Jesus had come or not. Irrespective of the coming of Jesus, the world has sin. The world has been sinful since the fall of Adam into sin. In Adam the world is guilty and worthy of condemnation. We know this because repeatedly throughout history, and even before the coming of Jesus, God punished sin: he punished individuals and he punished nations for sin. Take three obvious examples. God punished the world in Noah's day for sin, God punished Sodom and Gomorrah for sin, and God punished Pharaoh and the Egyptians for sin.

The one act of rebellion of Adam against God has developed into the manifold wickedness of human society in every age of human history. Adam's sin was like a deadly seed sown into Adam's nature, and that seed has produced very bitter and deadly fruit in all men and in all societies in every age. Before the coming of Jesus, the world lived in rebellion against God. The world transgressed God's commandments and the world refused to glorify God. The world murdered, lied, stole, fornicated, and worshiped idols. The world was guilty of greed, envy, malice, lust, and pride. This verdict is true of the world in every person, in every society, and in every age. This charge of sin applies to the Jews and the Gentiles, to the sophisticated Greeks and Romans, and to the barbarians and savages. The whole world is guilty before God because of sin and therefore worthy of death.

Jesus is not speaking absolutely in verse 22, but he is speaking relatively or comparatively. Jesus means that until he came, the world was not guilty of a particular sin, namely, the sin of the willful, hateful rejection of the Son of God. The sin of which Jesus speaks is the crowning pinnacle of sinful rebellion. We rightly view all sins as serious, but some sins are more serious than others. To steal an apple is a sin, but homicide is a worse sin. To commit adultery is a dreadful sin, but to abuse a child is a worse sin. To worship an idol is a terrible sin, but human sacrifice is a worse sin. Even human justice recognizes that: premeditated murder is punished more severely than petty theft.

The worst sin is the willful rejection of Jesus Christ. The worst sin is to hear the gospel of Christ and not believe it, for that sin condemns a man to the lowest place in hell. It would be better to live and die in the obscurity of heathendom than to be in a true church and refuse to believe the gospel, and it would be better never to be born than to hear the gospel and not believe it.

It is not unusual for Scripture to speak relatively or comparatively about sin. Jesus makes a similar point in John 9:39–41:

> 39. And Jesus said, For judgment I am come into this world, that they which see not might see; and that they which see might be made blind.
> 40. And some of the Pharisees which were with him heard these words, and said unto him, Are we blind also?
> 41. Jesus said unto them, If ye were blind, ye should have no sin: but now ye say, We see; therefore your sin remaineth.

The point Jesus is making is not that the spiritually blind Pharisees are guiltless or without sin, but that their guilt increases because they profess to see when, in fact, they cannot see. In Matthew 9:13 Jesus declares, "I am not come to call the righteous, but sinners to repentance." Jesus does not mean that there are righteous people, but he condemns the self-righteous hypocrites who view themselves as righteous. When Jesus calls his elect, he causes them to understand their sin. In Luke 15:7 Jesus says, "I say unto you, that likewise joy shall be in heaven over one sinner that repenteth, more than over ninety and nine just persons, which need no repentance." Jesus does not mean that there are people who need no repentance, but he is speaking of those who believe (wrongly) that they need no repentance. Jesus is concerned about his lost sheep who know by the power of the Holy Spirit that they are lost.

Paul declares to the men of Athens, "And the times of this ignorance God winked at; but now commandeth all men every where to repent" (Acts 17:30). It is not that God completely ignored the sins of people in the past, but he did not yet confront them with the solemn obligation to repent of sin and believe the gospel of Jesus Christ. Without the coming of Jesus Christ in the gospel, the world would not have sin, the particular sin of rejecting Christ in the gospel.

Jesus identifies the sin in verse 24: "But now have they both seen and hated both me and my Father." The sin of which the world was formerly not guilty, but of which the world is now guilty, is the sin of hating Jesus Christ and God. There was, of course, hatred for God in the world before the coming of Christ, but since the world did not yet know Christ, its sin was not so open and obvious. Before Jesus came, the Jews professed to love God and claimed to be looking for the Messiah. The Jews claimed that their God was the one true, living God. They professed to worship the Creator and to love him from the heart. The Jews were looking forward, they said, to the coming of the Messiah, for he was the hope of their fathers and their Scriptures promised his coming. The Jews had religious fervor, vibrant religious activity, and they kept God's commandments, they thought, strictly. An outside observer would have said, "These people love God; these people long for the coming of Christ." But it was only an appearance, for when Jesus came, they hated him.

The same is true of the Gentiles, although the situation is somewhat different. The Gentiles worshiped a variety of gods and lived in heathen idolatry. Nevertheless, many of the Gentiles, especially among the Greek philosophers, claimed to be moral. In Athens, for example, they had erected an altar "TO THE UNKNOWN GOD" (Acts 17:23). Surely, these people were open to being enlightened in the true religion. Surely, they were ready to embrace the true God when he would be revealed. Surely, the gospel of Christ would be good news to them. However, when the gospel of Jesus Christ came, they mocked the apostles: to the Greeks the message of Christ crucified was foolishness, while it was a stumbling block to the Jews. The coming of Christ revealed the world's sin.

The same applies to many unbelievers in our day. There is hatred in the unbeliever's heart for God and for Christ: "Because the carnal mind is enmity against God: for it is not subject to the law of God, neither indeed can be" (Rom. 8:7). Nevertheless, many unbelievers seem to be nice, moral people. They even seem to be interested in religious things and will chat amicably about them. But preach the gospel to them, and they respond to Christ with hatred. As long as God is abstract and theoretical, the unbeliever is cordial, but when he hears the gospel of Christ crucified, then the hatred of his heart is stirred up and comes to expression.

Here, then, is Jesus' devastating verdict upon the world, a verdict that he pronounces before he goes to the cross, and a verdict that he pronounces before the disciples are sent out to preach the gospel to that world: "Now have they both seen and hated both me and my Father" (v. 24). I start with the world's response to Jesus: "They have both seen and hated Jesus." What a devastating indictment of the world of men, of Jews and Gentiles alike! What a devastating indictment of fallen, sinful humanity!

In the Old Testament period they had not yet seen Jesus. Therefore, their guilt was not as great. Jesus was only a prophecy, one that they interpreted in various ways. It is easy to claim to desire the fulfillment of a prophecy.

But now the world has seen Jesus. The first reference is to the Jews, for they saw Jesus in the flesh. Some of the Gentiles, the Romans, for example, saw Jesus in the flesh too, when they crucified him. We have seen Jesus too: our world has seen Jesus. We have not seen him in the flesh, of course, but we have seen him. The unbeliever knows something about Jesus. The unbeliever who has heard the gospel knows a lot about Jesus, for Jesus is presented on the pages of Scripture and set forth in every sermon preached by the true church. Paul writes to the Galatians "before whose eyes Jesus Christ hath been evidently set forth, crucified among you" (Gal. 3:1).

When the world saw Christ, it hated him. When people today see Christ, they hate him. When they read of him in Scripture, they hate him. When they hear him preached, they hate him. When they understand his doctrine and his demands for a holy life, they hate him. They turn from him in disgust and walk in rank unbelief, or they form a different Jesus in their idolatry and worship him instead of the true Jesus. In any case, they hate Jesus, and without the irresistible, effectual grace of the Spirit working in our hearts we would hate him too. By nature we hate him, but God has given us new life, so that we love him, for God has shed his love abroad in our hearts (Rom. 5:5).

The world's response to Jesus is indicative of the world's response to God, for by hating Jesus, the world hates God, whom Jesus calls his Father. In verse 23 Jesus explains, "He that hateth me [with an ongoing, persistent hatred—present tense] hateth my Father also." He concludes in verse 24, "But now have they both seen and hated [one decisive act in the past with results in the present—perfect tense] both me and my Father."

We have encountered Jesus' relationship to the Father before. The Father in Scripture can sometimes be understood as the first person in distinction from the second person. John 1:1 is an example—God in distinction from the Word is the Father in distinction from the Son. More often, however, the Father is the triune God, for the triune God is the God and Father of our Lord Jesus Christ, which is the teaching of many passages in the New Testament. As a man, Jesus worshiped the triune God, trusted in the triune God, and prayed to the triune God. To hate Jesus' Father, therefore, is to hate the triune God, the one only true and living God, while to hate Jesus is to hate Jesus' Father because Jesus is the perfect revelation of God and the one whom the triune God perfectly loves.

This, too, exposes the sin of the world, for the world (whether of Jews or Gentiles) claimed to love God or a god or gods, but they hated Jesus. You cannot love God while hating Jesus, and you cannot believe in God while rejecting Jesus. "For the Father judgeth no man, but hath committed all judgment unto the Son: that all men should honour the Son, even as they honour the Father. He that honoureth not the Son honoureth not the Father which hath sent him" (John 5:22–23).

What, then, is this hatred? Remember the threefold definition of hatred from the previous chapter. Hatred is an intense disliking, loathing, or detestation. Hatred is ill will, a desire for the destruction of someone, and a determination to harm someone. Hatred is the thrusting away of someone and the refusal of fellowship with him or her.

When Jesus came, the world was finally confronted with true righteousness and holiness because the world was confronted with God in the flesh. Scripture puts it very simply: "And the light shineth in darkness; and the darkness comprehended it not" (John 1:5). "Light is come into the world, and men loved darkness rather than light, because their deeds were evil" (3:19). To his unbelieving brothers Jesus says, "The world cannot hate you; but me it hateth, because I testify of it, that the works thereof are evil" (7:7). Since Jesus is God in the flesh, when the world was confronted with Jesus, it was also confronted with God, and the world hated both Jesus and God. So great was the world's hatred for Jesus that it crucified him. Hatred for God is manifested in a refusal to glorify him, a refusal to obey him.

Now Jesus prepares to send his disciples into that world to preach Christ to a world that hates him. Surely, it is an impossible, even a pointless and fruitless, task to do so! But it must be done so that God's elect can be saved.

THE INEXCUSABLE NATURE OF THIS SIN

Three things Jesus has done to expose the hidden hatred in the world and to render the world inexcusable for its hatred against God and Christ. First, Jesus came: "If I had not come" (v. 22). Before Jesus came, the Messiah was an abstract concept for the Jews, but the Jews at least professed to welcome the then-future coming of the Messiah. The Jews had been looking forward to a messianic figure for centuries, even millennia: they expected him to be the son of David and a great king. Although their Scriptures also prophesied the suffering of the Messiah, by and large they neglected or ignored that aspect of divine revelation. Surely, therefore, the Jews would have been expected to receive the Messiah. One of Christ's parables expresses this expectation: "But last of all he sent unto them his son, saying, They will reverence my son" (Matt. 21:37).

But then Jesus came—the Messiah came not in the abstract, but in the flesh—and when he came, the Jews showed their true sentiments. To continue with Christ's parable, "But when the husbandmen saw the son, they said among themselves, This is the heir; come, let us kill him, and let us seize on his inheritance" (Matt. 21:38). Jesus was not the Messiah that the Jews wanted: they wanted an earthly king. Jesus was a spiritual king, but they desired a liberator from Roman oppression and occupation. Jesus promised salvation from sin. The Gentiles met Jesus with similar disdain: they sought wisdom and might and the solution to earthly problems. Jesus is a spiritual Savior, one who does not make the world a better place but who saves his people from sin and death.

The same is true today: if the message of the gospel was to end poverty, to solve homelessness, to feed the poor, to end all disease, and to save the environment, Jesus would be loved. The world hates

Jesus who saves sinners from sin. The Jesus of the Bible, the crucified Savior, the resurrected Lord, and the Savior from sin and death—such ideas are abhorrent to the world. Oh, it is easy to love Jesus in the abstract, but to love the Savior who actually came and who is set forth on the pages of the Scriptures is impossible for the world.

Second, Jesus spoke: "If I had not come and spoken unto them" (v. 22). When Jesus came, he was not silent; in fact, he was outspoken. Before Jesus spoke, the Jews claimed to honor the word of God, but Jesus came with a message that was strange and offensive to their ears. The Jews—especially the Pharisees—had taken the Scriptures away from the people. They had used the Bible as a legalistic guide to salvation, and they had added multitudes of rules and regulations, thus obscuring the true meaning of God's word. The Jews had done this, just as the medieval Roman Catholic Church did much later in history, in order to establish and maintain their own religious and moral authority over the people.

Jesus spoke the word of God authoritatively, so much so that the common people recognized it and were amazed. This brought Jesus into direct conflict with the scribes, Pharisees, Sadducees, and chief priests of that day. Throughout the sermon on the mount Jesus declared his authority: "But I say unto you" was his constant refrain. At the end of his sermon he declared, "And every one that heareth these sayings of mine, and doeth them not, shall be likened unto a foolish man" (Matt 7:26). The people's reaction was clear: "The people were astonished at his doctrine: for he taught them as one having authority, and not as the scribes" (vv. 28–29). Elsewhere Jesus claimed divine authority for his words: "My doctrine is not mine, but his that sent me. If any man will do his will, he shall know of the doctrine, whether it be of God, or whether I speak of myself" (John 7:16–17).

The Jews rejected the words of Christ. They hated Christ's words and they hated Christ and they hated God who sent Christ because Christ's words exposed their sin. It is easy to claim to love the Bible until you actually read it. When the world sees that the Bible is not only about love for the neighbor or being kind to the poor, but that it exposes man's sin and demands of him repentance and faith in the only Savior, then the world responds to the word of Jesus with hatred.

The third thing Jesus did was the most striking of all. He did works that proved the genuineness of the other two things he did: "If I had not done among them the works which none other man did" (v. 24). Jesus' ministry was not only a preaching ministry, but he also performed miracles. If Jesus had simply come and spoken the word of God to them, they might have made some excuse for not believing in him, but his miracles proved that he was the Messiah and that his words were the words of God. In fact, Jesus deliberately connected his miracles to the gospel that he preached.

A miracle is simply a work of God that draws attention to the wonder of God's grace and mercy in Jesus Christ. In a sense, every work of God is miraculous: the rising of the sun is a miracle, but we are so used to it that we are not impressed any longer. The flying of a bumblebee is a miracle, but such things simply pass us by. The world is so blinded in unbelief that it cannot see the miracles all around it. We, too, are so dull that many of God's works pass by us unnoticed. Therefore, God performs miracles, which are extraordinary signs and wonders for which man can give no explanation.

Jesus performed more miracles in his earthly ministry than any other man did: he performed greater works than Moses, Elijah, or Elisha, for example. He performed them by his own power. Each of Jesus' miracles confirms the truth of the gospel that Jesus preached, the truth of his identity as the Messiah, the truth of the gospel that the apostles preached in the name of Jesus, and the truth of the gospel that the church preaches today. Indeed, we do not need any new miracles after the apostles because the miracles recorded in Scripture are the authentication of the gospel. Faithful preachers today preach the gospel that has already been authenticated by many miracles.

Jesus called his critics who refused to believe his words to believe him for his works' sake: "If I do not the works of my Father, believe me not. But if I do, though ye believe not me, believe the works: that ye may know, and believe, that the Father is in me, and I in him" (John 10:37–38). Jesus healed the lame. Believe that as the Son of God he has the power to give spiritual strength to his people to walk in his commandments. Jesus cleansed lepers. Believe that as the Son of God he has the power to cleanse from sin. Jesus cast out devils. Believe that as the Son of God he has the power to deliver from Satan. Jesus raised the dead. Believe that as the Son of God he has the power to give life to the spiritually dead. Despite this, the world did not believe, for by and large the Jews rejected Jesus despite his coming to them, his speaking to them, and his miracles among them. This makes the world inexcusable in their wicked rejection of Jesus Christ.

Thus, says Jesus, "They have no cloke for their sin" (v. 22). A cloak is a covering, an excuse or a pretext with which a person hides his real intentions. A cloak covers up what a person truly thinks or believes. In Matthew 23:14 the word is translated "pretence," where the Pharisees "for a pretence make long prayer." The idea is that the Pharisees hide their cruelty, covetousness, and wickedness behind a cloak of piety. They make long prayers as a covering for their secret sins. In 1 Thessalonians 2:5 Paul defends his ministry: "For neither at any time used we flattering words, as ye know, nor a cloke of covetousness; God is witness." Paul did not use his ministry as a covering for greed or as a pretext to make money. Instead, Paul was faithful in the ministry.

Before Jesus came, spoke, and performed miracles, the world had a cloak to cover their sin, but now the cloak has been removed and their sin is obvious. Jesus did not create the wickedness and hatred of the world, he did not even promote or encourage it, but he simply removed the curtain to reveal it. As it were, the world was like a dark cave full of loathsome creatures, and then the light shone upon that cave and revealed the true horrors within. Our hearts are like that, for before the gospel comes, we might appear to be godly, but the gospel reveals the awful wickedness, pride, greed, lust, envy, malice, and other sins in our hearts and lives. We do not like that. We resent that. We hate that. That is why, for all the protestations of men that they love Jesus, when they finally encounter him in the gospel, they hate him. That is what the disciples would encounter, and for that hateful reaction the disciples must be prepared.

THE DIVINE PURPOSE IN THIS SIN

The world's hatred was not a surprise for Jesus or for the Father who sent him. It was prophesied and therefore it was foreordained in God's eternal counsel. It is not as if Jesus came into the world expecting to be welcomed with open arms. Jesus knew what the world's response would be. He knew that he would face opposition, hatred, and hostility from the world and that they would reject him. Jesus knew that his life would be one of intense, painful suffering, and yet he came.

Jesus refers to two passages of Scripture from the law of the Jews (when he says "their law," he shows that the term *law* is wider than the five books of Moses, for the passages are in the Psalms). "But this cometh to pass, that the word might be fulfilled that is written in their law, They hated me without a cause" (v. 25). In Psalm 35:7 we read, "For without cause have they hid for me their net in a pit, which without cause they have digged for my soul," and in verse 19 the psalmist cries, "Let not them that are mine enemies wrongfully rejoice over me: neither let them wink with the eye that hate me without a cause." In Psalm 69:4 we read, "They that hate me without a cause are more than the hairs of mine head."

Take note of two points in those verses: many hate David (and therefore the Messiah, who is David's greater son), and they do so without a cause, needlessly, and without any justification. We would speak of gratuitous hatred, hatred that has no valid reason in the one who is hated. "They hated me without a cause." Jesus was holy and they hated him. Jesus was righteous and they hated him. Jesus was good and they hated him. Jesus preached the truth and they hated him. Jesus healed the sick and they hated him. Jesus saved sinners and they hated him. None deserves hatred less than Jesus, yet none is hated as viciously and as gratuitously as Jesus is.

Prophetic Scripture is not mere prediction of future events, but prophecy is the revelation of the eternal counsel of God. Jesus was hated because God determined it. God's absolute sovereignty in the hatred of the world for his Son does not lessen the guilt of the world. It does not reduce it by one iota, for the world is inexcusable. The world cannot say, "Ah, but my hatred of Jesus was prophesied and purposed. Therefore, I am not guilty." We are not fully able to comprehend the relationship between man's sin and God's sovereignty. Nevertheless, we confess both: God decreed the hatred of the world for his own wise and good purposes, and the world is guilty for that hatred.

Finally, God's purpose with the hatred of the world is our salvation and his glory. Without a world to hate Jesus and to nail him to the cross, we would not be saved. Had Jesus been lauded as a great king and enthroned in Jerusalem, we would have perished in our sins. The hatred of the world for Jesus—hatred that was inexcusable and gratuitous—was necessary. Driven by that hatred to the cross, Jesus made atonement for our sins. Let us therefore love Jesus for his great love to us: "[He] endured such contradiction of sinners against himself" (Heb. 12:3). He did so for our salvation.

Chapter 18

The Comforter Testifying of Christ

(John 15:26–27)

26. But when the Comforter is come, whom I will send unto you from the Father, even the Spirit of truth, which proceedeth from the Father, he shall testify of me:
27. And ye also shall bear witness, because ye have been with me from the beginning.

Verses 18–25 of John 15 are troubling, and perhaps even frightening, because they concern the world's hatred of Jesus Christ and its hatred of the church. To experience someone's hatred is a deeply unpleasant feeling, especially when the hater is so powerful, the hated is so powerless, and the hatred is so cruel and so inexcusable. In some ways, we can bear being hated when we deserve it, when we have done something to make our neighbor hate us. In those situations, we confess the sin that has made us odious to our neighbor, we seek his forgiveness, and hopefully we enjoy reconciliation as we repent of our fault. However, the world's hatred is relentless and implacable, and there is no possibility of reconciliation, unless we forsake the faith and join the wicked world in its sin, which by God's grace the Christian will not do.

The disciples might have wondered: "How shall we witness to such a hostile world?" They might especially have wondered this because Jesus was going to leave them. "How can we witness to the world about Jesus, whom the world hates, when Jesus is not even with us?" they might have asked anxiously.

The answer to the disciples' anxieties and fears is the Holy Spirit. Twice already in the upper room discourse Jesus has given instruction about the Comforter or the Holy Spirit. In John 14:16 he promises another Comforter, and in verse 26 he promises that the Holy Spirit will teach. In chapter 16:7–15 he will explain the ministry of the Comforter in the world and as the one who shall glorify Christ.

In verse 26 Christ begins with the adversative conjunction "but": "But when the Comforter is come..." The word "but" indicates a contrast with the preceding: the world hates Christ and the church, and the world will persecute the church, yet the disciples must preach the gospel to the ungodly, hateful, persecuting world. The disciples must not fear: the Comforter will come, and he shall testify of Christ, and he shall enable them, despite their weaknesses, to bear witness of the Savior.

WHO HE IS

Much of the material in the first section of this chapter is review because Jesus has mentioned the Holy Spirit earlier in the upper room discourse. Nevertheless, repetition is good: "To write the same things to you, to me indeed is not grievous, but for you it is safe" (Phil. 3:1). Let us, then, review the doctrine of the Holy Spirit.

First, the Comforter is the Spirit or the Holy Spirit. "Spirit" is the Greek word *pneuma,* which means "breath." The Spirit, then, is not a physical thing. The Spirit is not material. He is breath. Because he is breath, the Spirit is also invisible and deeply mysterious: he works secretly, silently, and inwardly. The Spirit is able to "pervade the inmost recesses of the man,"[1] as the Canons explain it. Jesus speaks of the Holy Spirit as wind in John 3:8: "The wind bloweth where it listeth, and thou hearest the sound thereof, but canst not tell whence it cometh, and whither it goeth: so is every one that is born

1 Canons 3–4.11, in Confessions and Church Order, 168.

of the Spirit." Moreover, the Spirit is the Spirit—or the breath—*of God.* There are created spirits; for example, the angels are called spirits in Hebrews 1:14: "Are they not all ministering spirits, sent forth to minister for them who shall be heirs of salvation?" We, too, have spirits, although we are not spirits, for we also have bodies: our spirit is the immaterial aspect of our nature.

The Holy Spirit is the eternal, unchangeable, pure, and uncreated Spirit. The Holy Spirit has no beginning and no ending; the Holy Spirit is infinite, for he fills heaven and earth with the whole of his being; and the Holy Spirit is almighty, possessing the power of God. Since he is the Spirit of God, he has the power to regenerate dead sinners; sanctify unholy, depraved sinners; and defend and preserve the church.

Furthermore, he is the *Holy* Spirit or the Holy Ghost (the two names are used interchangeably in Scripture). Holiness is not only separation from and opposition to sin, but it is also (and mainly) consecration to God. The Holy Spirit is consecrated to God, and he hates and detests everything that is sinful. The Holy Spirit is consecrated to God because he is God: he is the holy consecration between the Father and the Son in the triune being of God. When we sin, therefore, we grieve the Holy Spirit: we make him indignant because he is holy. Bitterness, wrath, anger, clamor, evil speaking, and malice grieve the Spirit (Eph. 4:30–31). Because he dwells within us, we know when he is grieved: he grieves us by making us aware of his displeasure by withdrawing from us, so that we lose a sense of his favor.[2]

Second, the Comforter is a person. A person is not a thing, a power, a force, or an influence. A person is a conscious and self-conscious individual who wills, thinks, plans, speaks, and does the other activities associated with personhood. The Holy Spirit is the third person of the Trinity. The Father is the first person, the Son is the second person, and the Spirit is the third person. There is perfect equality between these three persons: each person is God,

2 Canons 5.5, in Confessions and Church Order, 174.

each person is eternal, and each person is glorious. They are coequal, coessential, and coeternal.

This makes the Holy Spirit highly unusual—or unique—breath. Your breath is not personal: your breath does not will, think, plan, or speak in distinction from you. Your breath is in a sense part of you: it is the product of your breathing. But God's breath—the breath of the Father and the breath of the Son—is personal. Jesus has already taught the personality of the Spirit, and the New Testament abounds with testimonies to the personality of God's holy breath. In John 14:26 the Spirit "shall teach you all things." Breath does not teach, but a person teaches. The Spirit shall "bring all things to your remembrance, whatsoever I have said unto you" (v. 26). Breath does not remind, but a person reminds. In chapter 15:26 the Spirit "shall testify of me." Breath does not testify, but a person testifies. In chapter 16:13 the Spirit "shall not speak of himself; but whatsoever he shall hear, that shall he speak: and he will shew you things to come." Breath does not speak and show, but a person speaks and shows.

In addition, the Bible testifies to the Spirit's personality by using the masculine personal pronoun "he" or "him." "He dwelleth with you" (John 14:17). "He shall teach you" (v. 26). "He shall testify" (15:26). "He will reprove the world" (16:8). "Whatsoever he shall hear, that shall he speak" (v. 13). We do not refer to the Holy Spirit with the pronoun "it," although the Greek noun *pneuma* is a neuter word. We refer to the Holy Spirit with the pronoun "he."

Those first two points—that the Spirit is the breath of God and that he is a person—are necessary for the next two points about the Holy Spirit.

Third, the Holy Spirit is the Comforter. The Comforter is a name that only Jesus gives to the Spirit, for the apostles never refer to the Spirit by this name in their epistles. "And I will pray the Father, and he shall give you another Comforter" (John 14:16). The Holy Spirit will be a comforter, as Jesus was. He will be another comforter of the same kind, not a completely different comforter. "But the Comforter, which is the Holy Ghost, whom the Father will send in my name, he shall teach you all things" (v. 26). The Holy Spirit will comfort God's people by teaching them the truth of the gospel, which he will enable the apostles to remember and to record infallibly in the Scriptures. "But when the Comforter is come, whom I will send unto you from the Father, even the Spirit of truth, which proceedeth from the Father, he shall testify of me" (15:26). The Holy Spirit comforts us by testifying to Jesus Christ. "If I go not away, the Comforter will not come unto you; but if I depart, I will send him unto you. And when he is come, he will reprove the world" (16:7–8). The Comforter will comfort us by reproving the world.

The Comforter is only an effectual comforter if he is both personal and divine. The Holy Spirit is the Comforter, which is the Greek *Parakletos*: the Greek word has the idea of one who comes alongside to help another. If the Comforter is impersonal, he is not a comforter at all. Only a person can comfort someone who is distressed; only a person can console the grieving and bereaved; only a person can strengthen the fearful; and only a person can encourage the perplexed. That is because only a person can know and understand the afflictions of another person to be able to bring him comfort. The Holy Spirit knows our deepest feelings, fears, and anxieties because he is not only a person, but he is also divine. Your friend, your spouse, or your child can bring comfort, but only in a limited measure. The Holy Spirit, who is infinite, almighty, and omniscient, brings complete, perfect comfort, comfort suited to every occasion and comfort designed to help in every trial.

Fourth, the Holy Spirit is the Spirit of truth. This is another name of the Holy Spirit unique to the upper room discourse. "And...the Father...shall give you...the Spirit of truth" (John 14:16–17). "But when the Comforter is come...even the Spirit of truth" (15:26). "Howbeit when he, the Spirit of truth, is come, he will guide you into all truth: for he shall not speak of himself" (16:13). Recall the meaning of truth by remembering the three words in an earlier definition of truth: reality, stability, and authority. The Spirit is the Spirit of truth in that he reveals reality: he does not bring fantasy or imaginary nonsense, but he brings truth. He works in the service of truth, he loves and delights in the truth, he brings the truth of God. This is because God is the most fundamental and the ultimate reality. The Spirit is the Spirit of truth in that he represents stability: although he is spiritual, he is not inconsequential. He brings that which is stable, solid, trustworthy, and firm. The Spirit is the Spirit of truth in that he speaks authority: what the Spirit brings and reveals has authority as the truth of God. It must be believed.

This, too, explains how the Holy Spirit comforts us: by bringing the truth. The Spirit does not comfort—or even sanctify—by whispering into our ears. He does not make us feel funny with fuzzy sensations, but he brings the truth. This is a condemnation of everything masquerading as the Spirit that does not bring the truth, that contradicts the truth, and that ignores the truth. The Spirit is the breath of God. He is personal, he is holy, he is almighty, he is the Spirit of truth who brings the truth, and by that truth he is the Comforter. Thus ends a review of Christ's teaching about the Spirit in these chapters.

HOW HE COMES

In verse 26 Jesus says, "When the Comforter is come." The Spirit therefore comes, but we need to understand how he comes. Jesus begins with the procession of the Spirit: "even the Spirit of truth, which proceedeth from the Father" (v. 26). The word "proceedeth" simply means "goes out" or "comes out." The Spirit proceeds, comes out of, or goes out from the Father. This is true with respect to the third person's procession from the first person. In theology, we call this the personal property of the Holy Spirit. The personal property of the Father is that he is not begotten or proceeding. The personal property of the Son is that he is begotten of the Father, where begetting is that act of the Father in love by which he brings forth one who is of the same essence as himself, but personally distinct from himself. The personal property of the Spirit is that he is breathed forth by the Father, so that he proceeds from the Father.

(He is breathed forth by, and proceeds also from, the Son, as shall be explained below.)

Be careful not to misunderstand this. This neither means nor implies that the Son or the Spirit is a creature, for the Father's begetting of the Son and breathing forth of the Spirit is eternal. The Spirit is the breath of God: when you breathe, your breath proceeds from you or comes out of you. You exhale when you breathe. But the Spirit is the breath of God: God's breath is eternal and the Spirit is the eternal breath of God. The Father breathes forth the Spirit: this eternal activity of God is reflected in the Spirit's activities in time. God breathes in eternity, therefore. God also breathed in creation. God breathed in the inspiration of Scripture. And God breathes when he regenerates us. But there is more to say: for if the Father breathes the Spirit in the being of God, to whom does he breathe his breath? Does he breathe him (not "it") only to himself, or does he breathe the Spirit to another?

The question of the procession of the Spirit exercised the church in the *filioque* controversy, which led to the Great Schism between the Eastern and Western churches in AD 1054. That controversy is the main explanation for the existence of the Eastern Orthodox Church today. The word *filioque* is the Latin for "and the Son." In AD 381 the Nicene Creed stated: "And I believe in the Holy Ghost, the Lord and Giver of life, who proceedeth from the Father, who with the Father and the Son together is worshiped and glorified, who spake by the prophets." However, the Western church added a phrase to the Nicene Creed in AD 589, without consulting the Eastern church. That phrase was "and the Son" (Latin: *filioque*). The creed reads, "Who proceedeth from the Father *and the Son*." By adding those words, the Western church confessed that the Spirit is not merely breathed forth by the Father in the being of God, but that in the being of God the Son also breathes forth the Spirit. The Spirit therefore is the holy, divine, eternal breath that the Father breathes to the Son and that the Son breathes to the Father. The Spirit is the holy, personal breath between the Father and the Son.

We know this because the Spirit also comes from the Son. Jesus does not say that in so many words (he says, "the Spirit of truth, which proceedeth from the Father"), but that is clearly his meaning and the meaning of Scripture. In John 15:26 Jesus says about the Spirit, "Whom I will send unto you from the Father." How can the Son send the Spirit unless he also proceeds from him: does the Father breathe the Spirit, and does the Son then send the Spirit, without the Son also breathing him forth? Again in chapter 16:7 Jesus says, "I will send him unto you." Even more conclusively, Jesus breathes the Spirit in chapter 20:22 after his resurrection: "And when he had said this, he breathed on them, and saith unto them, Receive ye the Holy Ghost." How can Jesus as the incarnate Son of God breathe the Spirit on the disciples in time if he does not breathe forth the Holy Spirit to the Father within the triune being of God in eternity?

The procession of the Spirit from the Father and the Son—or the breathing forth of the Spirit in love by the Father to the Son and by the Son to the Father—is the eternal activity behind the sending forth of the Spirit in time and history. What God does within his own being in eternity is reflected in his works in time and history. The emphasis in John 14–16 is not on the eternal procession of the Spirit within the being of God, but on the sending of the Spirit in time and history by Jesus Christ to the church. However, behind that sending is the eternal procession of the Spirit.

In some passages in John 14–16 emphasis is on the Father's sending the Holy Spirit. "I will pray the Father, and he shall give you another Comforter" (14:16). "But the Comforter, which is the Holy Ghost, whom the Father will send in my name, he shall teach you all things" (v. 26). In those passages the Father sends the Spirit, but always in association with the Son. The Spirit comes in response to the Son's prayer, he comes in the Son's name, he comes to testify of the Son, and he comes to glorify the Son.

Here in John 15:26, however, the emphasis is on Christ's sending the Holy Spirit. "But when the Comforter is come, whom I will send unto you from the Father, even the Spirit of truth, which proceedeth from the Father." The same is true in chapter 16:7: "If I go not away, the Comforter will not come unto you; but if I depart, I will send him unto you." In those passages the Son sends the Spirit but always in association—even in union—with the Father: he sends the Spirit from the Father, the Spirit proceeds from the Father, and the Spirit comes only when Jesus returns to the Father. In that sense, the Spirit is sent by the triune God. Here, then, is how the Holy Spirit comes: he proceeds from the Father and the Son, and at his ascension Christ receives the Spirit from the Father (that is, from the triune God), and then Christ gives the Spirit to the disciples and to the church.

Jesus Christ made a perfect sacrifice of his body on the cross. The purpose of Christ's sacrifice is to make atonement for our sins. But the purpose is also this: by his death on the cross Christ purchases the Holy Spirit for us, the Holy Spirit makes us partakers of Christ's benefits, and the Holy Spirit gives us faith, the pardon of sins, and eternal life. Listen to Galatians 3:13–14:

13. Christ hath redeemed us from the curse of the law, being made a curse for us: for it is written, Cursed is every one that hangeth on a tree:
14. That the blessing of Abraham might come on the Gentiles through Jesus Christ; that we might receive the promise of the Spirit through faith.

Jesus rose from the dead and ascended into heaven partly for this purpose, to receive the Holy Spirit. At the ascension the Spirit became Christ's Spirit, so that Christ sends the Spirit as a gracious gift to his church. Peter teaches that in Acts 2 when he expounds the prophecy of Joel 2: Jehovah promises, "I will pour out my spirit," and Jehovah does that when Jesus pours out the Spirit, proving, by the way, the divinity of Jesus. Jesus—who is Jehovah in our flesh—pours out the Spirit. "Therefore being by the right hand of God exalted, and having received of the Father the promise of the Holy Ghost, he [Jesus] hath shed forth [poured out] this, which ye now see and hear" (Acts 2:33). Jesus Christ is exalted, Jesus Christ received the Spirit, and Jesus Christ poured out the Spirit.

The Spirit came upon the church once and for all at Pentecost. The Spirit came upon the disciples at Pentecost. The Spirit comes to us when he regenerates us and unites us to the church: "For by one Spirit are we all baptized into one body, whether we be Jews or Gentiles, whether we be bond or free; and have been all made to drink into one Spirit" (1 Cor. 12:13).

Perhaps you might wonder: Why do we need to understand such deep theology as the double procession of the Spirit from the Father and the Son? Why is the *filioque* clause so important? Why was the Great Schism of AD 1054 so serious? And what is the consequence of denying the truth of the double procession for the Eastern Orthodox Church, which denies this truth?

The answer is this: if the Spirit proceeds only from the Father and not from the Son, he cannot be the Spirit of Christ, who, as the Spirit of truth, works in the church. In effect, the Spirit is severed from Christ, from the truth, and from the church. It is for this reason that Eastern Orthodoxy has suffered doctrinal stagnation for over nine hundred years. In the last nine hundred years there has been no doctrinal development in Eastern Orthodoxy: the Scriptures, which are the Holy Spirit's book, are not preached. Moreover, God is not worshiped in Spirit and in truth, but through worthless icons of Jesus and the saints. This is God's judgment on the church of the East: by denying the double procession, they severed the Spirit from Christ, so that the Spirit does not work salvation in the Eastern Orthodox Church. The Spirit of truth does not testify to Christ where he is denied, such as in Eastern Orthodoxy.

WHAT HE DOES

When the Spirit comes (as he proceeds from the Father and the Son and as he is sent by Christ), what shall he do? The answer is that he shall testify (v. 26). We have already seen some of the Spirit's works (he comforts, he teaches, and he reminds). Here he testifies. To testify is to give witness (as a person). A witness is one who speaks of what he has seen or heard. If you are a witness in a court, you do not give your opinion or your interpretation of events, but you simply testify to the truth. The Holy Spirit therefore is the perfect witness: first, he is omniscient, for he is God; and second, he is the Spirit of truth, so that he cannot lie. A very profound passage concerning the testimony of the Spirit is 1 Corinthians 2:10–11:

> 10. ...for the Spirit searcheth all things, yea, the deep things of God.
> 11. For what man knoweth the things of a man, save the spirit of man which is in him? even so the things of God knoweth no man, but the Spirit of God.

Of what does the Spirit testify, or of whom does the Spirit testify? The answer is that the Spirit testifies of Christ. The Spirit testifies of the Son, for he testifies of the person and work of Christ. The Spirit testifies of the deity of Christ, the Spirit testifies of the cross of Christ, and the Spirit testifies of the resurrection of Christ. In a word, the Spirit glorifies Christ.

The Spirit does not give testimony directly—he does not speak audibly of Christ—but he testifies through the word and through the church that preaches the word. This was Jesus' word to the disciples: "And ye also shall bear witness, because ye have been with me from the beginning" (v. 27). The eleven disciples are qualified to be witnesses, for they have been with Christ. They have been with Christ for his entire earthly ministry. He called them to be his disciples, and they have seen and heard many wondrous things. They will also see and hear many more wondrous things in the future. They will see him after his resurrection and shall testify to the truth of the resurrection of Christ.

That is why the disciples must not fear. The Spirit will come and will enable them to be witnesses for Christ, and he shall enable them even to be martyrs for Christ (in Greek a witness is a martyr). Jesus' words in Acts 1:8 are important here: "But ye shall receive power, after that the Holy Ghost is come upon you: and ye shall be witnesses unto me both in Jerusalem, and in all Judaea, and in Samaria, and unto the uttermost part of the earth." The same power by which the disciples were witnesses is present in us because the Spirit works through the preaching to save sinners. The Spirit uses our witness as a congregation and as individuals to glorify Jesus. The Spirit gives us power to witness even when the world hates and persecutes the church.

Therefore, the world might rage, but the Spirit—the personal, divine, holy breath of the Father and the Son, who proceeds from the Father and the Son, and who is sent by the Son, even the Spirit of truth, and the Comforter—is with us, and he testifies of Christ through us.

That is rich comfort to a church hated by the world.

PART THREE

Warnings and Encouragement about the Future

Chapter 19

The Disciples Cast Out and Killed

(John 16:1–4a)

1. These things have I spoken unto you, that ye should not be offended.
2. They shall put you out of the synagogues: yea, the time cometh, that whosoever killeth you will think that he doeth God service.
3. And these things will they do unto you, because they have not known the Father, nor me.
4. But these things have I told you, that when the time shall come, ye may remember that I told you of them.

With John 16 Christ reaches the conclusion to his upper room discourse, his farewell to his disciples. Within hours Jesus will be arrested in the garden of Gethsemane by a mob led by Judas Iscariot; tried before the Jewish Sanhedrin, the highest religious court in Israel, which will treat him abysmally by spitting on him, beating him, and mocking him; and delivered to Pontius Pilate, the cowardly, self-seeking Roman governor. Pilate will find no fault in the innocent, righteous Jesus, but the Jews, at the instigation of their leaders, will demand his death and the release of the murderous insurrectionist Barabbas. Pilate will then pass sentence, even as he tries to wash his hands of Jesus, and deliver the Son of God to the base cruelty of his soldiers. Those heathen men will beat him, mock him, and scourge him. Finally, Jesus will be led away as a condemned criminal to be crucified on the hill of Calvary or Golgotha.

While Jesus is suffering these things, his eleven disciples will forsake him, unable and unwilling to stand with him at his darkest hour. One of his disciples, Judas Iscariot, the traitor, will commit suicide and go to his own place, everlasting perdition; while another, the boastful Peter, will in a moment of terrible weakness deny three times that he knows Jesus. Only the marvelous grace of the Savior will preserve Peter from the same despair that drove Judas to hang himself, for Jesus will forgive and restore the unworthy Peter.

As Jesus contemplates all these things, which will bring intense suffering to him in his body and soul, he has some words of farewell for his disciples.

I have tried to identify a theme for each of these three chapters: the theme of chapter 14 was "The Disciples' Advantage in Jesus' Departure"; the theme of chapter 15 was "Spiritual Fellowship with Jesus Christ"; and now the theme of chapter 16 is "Warnings and Encouragement about the Future."

At the end of chapter 15 Jesus warned his disciples about the hatred with which the world of ungodly men would treat them. The world hated Jesus with an intense but utterly inexcusable hatred. The disciples should not expect to receive better treatment. In fact, Satan, enraged at his failure to destroy Jesus on the cross, will direct his fury against Christ's disciples and will enlist the world as the willing instrument of his cruelty. Nevertheless, the disciples must not be anxious: "Fear not, little flock; for it is your Father's good pleasure to give you the kingdom" (Luke 12:32). That kingdom, we learn elsewhere, is entered through much tribulation (Acts 14:22).

The sixteenth chapter begins and ends with a dark cloud: "They shall put you out of the synagogues" (v. 2); and "In the world ye shall have tribulation" (v. 33). This chapter also gives more instruction on the ministry of the Holy Spirit, especially his ministry in the world. Therefore, the chapter is not gloomy, for in the midst of the dark clouds of persecution Jesus promises joy and hope: "Be of good cheer; I have overcome the world" (v. 33). The chapter begins with Jesus' prophecy concerning the persecution of the disciples by the Jewish leaders. Such persecution is really a pattern of the persecution of the church by the world in every age. The world shows the church that there is no room for her in its midst: we are rejected and cast out, but the Lord shall take us up.

THE FEARFUL REALITY

In John 15:18–25 Jesus warned about the hatred of the world in general. Now he becomes more specific in describing the persecution that his disciples must endure at the hands of their fellow Jews, their brethren according to the flesh.

First, "they shall put you out of the synagogues" (v. 2), literally, "they will make you 'dis-synagogued.'" We might say disfellowshiped or excommunicated. To be put out of the synagogue was a fearful punishment for any Jew. The synagogue was the place of public worship in every Jewish community. In every city where there were at least ten Jewish men, a synagogue was established. The synagogue was the heart and center of Jewish social and religious life. Therefore, to be "dis-synagogued" was to be cast out of Jewish society. It was to be made a pariah.

The process of disfellowshiping or discipline had three main steps. It began with the *Neziphah* or rebuke, which was expulsion from the synagogue for seven days. It progressed to the more serious *Niddui* or thrusting out, which was expulsion for thirty days and was pronounced by an assembly of ten men. It culminated in the fearful *Cherem* or final excommunication, which was a ban of permanent duration accompanied by curses.[1]

A "dis-synagogued" Jew was a miserable wretch. He was viewed as dead in the eyes of his fellow Jews, worse than a Samaritan or a heathen Gentile, so that no fellowship was possible with him. Because

---

1 Alfred Edersheim, *The Life and Times of Jesus the Messiah* (Peabody, MA: Hendrickson Publishing Inc., 2006), 601-602.

such a Jew lived in a community of Jews, his being "dis-synagogued" meant that his family and friends shunned him. In addition, he forfeited his job and his livelihood; and if he owned a business, his fellow Jews boycotted him. He was permitted only to buy the basic necessities of life, and no Jew would eat with him or drink from the same cup that he had used. A "dis-synagogued" Jew was viewed as under the anathema or curse of God.

Undoubtedly, Jesus refers to the third step, the *Cherem*. For the great crime of confessing Jesus as Messiah, and even preaching him as such, the disciples would be expelled from the synagogues. During Jesus' public ministry this was already beginning: the man born blind was "dis-synagogued" in John 9:35, and in chapter 12:42 we read of some who out of fear of this punishment neglected to confess Christ openly. This would continue because the Jews would, by and large, reject Jesus. After they had condemned Jesus, they would inflict their wrath upon those who dared confess him and preach him as the Messiah of God.

The same punishment is inflicted upon Christians in every age. It is always the response of the false church, and apostate Judaism was the false church of that day, to persecute the true followers of Jesus Christ. The Belgic Confession defines the false church as the persecutor of the true church. "As for the false church, she ascribes more power and authority to herself and her ordinances than to the Word of God…and [she] persecutes those who live holily according to the Word of God, and rebuke her for her errors, covetousness, and idolatry."[2] This was how the apostate Jewish Sanhedrin behaved when they cast out Christ and when they cast out the apostles. This is also the behavior of the false church of our day when they cast out faithful and conscientious Christians.

Such persecution occurred, for example, in the Middle Ages and at the time of the Reformation. The false church then, and now, was the Roman Catholic Church. The pope declared believers in Christ

2 Belgic Confession 29, in *Confessions and Church Order*, 64.

to be heretics, and he excommunicated and even anathematized them. At the time of the Reformation, Rome excommunicated and anathematized Luther. This excommunication of believers in Christ occurred because they dared teach contrary to Rome's errors. This was Rome's casting them out of the church and counting them as worthy of eternal damnation in hell. Because they were no longer under the church's protection, they were, as far as the priests, monks, and people were concerned, unworthy of life. This happens also in apostate Protestant and evangelical churches. A true believer is liable to be cast out if he remains faithful to the Scriptures. The more liberal a church becomes, the more intolerant the leaders are of the truth of Jesus Christ.

The second warning is more serious than the first. Not merely being "dis-synagogued" but also death awaits the disciples: "Whosoever killeth you" (v. 2). If being "dis-synagogued" is the most extreme ecclesiastical punishment, then the death penalty is the most extreme punishment inflicted by the state. In Jesus' day the state and religious authorities were intertwined. In Israel, for example, the Jews might "dis-synagogue" a man and then stone him to death. They did not always have the authority to do so, but they often did, while the Romans turned a blind eye. Stephen in Acts 7 is an example. In fact, Jesus himself endured such ecclesiastical and civil punishment: he was condemned as a false prophet, a deceiver, a blasphemer, and a counterfeit Messiah (excommunication); then he was delivered to the Romans to be crucified (execution). This also happened among the pagans: a Christian was accused of a crime against the gods (excommunicated from the religious community), and then he was executed under the authority of the state (cut off from this life).

This has often occurred in the history of the church, especially in the medieval and Reformation periods, when the pope wielded both religious and civil power. A Christian was first condemned in an ecclesiastical court, where the sentence was usually excommunication and anathematization. An excommunicated and anathematized person forfeited all protections under the civil law as well, so that the Inquisition delivered such a person to the state to be burned at the stake. In this way, Rome tries to absolve herself of guilt: she claims, falsely, that she did not put any Christians to death. She simply handed them over to the state, which then executed them. That is a vain subterfuge, for the state was at that time in the pocket of the pope. Magistrates did the pope's bidding, and the pope's bidding was the execution of Bible believers, whom the pope, his priests, and his monks deemed heretics who were not fit to live.

As far as we know, all the apostles except John died as martyrs: all of them suffered at the hands of the ecclesiastical, religious, and civil authorities for the sake of Christ. Millions of Christians have followed in their footsteps. The history of the church is a trail of blood, as Christians have willingly died for the truth.

Between these two extremes—the extreme ecclesiastical censure of being "dis-synagogued" and "excommunication" and the extreme civil punishment of death—were many other punishments suffered by the disciples and other Christians. Paul mentions some of these in 2 Corinthians 11. "Of the Jews five times received I forty stripes save one" (v. 24). According to Deuteronomy 25:3 the limit of stripes permitted was forty, but the Jews in their religious scrupulosity administered thirty-nine stripes to the worst offenders, lest they exceed forty. Paul received this punishment five times. "Thrice was I beaten with rods" (2 Cor. 11:25). The rod was a Roman punishment. Paul endured this punishment in Philippi (Acts 16:22–23), but he mentions two other times not recorded in Acts. "Once was I stoned" (2 Cor. 11:25). Paul suffered stoning in Lystra in Acts 14:19. Then there was imprisonment of various degrees of severity. Paul writes, "in stripes above measure, in prisons more frequent, in deaths oft" (2 Cor. 11:23). Some believers suffer also the confiscation of goods (Heb. 10:34).

The book of Acts records much of the persecution suffered shortly after Jesus' death, resurrection, ascension, and outpouring of the Holy Spirit. The Holy Spirit was poured out on Pentecost as recorded in Acts 2, and at the end of that chapter the church still met in the temple and enjoyed favor with the people (vv. 46–47).

However, threats of persecution began in chapter 4 after the healing of a lame man; in chapter 5 the disciples were beaten and imprisoned; and in chapter 7 Stephen, the first martyr, was stoned to death. Persecution heats up in chapter 8 until Saul the persecutor is converted, but soon Paul, the former persecutor of the church, is himself the target of persecution. In Acts 12 James is martyred and Peter is imprisoned, while the rest of the book records the missionary labors—and sufferings—of the apostle Paul. It did not take long for Jesus' warning to be realized, and the history of the church has always been the history of persecution: "Yea, and all that will live godly in Christ Jesus shall suffer persecution" (2 Tim. 3:12).

THE SOBERING REASONS

There are two main reasons for the disciples' excommunication and martyrdom: one is the reason claimed by the persecutors, while the other is the underlying spiritual reason.

The first reason is religious fanaticism: "The time cometh, that whosoever killeth you will think that he doeth God service" (v. 2). What the persecutors do is objectively evil, but they view it as a righteous act. It is a grossly evil thing to cast a believer out of the church; to confiscate his goods; to destroy his property; to separate him from his family; and to imprison, torture, and kill him. It was a desperately evil thing for the Jews to stone Stephen to death. It was a grossly wicked and abominable deed for Saul of Tarsus before his conversion to hunt down, imprison, and kill Christians. It was monstrously wicked for the Roman Catholic authorities to condemn Jan Hus, to cast him into a dungeon, and to burn him alive in 1415. It was abominable cruelty and wickedness for the authorities to strangle and burn William Tyndale in 1536. It was devilish for the Spanish Inquisition to arrest, imprison, and hang Guido de Brès, the author of the Belgic Confession, in 1567. Millions of Christians have died at the hands of such desperately wicked men.

Jesus reveals the motivation of such wicked men: they believed that they were doing God a service (v. 2). When the Jews took up stones to pelt at Stephen until he died in a heap of mangled flesh, they did so, they believed, in order to honor God. Paul explains his own motivation in Acts 26:9–11:

> 9. I verily thought with myself, that I ought to do many things contrary to the name of Jesus of Nazareth.
> 10. Which thing I also did in Jerusalem: and many of the saints did I shut up in prison, having received authority from the chief priests; and when they were put to death, I gave my voice against them.
> 11. And I punished them oft in every synagogue, and compelled them to blaspheme; and being exceedingly mad against them, I persecuted them even unto strange cities.

Paul believed that by killing Christians he was doing God a service. When the Roman Catholic Council of Constance condemned Jan Hus, they did so, they thought or they claimed, to the glory of God. Hus was a heretic in their eyes: he deserved to burn in the fires of hell. Therefore, to prevent the spread of heresy in the church, they sent him (they thought) to hell via the stake. The Spanish Inquisition was largely made up of sincere Roman Catholics who imagined that they were doing God's will by exterminating heretics. And almost everyone agreed with these actions, for almost no one in that day viewed them as murder, but as deeds glorifying to God. Therefore, Christians were stoned to death or condemned to the stake with the enthusiastic approval of the whole city.

The same thing is true of the heathen religions: their motivation, too, is religious fanaticism and devotion to their false gods. Many of the disciples died as martyrs not because the Jews killed them, but because the Romans, the Greeks, the barbarians, or the pagans killed them. Many Christians perished in fires, on crosses, and in the mouths of lions because superstitious pagans believed that the Christians had offended the gods, who could only be propitiated through the death of the Christians. Polycarp, an eighty-six-year-old Christian, was burned at the stake and pierced with a spear in AD 156 because he refused to deny Christ by offering incense to the gods on behalf of the emperor. Polycarp had, the people said, blasphemed the gods, and the pagans eagerly offered him up to the gods, hoping thereby to appease their wrath. Even today Christians are killed in order to please Allah, the pagan god of Islam, or one of the Hindu gods as fanatical religion continues to fuel persecution.

What Jesus says in verse 2 is horrifying but true. Persecutors have a zeal for God, but not according to knowledge. God warned the Jews, "I will have mercy, and not sacrifice" (Matt. 12:7), yet the persecutors believe that the merciless slaughter of Christians pleases him. God desires a broken heart and a contrite spirit, sacrifices acceptable to him by Jesus Christ, but the persecutor thinks that God wants Christian blood. Christians who are loyal citizens, gentle and kind souls, and honest and trustworthy employees are counted as the scum of the earth. About Christians the cry of godless persecutors is, "Away with such a fellow from the earth: for it is not fit that he should live" (Acts 22:22).

As the reign of antichrist approaches, fanatical persecution of Christians shall increase: Christians will be killed in the name of religious tolerance because they refuse to recognize the beast as God. But listen to the Belgic Confession, written by the martyr Guido de Brès.

> "Their cause, which is now condemned by many judges and magistrates as heretical and impious, will then be known to be the cause of the Son of God. And for a gracious reward, the Lord will cause them to possess such a glory as never entered into the heart of man to conceive."[3]

The idea that the persecutors of Jesus' disciples are doing God service, that is, offering him worship in so doing, is pretentious nonsense. Jesus gives the real reason in verse 3: "And these things will they do unto you because they have not known the Father, nor me." The reason for religious fanaticism and persecution is ignorance. Of

---

3 Belgic Confession 37, in *Confessions and Church Order*, 80.

course, this is culpable ignorance, not ignorance for which the persecutors of the church have any excuse.

The Jews, for all their religious pretension, did not know God. If they had known God, they would have recognized Jesus Christ. Instead, when they saw Jesus Christ, they hated him. He was not the kind of Messiah that they sought, and their carnal hopes were dashed in Jesus Christ. What they should have done was to embrace Jesus as the promised Messiah, turn from their sins, and serve him as the Son of God. But they could not do that, for they were slaves to sin and death. Besides that, it was not God's purpose that they would do so, for Jesus must not be hailed as the Messiah but rejected, so that he could make atonement for our sins on the cross. Notice again that Jesus equates ignorance of God with ignorance of himself. One cannot reject Jesus Christ and still know the true God. One knows the true God only through Jesus Christ.

The same is true for persecutors in every age. A person who can calmly torture his fellow human being, who can throw his fellow human being to the lions, or who can burn his fellow human being alive only because he disagrees with his theology does not know God or Jesus Christ. Such a person might claim some devotion to God: he might seem to be religious, but he does not know the God and Father of our Lord Jesus Christ. About such a person John warns, "Whosoever hateth his brother is a murderer: and ye know that no murderer hath eternal life abiding in him" (1 John 3:15). The bishops who condemned Jan Hus, the authorities who murdered Tyndale and de Brès, and the Spanish Inquisition and the popes who orchestrated the burning of many millions of Christians did not know God. Beware of religious fanaticism: zeal for God must be according to knowledge, knowledge founded and grounded in the truth of the gospel of grace.

This, too, should be of some comfort to the disciples. When the Jewish authorities turned against them, they might have wondered: Have I done something wrong? When Christians were persecuted by what called itself church, they might have wondered: Am I right, or am I actually a heretic, as the church seems to teach? What might the disciples have thought after being beaten and disfellowshiped? Jesus would have them know that it is not because God is displeased with them. Jesus would have them remember when they sat in dank prisons that their persecutors do not know God. They do not know me, but you know me, and I am with you. They learned this lesson also: "And they departed from the presence of the council, rejoicing that they were counted worthy to suffer shame for his name" (Acts 5:41). "For the which cause I also suffer these things: nevertheless I am not ashamed: for I know whom I have believed, and am persuaded that he is able to keep that which I have committed unto him against that day" (2 Tim. 1:12).

Of course, we must always distinguish true persecution, which is persecution for the truth of God's word and the gospel of Jesus, from suffering because of one's foolish and sinful behavior. The disciple, even when he contends for the truth, must be above reproach as far as his personal conduct is concerned. Peter explains the difference between suffering for righteousness' sake and suffering because of one's own sinful behavior:

> 11. Dearly beloved, I beseech you as strangers and pilgrims, abstain from fleshly lusts, which war against the soul;
> 12. Having your conversation honest among the Gentiles: that, whereas they speak against you as evildoers, they may by your good works, which they shall behold, glorify God in the day of visitation…
> 20. For what glory is it, if, when ye be buffeted for your faults, ye shall take it patiently? but if, when ye do well, and suffer for it, ye take it patiently, this is acceptable with God.
> 21. For even hereunto were ye called: because Christ also suffered for us, leaving us an example, that ye should follow his steps:
> 22. Who did no sin, neither was guile found in his mouth:
> 23. Who, when he was reviled, reviled not again; when he suffered, he threatened not; but committed himself to him that judgeth righteously. (1 Pet. 2:11–12, 20–23)

14. If ye be reproached for the name of Christ, happy are ye; for the spirit of glory and of God resteth upon you: on their part he is evil spoken of, but on your part he is glorified.
15. But let none of you suffer as a murderer, or as a thief, or as an evildoer, or as a busybody in other men's matters.
16. Yet if any man suffer as a Christian, let him not be ashamed; but let him glorify God on this behalf. (1 Pet. 4:14–16)

Similarly, Paul defends his behavior before the Jews and the civil authorities, while he contends righteously for the truth:

> And Paul, earnestly beholding the council, said, Men and brethren, I have lived in all good conscience before God until this day. (Acts 23:1)

10. Then Paul, after that the governor had beckoned unto him to speak, answered, Forasmuch as I know that thou hast been of many years a judge unto this nation, I do the more cheerfully answer for myself:
11. Because that thou mayest understand, that there are yet but twelve days since I went up to Jerusalem for to worship.
12. And they neither found me in the temple disputing with any man, neither raising up the people, neither in the synagogues, nor in the city:
13. Neither can they prove the things whereof they now accuse me.
14. But this I confess unto thee, that after the way which they call heresy, so worship I the God of my fathers, believing all things which are written in the law and in the prophets:
15. And have hope toward God, which they themselves also allow, that there shall be a resurrection of the dead, both of the just and unjust.
16. And herein do I exercise myself, to have always a conscience void of offence toward God, and toward men. (Acts 24:10–16)

> 10. Then said Paul, I stand at Caesar's judgment seat, where I ought to be judged: to the Jews have I done no wrong, as thou very well knowest.
> 11. For if I be an offender, or have committed any thing worthy of death, I refuse not to die: but if there be none of these things whereof these men accuse me, no man may deliver me unto them. I appeal unto Caesar. (Acts 25:10–11)

What might we think when the whole world, the false church and the wicked world, turns against us because we confess the truth of the gospel and because we defend Christian morality and insist upon godly behavior, especially in our day when we oppose abortion and same-sex relationships? The false church will increasingly say of faithful Christians, "Those people are bigots. They are intolerant. Jesus is inclusive and tolerant." When the world comes to arrest Christian pastors, the false church, which has sold its soul to the devil for the price of popularity, will applaud. Then we will remember Jesus' words: "They have not known the Father"—but you know him. "They have not known me"—but you know me. "And in nothing," says Paul, "terrified by your adversaries: which is to them an evident token of perdition, but to you of salvation, and that of God" (Phil. 1:28).

THE FAITHFUL WARNING

Jesus gives two reasons for this warning: first, to protect the disciples from apostasy; and second, as an encouragement to their faith.

"These things have I spoken unto you, that ye should not be offended" (v. 1). Jesus speaks about these things in order to protect his disciples against apostasy. To be offended is not the same as being merely upset or annoyed. It is much more than that. Jesus refers to a scandal, which is something that causes a person to stumble. A scandal in the Bible is part of a trap. It is the stick that triggers the trap, snapping the trap shut upon the unsuspecting prey and killing it.

Jesus did not lure his disciples into a trap or a snare. He did not entice them to follow him by carefully hiding the unpleasant consequences of discipleship. Jesus was faithful and true. Yes, I prepare a place for you, but the world will have no place for you. Yes, I give you peace, but the world will give you tribulation. Yes, I love you and make you my friends, but the world will hate you and view you as its enemies. Yes, I give you joy, but the world will inflict misery upon you. Yes, I give you my Comforter, but the world will give you no comfort.

Expect, warns Jesus, the reality of persecution. Your friends and family will reject you. Your community will ostracize you. The authorities will persecute you. So fanatical will be their hatred of you that they will kill you, thinking that they do God religious service. Do not be scandalized, therefore.

We must take this warning seriously also. Perhaps our experience of persecution will be less severe, but we must always be prepared to suffer as Christians. Do not say that Christ has never warned you: "But he that received the seed into stony places, the same is he that heareth the word, and anon with joy receiveth it; yet hath he not root in himself, but dureth for a while: for when tribulation or persecution ariseth because of the word, by and by he is offended" (Matt. 13:20–21).

"But these things have I told you, that when the time shall come, ye may remember that I told you of them" (v. 4). The second reason for Jesus' teaching is to prove his care for his disciples in forewarning them. Jesus did not hide from the disciples what the future would bring for them. When they were put out of the synagogues, they would remember, "Jesus told us this. His word is faithful and true." When they were cast into prison, they would remember, "Jesus told us this. His word is faithful and true." When the sword was about to fall upon their necks, they would remember, "Jesus told us this. His word is faithful and true."

If Jesus' warnings about persecution can be trusted, so can his promises. If the warnings about persecution are true, his teaching about the Holy Spirit is also true. If the warnings about excommunication are true, the love of Christ is also true. Christ's word is always true and faithful.

Finally, consider the time: Jesus speaks in verse 4 of the time, or literally, the hour. The hour in the gospel according to John is a reference to the hour of Jesus' death. Often John writes, "His hour was not yet come." Repeatedly Jesus says, "Mine hour is not yet come." Now the hour is very close: it is almost here. Jesus does not leave his disciples to face excommunication and martyrdom without comfort. Jesus faces persecution and death first himself. The Sanhedrin will put him out of Israel. They will curse him. Pilate will condemn him to death. But worse for Jesus is not the fury of men, but the wrath of God, for Jesus must face the wrath of his offended Father, who is offended because of our sins. On the cross Jesus must bear the full burden of that wrath in our place. And by virtue of that death on the cross, Jesus accomplished our salvation. Therefore, any suffering that we endure for his sake is not satisfaction for our sins, but it is simply fellowship with Jesus in his sufferings, which we endure out of love for him, who first loved us.

Chapter 20

Christ's Expedient Departure

(John 16:4b–7)

4. And these things I said not unto you at the beginning, because I was with you.
5. But now I go my way to him that sent me; and none of you asketh me, Whither goest thou?
6. But because I have said these things unto you, sorrow hath filled your heart.
7. Nevertheless I tell you the truth; It is expedient for you that I go away: for if I go not away, the Comforter will not come unto you; but if I depart, I will send him unto you.

The immediate context of these words is the dark prophecy of persecution. The world that already hated Jesus would soon vent its hatred upon Jesus' disciples. Because the eleven disciples were Jesus' closest followers, they would bear the brunt of the world's anger and scorn. That hatred would begin almost immediately after the resurrection and especially after Pentecost. This is because the Jewish leaders who had plotted to kill Jesus, and who imagined that they had been successful in that endeavor, would be infuriated at the disciples' preaching that Jesus had risen from the dead. From the disciples' position in the upper room, their future persecution by the world, even by the religious world, was deeply unsettling; and they did not yet understand the meaning of the death and resurrection of their Lord.

The disciples had grasped two things, however. First, the disciples understood, even if they preferred to dismiss it from their minds, that their future would be one of persecution. Jesus was forewarning and preparing them. It is not a pleasant subject for us either, but it is one that we need to hear because persecution draws ever closer as the end of the world is near. Before Jesus comes in glory, the church must fill up the cup of suffering that the Lord has appointed.

Second, and worse than that, the disciples understood that Jesus was departing from them. Would they, then, have to face a cruel, persecuting world alone? To comfort and reassure them Jesus returns to an earlier theme, really the main theme of these chapters: his imminent departure. In a matter of hours, Jesus will be taken from the disciples, arrested, tried, and crucified. The disciples must understand the necessity of this departure for the coming of the Comforter: "It is expedient," says Jesus, "for you that I go away" (John 16:7). It is not only necessary for Jesus, but it is also expedient for the disciples, and that is how they should view his departure: not as misery for them, but as glory for Jesus and as a blessing for them.

THE FACT OF CHRIST'S DEPARTURE

Christ's departure belongs to the "these things" of verse 4: "But these things have I told you…And these things I said not unto you at the beginning." "These things" are a reference to the entire preceding discourse; I briefly list the following by way of review. "These things" include the fact of the departure itself, which is really the theme of the entire discourse: Christ is preparing his disciples for his departure. They include the promise of a place in the Father's house, as well as an explanation concerning the way to the Father: he is the Way (John 14:6). They include the promise of the Comforter, who is the Holy Spirit, as well as the advantages that they will enjoy when the Comforter comes. They include the union that the disciples enjoy with Christ as branches in the vine, as those who abide in Christ's love, as his beloved, chosen friends, which union will not be severed even when he departs from them. And they include the reality of the future hateful persecution of the world, which will take place after he departs from them.

Central to "these things," however, is the fact of the departure of Christ. Recall the references to this truth already in these chapters: "I go" (14:2), "And if I go" (v. 3), "And whither I go ye know" (v. 4), "I go unto my Father" (v. 12), and "I go away...I go unto the Father" (v. 28). In chapter 15 Jesus drops the subject, but he picks it up again in chapter 16:5: "But now I go my way." In verses 4b–5 Jesus expresses a contrast: "I was with you, but now I go my way to him that sent me." "These things" therefore concern the disciples' future without the physical presence of Jesus in their midst.

In fact, Christ's departure gives significance to the other things: a place is prepared in the Father's house for them because Jesus is departing from them. They need to know the way to the Father because Jesus is departing from them. They need the promise of the Comforter, which is the Holy Spirit, as well as the advantages of the Spirit's presence, because Jesus is departing from them. They need the assurance of their union with Christ the vine, assurance that they abide in Christ's love, and assurance that they are Christ's beloved, chosen friends because Jesus is departing from them. And they will face the hateful persecution of the world exactly because of Jesus' departure from them.

Jesus makes his destination specific in verse 5: "But now I go my way to him that sent me." Jesus speaks as a servant returning to his master although he is greater than a servant, for he is also the Son. The Father gave him a commission to fulfill (he "sent me") and he has now completed it. This is a common manner of speech, especially in the gospel according to John. The Father sent his Son into the world and the Son willingly came. Read, for example, John 6:38–40:

38. For I came down from heaven, not to do mine own will, but the will of him that sent me.
39. And this is the Father's will which hath sent me, that of all which he hath given me I should lose nothing, but should raise it up again at the last day.

40. And this is the will of him that sent me, that every one which seeth the Son, and believeth on him, may have everlasting life: and I will raise him up at the last day.

Now Jesus returns to his Father; and he can say, "Mission accomplished. I have finished the task that thou gavest me to do. I have glorified thee, and I have accomplished the salvation of my beloved church."

Jesus speaks this way because, as far as he is concerned, the work is as good as done. He speaks similarly in his prayer in John 17:4: "I have glorified thee on the earth: I have finished the work which thou gavest me to do." Of course, in reality the work was not finished when Jesus spoke these words in John 16–17. He had almost finished his earthly ministry with the disciples, but his greatest and most difficult work lay ahead of him. As Jesus spoke, Judas and the chief priests were gathering for his arrest and Satan was marshaling his forces.

However, the cross was decreed and prepared, and Jesus was determined to go the way of the cross. Nothing could deter him or deflect him from that path. That is what is meant by "I go my way to him that sent me." Ultimately, Jesus returns to heaven, but he does so via the cross, the resurrection, and the ascension, all of which events lay before him. That gives us great confidence. If Jesus could speak of a finished work even before he went to the cross, we can be even more confident that his finished work of atonement on the cross has fully accomplished our salvation, now that he has actually gone to the cross and is risen from the dead.

That leads to the question, perhaps a question on the disciples' minds, "Why did Jesus not tell us this earlier?" Jesus answers that question in verse 4: "And these things I said not unto you at the beginning, because I was with you." When the disciples began to follow Jesus, there were many things he did not yet tell them. The disciples followed Jesus convinced that he was the Messiah sent from God. However, their conceptions of what that meant were not immediately clear: they had to learn—and Jesus patiently taught them—the implications: who Jesus is, what kind of kingdom Jesus was preparing, and what the future would hold for Jesus and for the disciples. The disciples had been Jesus' apprentices for some three and a half years. Jesus had not, however, left them altogether in the dark, for he had mentioned some of these themes before. They knew something about the Father's house. They had received some instruction on the Holy Spirit. They had some expectation of persecution.

Nevertheless, now things would come to a head, for after Jesus' death and resurrection persecution would increase and intensify. The time had now come for detailed instruction on what the future would hold for the disciples. At this time, Jesus provides the explanation for why he did not speak of these things earlier: "And these things I said not unto you at the beginning, because I was with you" (v. 4).

In a comparison of the gospel accounts with the book of Acts, you see the contrast. When Christ was with the disciples, they were not yet persecuted. Christ bore the brunt of the Jews' opposition, hatred, and persecution. The disciples stood on the sidelines. When the disciples were criticized, Jesus defended them. When the disciples were in danger, Jesus protected and shielded them. But that was about to change: when Jesus was put to death, the Jews were on the lookout for his followers. When Jesus rose again, the Jews would persecute the apostles for preaching about him. The Jews, we read in Acts 4:13, "took knowledge of them, that they had been with Jesus."

The disciples had not reckoned with Christ's departure. They expected the Messiah to live forever, for they expected an everlasting, earthly kingdom. They did not expect the Messiah's death, resurrection, and ascension to heaven, and they did not expect Jesus to sit at God's right hand. Now that Jesus was predicting a difficult future for them, including the hatred and persecution of the world, without his presence, they did not understand. They were confused, perplexed, and bewildered. Jesus was supposed to stay with them.

We learn from this a valuable lesson: Jesus reveals to us the truth when we need to know it. Jesus prepares us for the battle when we enter it, and not earlier. Jesus gives grace not in advance, but exactly at our time of need. We see this contrast also between the gospels and Acts. When Jesus was with them, the disciples were not ready for persecution, but when Jesus sent the Spirit, they were as bold as lions.

THE DISCIPLES' ATTITUDE TO CHRIST'S DEPARTURE

The disciples' attitude in John 16 could be summed up in two words: sorrowful self-absorption. For that reason, Jesus issues a twofold rebuke, gently but firmly expressed in verses 5–6. The first rebuke is found in verse 5: "None of you asketh me, Whither goest thou?"

Perhaps two of the disciples could have contradicted Jesus on that point. In John 13:36 Peter asked, "Lord, whither goest thou?" But Peter's question was not a serious question, for he merely asked about the destination of Jesus, which he perceived wrongly as an earthly place. Peter sought to know where Jesus was going, so that he could follow him. Peter boasted in Luke 22:33, "Lord, I am ready to go with thee, both into prison, and to death." But Jesus had already warned in John 13:33, "Whither I go, ye cannot come." Peter imagined a destination such as the region beyond the Jordan River, or a city or country of the Gentiles. He did not imagine the cross, the resurrection, and the ascension, with the ultimate destination of the Father's house. Therefore, Peter's question betrays his lack of comprehension. He did not ask about the meaning of Christ's departure, for he did not truly grasp it, and he did not ask any follow-up questions in order to come to a better understanding about it.

In John 14:5 Thomas asked, "Lord, we know not whither thou goest; and how can we know the way?" But Thomas' question was not a serious inquiry either: it was simply the expression of his gloomy pessimism. When Jesus explained that he was the "way" to the Father in verse 6, Thomas did not pursue it but dropped the subject. After Thomas, a few other disciples, namely Philip in verse 8 and Judas, not Iscariot, in verse 22, asked questions, but not about

Jesus' destination or the manner of his departure. And there are no questions at all in chapter 15. Jesus therefore is right: "None of you asketh me, Whither goest thou?"

If the disciples had grasped what Jesus was saying, they could have asked intelligent and insightful questions and they could have learned a great deal, but since they were so dull, Jesus did not tell them what they could not yet bear. They could have asked questions like these: "Lord, what is the Father's house like?" "Lord, what is your kingdom like?" "Lord, tell us about your future glory." "Lord, tell us more about the Father's greatness." "Lord, tell us about your sufferings—what do they mean, why are they necessary, and what is their relationship to your glory?" "Lord, explain to us the resurrection of the dead."

If they had understood—or at least understood enough to ask the right questions—they would have rejoiced. Recall Jesus' words in John 14:28: "Ye have heard how I said unto you, I go away, and come again unto you. If ye loved me, ye would rejoice, because I said, I go unto the Father: for my Father is greater than I." The Father's greater position in glory and the Son's future exaltation in the Father's presence should have been reasons for joy—they should have been happy for Jesus, thrilled at his coming exaltation—but instead they were only concerned about themselves: what does Jesus' departure mean for us? Jesus' departure affected them—it upset them. That was their only concern at this time.

But Jesus is merciful. He knew their dullness and he made accommodations for it. He bore with them in their dullness, he was patient with them in their dullness, and he did not overtax them, for he knew that they could not yet understand. When the events take place—the cross, the resurrection, the ascension, and especially the outpouring of the Spirit—then they will understand.

Jesus is a wonderful example for teachers everywhere in the patient, gentle instruction that he gives to his weak, foolish people. Are we as patient with those whom we seek to instruct in the truth? Are we as kind to those who "do not get it" the first, second, or third time? Are we gentle in our rebukes, not browbeating our listeners but accommodating ourselves to their weaknesses? "But we were gentle among you, even as a nurse cherisheth her children: so being affectionately desirous of you, we were willing to have imparted unto you, not the gospel of God only, but also our own souls, because ye were dear unto us...As ye know how we exhorted and comforted and charged every one of you, as a father doth his children" (1 Thess. 2:7–8, 11).

The second rebuke is found in verse 6: "But because I have said these things unto you, sorrow hath filled your heart." The rebuke is not for sorrow, but for excessive sorrow. Jesus will return to the subject of sorrow later in chapter 16, but now he says, "Sorrow hath filled your heart." In verse 20 Jesus prophesies, "Verily, verily, I say unto you, That ye shall weep and lament...ye shall be sorrowful." In verse 21 he compares their temporary sorrow to the pain of childbirth. In verse 22 he says, "And ye now therefore have sorrow: but I will see you again, and your heart shall rejoice." Jesus' words here are an observation and a rebuke. Jesus knows the state of their hearts. In chapter 14:1 he said, "Let not your heart be troubled." In verse 27 he repeated, "Let not your heart be troubled, neither let it be afraid." And now he looks into their hearts, the sorrow of which is probably etched on their faces, and says, "But because I have said these things unto you, sorrow hath filled your heart" (16:6).

Their sorrow is because of Jesus' words concerning his departure. For the disciples, despite Jesus' teaching to the contrary, the departure of Jesus is only negative. They see no advantage in it, and they see no glory in it, for it simply makes them sad. That the disciples have sorrow is understandable: they love Jesus and they do not want him to leave them. Yet their sorrow preoccupies them and is evidence of their self-absorption. They are not concerned about Jesus' glory, they do not care what is best for Jesus, but they are only concerned about the effect upon them. The source of comfort was with them—Jesus had been explaining it to them—but they could not grasp it. They did not understand the cross and the forgiveness of sins and everlasting righteousness and justification. They did not understand the resurrection and eternal life. They did not understand the ascension, Christ's glory at God's right hand, or the coming of the Holy Spirit. Furthermore, they made no effort to understand or to ask questions of the one who could explain these things.

Instead, sorrow overwhelmed them: "Sorrow hath filled your heart" (v. 6). Sorrow dominated them, sadness controlled them, grief blinded them, and they were under sorrow's power. Sorrow so filled their hearts that there was little to no room for anything else: no room for understanding, no room for comfort, and no room for peace or joy. They were simply fixated on their sorrow. This is a temptation for the Christian in trials: sorrow fills our hearts. We dwell upon those gloomy realities of life, and we refuse to see those things that should comfort us. Paul writes, "But I would not have you to be ignorant…that ye sorrow not, even as others which have no hope" (1 Thess. 4:13).

And yet, although the disciples are self-absorbed and fixated on their sorrow, Jesus is not fixated on his own sorrow. He could be, for after all, he faces the cross. Instead, Jesus takes the time in his tender mercy to comfort them by revealing to them yet again the advantage that they will enjoy in his departure. Jesus' departure is not a cause for sorrow, but it is expedient for the disciples.

THE EXPEDIENCY OF CHRIST'S DEPARTURE

To comfort his disciples, Jesus raises their thoughts yet again to the subject of the Holy Spirit, the Comforter. The Holy Spirit is one of the major themes of these chapters. Recall the times where Jesus has already promised the Holy Spirit in this discourse. In chapter 14 the emphasis is on the Father's sending of the Spirit in the name of the Son and in response to the prayers of the Son: "And I will pray the Father, and he shall give you another Comforter, that he may abide with you forever" (v. 16). "But the Comforter, which is the Holy Ghost, whom the Father will send in my name, he shall teach you all things" (v. 26). In chapters 15–16 the emphasis is on the

Son's sending the Spirit from the Father: "But when the Comforter is come, whom I will send unto you from the Father, even the Spirit of truth, which proceedeth from the Father, he shall testify of me" (15:26). "If I go not away, the Comforter will not come unto you; but if I depart, I will send him unto you" (16:7).

Now Jesus explicitly connects the coming of the Holy Spirit to his own departure. "If I go not away, the Comforter will not come unto you" (v. 7). "But if I depart, I will send him unto you" (v. 7). Jesus does not explain the connection: he simply states it with the introductory words, "Nevertheless I tell you the truth" (v. 7). This explains the expediency of Christ's departure: "It is expedient for you that I go away." The word "expedient" has negative connotations today: something is expedient when it is convenient or practical, but it could be improper or even immoral. We speak of "political expediency," for example. There are no negative connotations in the word as Jesus uses it. It simply means advantageous or beneficial: "My departure is for your advantage or benefit."

The disciples need to be convinced on this point. Jesus has emphasized the advantages throughout these chapters. Jesus goes to prepare a place for them in the Father's house. When Jesus departs, the disciples will be enabled to perform greater works than Jesus performed (the gathering of the church through the preaching of the gospel). When Jesus departs, he will pray for the gift of the Spirit, which the Father shall send to them. When Jesus departs, he will return to them in a richer, deeper, more intimate and spiritual manner. When the Spirit comes, he shall teach them and give them peace. "Nevertheless I tell you the truth; It is expedient *for you* that I go away."

Notice Jesus' utter selflessness. The disciples should have been concerned about how Jesus' departure benefits their Lord, but instead, Jesus is concerned with teaching his disciples how his departure benefits them. "It is expedient *for you*."

What, then, is the advantage or the expediency in Jesus' departure, in Jesus' death, resurrection, ascension, and sitting at God's right hand? Negatively, without Jesus' departure there is no coming of the

Holy Spirit. Jesus does not explain why that is the case, but he simply states it as the truth. To understand the relationship, recall the role or the function of the Holy Spirit. Fundamentally, the Holy Spirit glorifies Christ by applying the benefits of Christ, earned on the cross and sealed in the resurrection, to God's people. Unless Christ departs from the disciples to go to the cross, there are no benefits to apply. Unless Christ rises from the dead and ascends to heaven, there are no benefits from his work of redemption. Only at the exalted position at God's right hand does Jesus pour out the Holy Spirit and make us partakers of his riches and gifts. Peter, who is clueless and filled with sorrow in John 14–16, understands this perfectly on Pentecost: "Therefore being by the right hand of God exalted, and having received of the Father the promise of the Holy Ghost, he hath shed forth this, which ye now see and hear" (Acts 2:33). The other disciples will also understand this wonderful truth when the Spirit comes.

Positively, when Jesus departs, he sends the Holy Spirit. This is Christ's answer to all those who pine for his physical presence. If only Jesus were present in our midst, we say: "If only I could touch his hand or see his smile, then I would be comforted." Jesus insists in John 16:7 that it is better for us that he is physically absent but present by his Spirit. The Spirit's presence in the church is better, says Jesus, than his physical presence with the church.

If the disciples had gotten their preference, which was a short-sighted and foolish preference, they would still be in their sins because Jesus would never have died, the cross would never have occurred, the resurrection would never have happened, the Spirit would never have come, and we would all have perished. What is your preference, a kingdom of Christ on earth or a place in the Father's house? A humiliated Christ in the midst of sin and death or a crucified and exalted Christ, a Christ whose work is never completed or a Christ who cries out on the cross, "It is finished," and a Christ risen and exalted to highest glory? Think of what Christ can accomplish, and has accomplished, because he departed and sent his Spirit! About the Spirit's work we learn more in the next chapter.

Chapter 21

The Comforter Reproving the World

(John 16:8–11)

8. And when he is come, he will reprove the world of sin, and of righteousness, and of judgment:
9. Of sin, because they believe not on me;
10. Of righteousness, because I go to my Father, and ye see me no more;
11. Of judgment, because the prince of this world is judged.

As Jesus prepares to depart, he leaves his disciples an impossible task. They must be his witnesses: "And ye also shall bear witness" (John 15:27). The object of their witness is the world. However, that world would not offer the disciples a friendly ear. Instead, the world hated Jesus and would also hate his disciples, even persecuting and killing them. Yet Christ's command is clear: preach the gospel to the world, first to the Jews, and then to the Gentiles, and to the uttermost parts of the earth. Moreover, the disciples must preach the gospel to the hostile world without the comforting, physical presence of Jesus, for Jesus would depart and return to his Father.

The disciples must not fear, however, but they must be confident, for Jesus would be with them in a richer, deeper, and more intimate way by the presence of the Holy Spirit. In order for the Spirit to come, Jesus must depart: he must be crucified, raised, and ascend into heavenly glory. Therefore, Jesus' departure is expedient for the disciples and for us. When the Spirit would come, he would operate powerfully in two spheres: in the world and in the church. In these verses Jesus describes the Spirit's ministry in the world, a ministry and testimony that the world will not be able to withstand. That will lead to further instruction on how the Spirit operates among the disciples and in the church. The Spirit operates in the world to judge and condemn, while the Spirit works in the church to enlighten, illuminate, and save. In both spheres the Spirit is irresistible.

THE REPROOF

A number of questions occur to us when we read these words, answers to which are necessary for a proper understanding of the text.

First, who reproves in the text? The answer is the Comforter, who is the Holy Spirit. We have encountered the Comforter before in John 14:16–17, 26, and 15:26. The Comforter is the Holy Spirit or the Spirit of truth. The Comforter is a person. We know this because Christ uses the pronoun "he" to refer to the Comforter: "When he is come, he will reprove" (v. 8); and "Howbeit when he, the Spirit of truth, is come, he will guide" (v. 13). We also know this because the activity of reproving is the activity of a person. One with intelligence, consciousness, and volition reproves, while an impersonal power, force, or influence does not reprove.

The text therefore describes the work of the Holy Spirit on and after Pentecost: "When he is come, he will reprove" (v. 8). This is the work of the Spirit after Jesus is crucified, is resurrected, ascends to the right hand of the Father in heaven, and pours out the Spirit on the church. Christ returns to the Father in order to send the Comforter, and when the Spirit comes, this will be one of his great works: "And when he is come, he will reprove" (v. 8).

Second, whom does the Comforter reprove in the text? The answer is that the Spirit reproves other persons. These persons constitute the world (v. 8). That leads to another question: Who or what is the world? Or consider a related question: Does the Spirit reprove the world unto condemnation, or does the Spirit reprove the world unto salvation? If we answer that question, we can better identify the world of verse 8.

There really are two main possibilities. One option is that the world that the Spirit reproves is the world of the ungodly, which perishes in its sin because it refuses to heed the reproof of the Spirit. The world that the Spirit reproves hates and persecutes the disciples and the church. Alternatively, the world that the Spirit reproves is the world of God's elect, the world that is the object of God's love, and the world that God saves. The term "world" has both meanings in Scripture, especially in the gospel according to John. Therefore, the context must decide the answer to the question.

The main meaning of "the world" *in this text* is the world of the ungodly, which becomes clear when we examine the context. The other meaning is not entirely excluded, but it does not receive the emphasis in this passage.

There is a clear contrast between this text and verse 13: "Howbeit when he, the Spirit of truth, is come, he will guide you into all truth." Verses 13–15 concern the Spirit's activity and operation among the disciples and in the church, which he guides into all truth. The Spirit's activity and operation in the world, on the other hand, is to reprove. There is also a contrast between the world ("They believe not on me," verse 9) and the church ("He will guide you into all truth...he will shew you things to come...He...shall shew it unto you," verses 13–14). The Spirit's reproving ministry in the world is different, very different, from his ministry in the church.

In addition, the context of these chapters demands that the world be understood as the ungodly. Never in John 14–16 does Jesus speak of the world as the object of the love, grace, and salvation of God. Always in these chapters the world is contrasted, sharply contrasted, with the disciples. Notice these references to the world: "The Spirit of truth; whom the world cannot receive" (14:17). Judas, not Iscariot, asks the question, "Lord, how is it that thou wilt manifest thyself unto us, and not unto the world?" (v. 22). Jesus speaks of the "prince of this world," who is Satan (v. 30). In chapter 15:18 the world hates the disciples. In chapter 16:20 the world rejoices over the death of Jesus. In verse 33 the world inflicts tribulation upon us.

I conclude, therefore, that the world is the world of the ungodly in which the Spirit operates to reprove the world after the death and resurrection of Christ. This reproof is not gracious, nor does it bring about the salvation of the reproved. Rather, the reproof, as administered powerfully by the Spirit, leaves the world without excuse. It is not impossible that some of those whom the Spirit reproves do come to faith and repentance through the Spirit's reproof, but that saving work of God is not on the foreground of the text.

The third main question is simply this: what is a reproof, or what is the meaning of *reprove*? Or what does the Spirit do when he reproves, and how does he do this? That is a difficult question to answer because there are different kinds of reproofs. You might rebuke someone—say, a child—for bad behavior, but that reproof has no effect. The child does not turn from his bad behavior. Since you have not reached the child's conscience, he feels no shame or guilt for what he did. Or perhaps you rebuke the child so that your reproof reaches his heart. The child feels shame, he knows what he has done, for you prove with compelling reasons the guilt of the child so that he is thoroughly exposed, and even convinced and convicted concerning his sin. The second example is the case here.

A better example is a legal context, for the word *reprove* has legal overtones. A prosecutor reproves in this sense: he lays out with unmistakable evidence the guilt of the accused so that the criminal is confronted with his guilt. This does not necessarily mean that the reproved person will admit to you or to others that he is guilty, or that he will be remorseful for his crime, or that he will turn from his crime. Nevertheless, he will be convicted of his guilt before his own conscience. Therefore, a good translation of *reprove* is "convict" or "convince."

Several examples of the use of this word will illustrate the meaning of this verb. In Luke 3:19 John the Baptist brings before the conscience of Herod his undeniable guilt, so that Herod is thoroughly convicted. Nevertheless, Herod, despite this convicting reproof, does not repent of his sin. In Matthew 18:15 the calling of the Christian is to bring the brother's sin before him so that he is compelled to forsake his sin or so that he angrily refuses to hear: in both scenarios the reproof is such that his conscience is convicted. In John 8:9 the Pharisees, for all their self-righteousness and pride, are convicted or convinced of their sin even to the point of shame. Yet they do not turn from their sin or seek mercy in Jesus Christ: instead, they sneak away convicted and ashamed, but without excuse. Finally, in chapter 8:46 Jesus challenges his enemies not merely to accuse him of sin, but to bring forth an indictment by which they can unmistakably prove that Jesus is guilty of something—anything! Indeed, Jesus is the only person who cannot be reproved in the sense of the text. To speak with all due reverence, not even the Spirit himself can reprove Jesus of sin, for he has no sin.

Such a reproof—a convicting, convincing, conscience-piercing, sin-exposing reproof—the Spirit will administer to the world, not to the world of men head for head, but to Jews and Gentiles in all nations who hear the preaching of the gospel. We must understand this: the Spirit reproves only through the word. The Spirit does not work independently of the word, for it is his instrument. When the gospel is preached with power (by the apostles and all true preachers in the post-Pentecost New Testament age), the Holy Spirit reproves: he convicts, he convinces, he presses upon the conscience, he exposes, he forces the truth powerfully upon the mind and heart, and he silences the objections of the listeners. Where the Spirit's reproof does not convert and save by bringing the reproved listener to repentance and faith, the Spirit's reproof hardens, condemns, and damns, leaving the reproved hearer without excuse in his guilt before God.

Of course, we must be careful not to conclude that every reproof that comes from the pulpit is the Spirit's reproof. If the preaching is faithful, it certainly is the Spirit's reproof. When Nathan reproved David with those famous words, "Thou art the man" (2 Sam. 12:7), David knew that the reproof came from the Lord, and God used that convicting word to bring David to repentance. When John the Baptist reproved Herod in Mark 6:18, "It is not lawful for thee to have thy brother's wife," he brought the Spirit's reproof, which Herod refused at his peril. When Peter reproved Ananias and Sapphira in Acts 5 for lying to the Holy Ghost, he did so under divine inspiration, with the result that those two wicked people died. When Paul reproved Peter to his face in Galatians 2, he acted lawfully and charitably, warning his beloved brother that his conduct was unbecoming of the gospel.

A pastor today may not mount the pulpit and make specific, personal reproofs to the congregation, as if he were an inspired prophet of the Lord. Certainly, he can and must admonish them from the word of God concerning many sins, and his exhortations and rebukes must be pointed and sharp. Nevertheless, he does not enjoy the gift of divine inspiration: he may not, for example, admonish a member *by name* from the pulpit concerning a sin about which only he (or perhaps also the consistory) is aware. Paul, for example, did not mount the pulpit in Antioch to denounce Peter as a man who was not (or had not been) walking according to the truth of the gospel. He approached Peter directly, albeit in a public meeting, and he did so with meekness, with the result that Peter, Barnabas, and others were brought to repentance. The proper way to deal with known sin by a particular individual is the way of Matthew 18.

> 15. Moreover if thy brother shall trespass against thee, go and tell him his fault between thee and him alone: if he shall hear thee, thou hast gained thy brother.
> 16. But if he will not hear thee, then take with thee one or two more, that in the mouth of two or three witnesses every word may be established.
> 17. And if he shall neglect to hear them, tell it unto the church: but if he neglect to hear the church, let him be unto thee as an heathen man and a publican. (Matt.18:15–17)

THE CONTENT OF THE REPROOF

The Comforter or the Holy Spirit reproves the world concerning three things: "of sin, and of righteousness, and of judgment" (v. 8). These are the Spirit's three indictments against the world for which he reproves the world.

First, the Spirit reproves the world "of sin, because they believe not on me" (v. 9). Sin is the deliberate refusal of man in his rebellion to live to God's glory. We know this because the biblical word translated "sin" is missing the mark. If I gave you a bow and arrow, pointed at a target, and said, "Shoot at the bull's-eye," you could do a number of things. You could attempt to shoot but miss. You could hit the target if you are a skilled archer. Or you could deliberately shoot at a different target and miss.

The last option is an illustration of sin. God says, "Seek my glory in all things." The sinner says, "No, I will not. I will seek my own pleasure, my own glory, my own power, my own wealth, or my own ambition." That, fundamentally, is what sin is. The world is steeped in sin, for the world tramples underfoot the law of God, the world lives in defiant rebellion, and the world consists of totally depraved sinners. We are sinful also, for both in nature and in practice we miss the mark of God's glory in our lives, although by virtue of regeneration we have by the grace of God a small beginning of the new obedience.

The Spirit reproves the world of sin: the Spirit convinces, convicts, and drives home to the world's conscience that it is guilty of sin. This is necessary because, although the world is full of sin, it does not want to acknowledge its sin, and it refuses to be reproved for its sin. "And this is the condemnation, that light is come into the world, and men loved darkness rather than light, because their deeds were evil. For every one that doeth evil hateth the light, neither cometh to the light, lest his deeds should be reproved" (John 3:19–20). The world of sinful men hates to have its sin reproved or exposed. The world will not acknowledge its sin or turn from it. Therefore, the Comforter or the Holy Spirit must "reprove the world of sin" (v. 8).

But what evidence does the Spirit bring of the world's inexcusable, undeniable, and unavoidable guilt? How does the Spirit convict the world of sin? If the Spirit wrote an indictment in order to press charges against the world, what would the Spirit's indictment say? If you were a prosecutor tasked to investigate and indict the world, how would your indictment read? Would you indict the world of murder (the world is full of murder: think only of the murder of the unborn; think of the cruelty, bloodshed, warfare, violence, and persecution of which the world is guilty)? Would you indict the world of uncleanness (think of the world's fornication, adultery, and sexual deviancy)? Would you indict the world of idolatry (think of the world's false religions, greed, and covetousness)? These are some of the gross sins of the world, but Jesus does not mention them; instead Jesus focuses on unbelief: "Of sin, because they believe not on me" (v. 9).

The world's cardinal sin, the world's damning sin, is unbelief, unbelief in Jesus Christ. The proof of the world's sin, which the Spirit drives home to the conscience of those who hear the preaching with convincing, convicting power, is that the world does not believe in Jesus Christ. Every person who has heard the preaching of the gospel and who knows anything about Jesus from living in proximity to the church knows that his calling is to believe in Jesus for salvation. "Believe on the Lord Jesus Christ, and thou shalt be saved, and thy house" (Acts 16:31). "He that believeth on the Son hath everlasting life" (John 3:36). The Spirit accuses the unbeliever: "You do not believe in Jesus. You must believe in Jesus. God commands of you, he demands of you, that you believe in Jesus. Because you do not believe in Jesus, you will perish. Salvation is only through faith in Jesus." Only the Spirit can convince the world that unbelief in Jesus is sin, the great, cardinal, damning sin, of which the world is guilty. The world says, "I have no sin and you cannot convince me of sin." The Spirit says through the preaching to the world, "Here is your sin: your unbelief in Jesus!"

Second, the Holy Spirit reproves the world "of righteousness, because I go to my Father, and ye see me no more" (v. 10). Righteousness is conformity to, or harmony with, a standard. In Scripture, righteousness is conformity to, or harmony with, God's standard. That standard, which is God himself in his perfect character, is revealed in his law.

Righteousness in the Bible could refer to righteous behavior, that is, behavior that is in conformity to, or in harmony with, God's law. That is the meaning in 1 John 3:7: "Little children, let no man deceive you: he that doeth righteousness is righteous, even as he is righteous." In that text the issue is the doing of righteousness. Righteousness could also refer to the righteousness that a believer has in justification, which is the declaration of God based upon the imputed righteousness of Jesus Christ that the believer is righteous. Paul speaks of this in Romans 3:26: "To declare, I say, at this time his righteousness: that he might be just, and the justifier of him which believeth in Jesus." The meaning could be that the Spirit reproves the world for its unrighteousness, for its behavior out of harmony with God's standard; or that the Spirit reproves the world for its lack of Christ's righteousness in justification and for its need of Christ's righteousness in justification.

While those things are true, that meaning does not fit here; it does not fit the parallel between verses 9 and 10. If the Spirit convinces the world of sin in verse 9, how can he convince the world of its lack of righteousness in verse 10? Or does the world in verse 10 have righteousness of which it must be reproved or convicted?

A better understanding is that the world has wrong notions about righteousness. The world, which even boasts of righteousness, must be reproved, convinced, or convicted concerning what righteousness is because it does not know righteousness. Consider what passes for righteousness in the world. Everyone claims to be righteous and to have a righteous cause. Terrible atrocities and gross wickedness are committed in the name of a righteous cause or righteousness. Ask people on the street: What is righteousness?

The world equates righteousness with equality, equal rights, the promotion of various social causes, the redistribution of wealth, even climate justice or reproductive justice, which are euphemisms for radical left-wing socialism and the murder of unborn children. Even the religious people of the world are clueless about righteousness: they equate righteousness with doing good deeds to earn God's favor, or they equate it with building the kingdom of heaven on earth, or with making the world a better place.

The second clause of verse 10 sheds light on Jesus' meaning: "Of righteousness, because I go to my Father, and ye see me no more." This is a reference to Jesus' death, resurrection, and ascension to the right hand of the Father. In this the world showed its false conviction concerning righteousness. The only righteous man who ever lived appeared before them, but they judged him as unrighteous and worthy of death. They rejected and crucified him, but they did not reckon with his glorious exaltation in the resurrection and ascension.

While the world crucified Jesus as if he were unrighteous, God glorified him as his righteous Son. The resurrection is proof of the righteousness of Jesus. The ascension is proof of the righteousness of Jesus. The outpouring of the Spirit is proof of the righteousness of Jesus. Moreover, the only righteousness that avails is not the righteousness of man (man's good works or law-keeping), but the heavenly, unseen righteousness of Jesus, imputed to believers by faith alone.

The Spirit reproves the world of righteousness: he brings home to the world, driving it into the world's conscience, that Jesus is the righteous one, so that the world is convicted. The Spirit indicts the world for having crucified Christ and drives home to the world the great truth that God raised him from the dead. The world says, "I am righteous and I have a righteous cause." The Spirit says through the preaching to the world, "You know nothing of righteousness. You rejected the only righteous one, Jesus Christ. But God raised him from the dead, and the only way you can be righteous in God's sight is through the righteousness of Jesus, who is no longer on earth but in heaven at God's right hand. Believe in Jesus and you shall be saved. But continue in your sin and you shall be damned."

Third, the Holy Spirit reproves the world "of judgment, because the prince of this world is judged" (v. 11). Judgment is a judicial term: it belongs to the realm of the law and courtrooms. In Scripture judgment can refer to a number of things. It can refer to the verdict or decision of the judge after an examination or investigation has taken place and the evidence has been considered. Then the judge issues a judgment. More specifically, judgment is the sentence of condemnation inflicted upon the guilty. The meaning here is this: the Spirit reproves the world of judgment, the Spirit convinces and convicts the world of judgment, and the Spirit drives home to the conscience of the world the inescapable judgment of God that will fall upon the world, except the world repents and believes in Jesus Christ.

This, too, is necessary because the world is at fault here: the world is at fault with respect to sin (it is guilty of sin but denies its sin); the world is at fault with respect to righteousness (it has no righteousness, it rejects true righteousness, but it boasts in its righteousness, which is unrighteousness); and the world is at fault with respect to judgment. Therefore, the Spirit must reprove the world here also.

The world lives in denial concerning judgment; therefore, the Spirit convicts the world. The world is utterly unable to judge because the world is at enmity with God and it judges contrary to the truth. The world judges that good is evil and that evil is good. The world denies the judgment to come and refuses to acknowledge the just judgment of God that shall fall upon it. Therefore, the Holy Spirit reproves, convinces, and convicts the world of judgment. The Spirit reproves the world of judgment: it does not reprove the world for its lack of judgment, but it reproves the world of the truth or fact of judgment. In the preaching of the gospel the Spirit confronts the world with the truth concerning the judgment, driving that truth home with undeniable force to the world.

Jesus explains how the Spirit does this: "Of judgment, because the prince of this world is judged" (v. 11). Jesus uses the perfect tense: "has been judged." We have met the prince of this world before. In John 12:31 Jesus declared, "Now is the judgment of this world: now shall the prince of this world be cast out." In chapter 14:30 Jesus said, "Hereafter I will not talk much with you: for the prince of this world cometh, and hath nothing in me." Now Jesus says, "The prince of this world is judged" or "has been judged."

The judgment of the prince of the world happened at the cross where Jesus died. Jesus speaks of this event in the perfect tense, as if it had already happened, because it is certain to happen. What seemed to be the defeat of Jesus was actually the defeat of Satan. On the cross Jesus did what God promised: he crushed the old serpent's head. He did so by making satisfaction for our sins, thus delivering the church from the power of Satan and procuring for the church the pardon of her sins.

The Spirit reproves the world of judgment, therefore, by driving this truth home. The prince of the world has been judged, found guilty, and sentenced to everlasting punishment. The only thing left to do is to cast the devil into the lake of fire (Rev. 20:10). And since Satan is the prince of the world, the world that follows him is also condemned, except they repent and believe in Jesus Christ. The world says, "There is no judgment." The Spirit says to the world through the preaching, "Judgment is certain and inevitable. Your prince was judged at the cross. In his judgment you must see your judgment. Your doom is sealed unless you repent and believe in the Lord Jesus Christ."

THE EFFECT OF THE REPROOF

The effect of the Spirit's reproof is the conviction of the world. The Spirit brings three truths to bear upon the world: sin, righteousness, and judgment. In each case, the Spirit's reproof is unmistakable and undeniable. This does not mean, however, that the world, by and large, is won through the Spirit's reproof. Many who hear the Spirit's reproof reject it. However, what they cannot do is deny the truth of the Spirit's reproof. They can claim to deny it, but in their conscience they know the truth of the Spirit's reproof. God insists that they know. The effect is the hardening of the world in unbelief so that the world is without excuse when God condemns the world in perfect righteousness.

Although this truth is not on the foreground of the text, the Spirit also reproves the elect within the world. When he does so, they are brought to repentance. We see this beautifully illustrated on Pentecost when the Comforter comes. He came with great power, mighty miracles, and especially this, with preaching. The Spirit used the words of Peter's sermon to drive home with unmistakable power and clarity the guilt of the people of Israel, whether they confessed it or not. The Spirit reproved the men of Jerusalem in that first Pentecostal sermon of sin, righteousness, and judgment. And many believed. "Therefore let all the house of Israel know assuredly, that God hath made that same Jesus, whom ye have crucified, both Lord and Christ" (Acts 2:36). Through those words the Spirit pricked the hearers in their hearts, and many of them repented, believed, and were baptized: "Now when they heard this, they were pricked in their heart, and said unto Peter and to the rest of the apostles, Men and brethren, what shall we do? Then Peter said unto them, Repent, and be baptized every one of you in the name of Jesus Christ for the remission of sins, and ye shall receive the gift of the Holy Ghost" (vv. 37–38). The Spirit used other sermons in the book of Acts also. Think of these words: "But ye denied the Holy One and the Just, and desired a murderer to be granted unto you; and killed the Prince of life, whom God hath raised from the dead; whereof we are witnesses...Repent ye therefore, and be converted, that your sins may be blotted out" (3:14–15, 19).

The disciples must not fear, therefore. In their own strength, they cannot withstand the world, but the almighty Comforter is with them to reprove, convict, and confound the world, and to save and convert the elect and bring them into his church.

Chapter 22

The Spirit Guiding Into All Truth

(John 16:12–15)

12. I have yet many things to say unto you, but ye cannot bear them now.
13. Howbeit when he, the Spirit of truth, is come, he will guide you into all truth: for he shall not speak of himself; but whatsoever he shall hear, that shall he speak: and he will shew you things to come.
14. He shall glorify me: for he shall receive of mine, and shall shew it unto you.
15. All things that the Father hath are mine: therefore said I, that he shall take of mine, and shall shew it unto you.

Two troubling realities are highlighted in the opening verses of John 16. The first is that the disciples must prepare for persecution, greater opposition than they have experienced before. That persecution will begin close to home: they will be disfellowshiped, excommunicated, and even killed by their fellow Jews. Persecution will spread, so that wherever they preach the gospel, Satan will stir up opposition against them. Persecution causes intense suffering, and nobody likes to suffer. We would much prefer for our message to be gladly received than to suffer persecution on account of it.

The second troubling reality exacerbates the first, for while this persecution takes place Jesus will no longer be with them. He is preparing to depart from them and to return to the Father. It is one thing to face persecution, but it is quite another thing to face persecution alone, without the reassuring presence of Jesus.

The disciples are mistaken, however. They will not be alone. Yes, Jesus will no longer be with them in the flesh, but he will still be with them. In fact, he guarantees by his departure a richer and more intimate presence with them, namely, by the Holy Spirit. Therefore, as Jesus prepares to depart, he promises a gift, the Holy Spirit, who came on Pentecost.

This is the fifth and final passage about the Holy Spirit in the upper room discourse. In John 14:16–18 Jesus promises a Comforter, one who will dwell with them forever, and through whom Jesus himself will continue to be with them. In verses 26–27 Jesus promises a divine Teacher, who will remind them of the words of Jesus and who will impart peace to them. In chapter 15:26–27 Jesus promises a divine Testifier, who will testify of Christ even against the hostility, enmity, and hatred of the ungodly world. In chapter 16:7–11 Jesus promises one who will reprove, convict, or convince the world, so that the world will not be able to withstand the message of the gospel.

In this text, Jesus moves from the Spirit's ministry in the world of the ungodly and promises a guide to the church, a guide who will lead the church into all truth. Surely, then, the disciples have no reason to fear the departure of Jesus.

THE GUIDE

A guide is one who leads another person along a path or a way. The verb that Jesus uses in verse 13 expresses that idea, for it contains the Greek word for "path" or "way." A guide has certain necessary characteristics or qualifications. First, a guide is personal, for he has intelligence and will. A guide is not a map or a GPS. While those are helpful tools, they are not guides. Besides, a map was drawn by a person, a cartographer, while a GPS was designed by a person. Even the voice inside a GPS is computer generated and created by a person.

The guide promised in verse 13 is the Spirit of truth, a person.

Jesus refers to him with the pronoun "he," not "it." The Spirit—as a person—does additional things that only a person does: he speaks, he hears, he receives, he takes, he shows, and he glorifies. These activities require the personal qualities of intelligence and will. Jesus has emphasized the personality of the Spirit before.

Second, a guide has knowledge, for a guide without knowledge is worthless. He is a blind guide. One who follows the blind guide falls into the ditch (Matt. 15:14). If you travel to an unknown place, you desire a guide with local, expert knowledge of the area. He should be familiar with the territory and the terrain through which you travel. Ideally, such a guide should know the local language and the local customs. He should be familiar with the local laws. He should be able to warn you about dangers and pitfalls in the area and to prepare you accordingly. Without such a guide you are liable to get lost, to stumble into danger, to violate the rules and customs, and even to be killed in an encounter with a wild animal or to die because you eat something poisonous, for example. The Holy Spirit is the expert guide, for not only is he personal, but he is also God. As God he is omniscient and perfectly wise.

The territory into which and the terrain through which the Spirit guides us is "truth," and even "all truth." "Howbeit when he, the Spirit of truth, is come, he will guide you into all truth" (v. 13). Think of truth as a strange but wonderful country. We stand outside this country called truth because we are by nature strangers to truth. Truth is foreign and unfamiliar to us. Therefore, the Spirit comes to us and brings us through the gate into the glorious land of truth. Having brought us into the truth, he guides us along the many wonderful avenues of truth; he shows us the riches of the truth: the highways and byways, the forests, the mountaintops, the valleys, the rivers, and the lakes. We explore the land of truth with the Spirit as our guide.

The Spirit explains the truth to us. He explains the one central truth in Jesus Christ, and he expounds the various doctrines that make up the truth. He relates the various doctrines to the central truth and the various doctrines to one another, so that we understand the beautiful harmony of the truth.

This presupposes that we are ignorant of the truth and that we are not competent of ourselves to comprehend the truth. As the Ethiopian eunuch asked Philip in Acts 8:31, "How can I, except some man should guide me?" so we ask, "How can I know the truth except the Holy Spirit guide me?" This was certainly true of the eleven disciples in the upper room. Although they were familiar with some of the truth, they were very amateurish in their understanding of the truth. Jesus takes note of this in verses 12–13: "I have yet many things to say unto you, but ye cannot bear them now. Howbeit when he, the Spirit of truth, is come, he will guide you into all truth." The disciples could not yet understand or receive the truth of the cross, resurrection, or ascension, but the Spirit would guide them into the truth, even all truth, concerning those things.

This deficiency is true of the whole church of all ages. Where would the church be without the Spirit guiding her into all truth? How could the Bible have been written without the Spirit? How could the church have defined dogmas such as the Trinity without the Spirit? How could the church have combated error and developed dogma without the Spirit? What a precious promise is this: "He shall guide you into all truth"!

But what is the truth, this wonderful thing into which the Spirit guides the church? We have encountered this idea before, especially in connection with John 14:6, 17, and 15:26, so I do not need to give a detailed explanation here. Remember that truth is three things: reality, stability, and authority. Truth concerns God: he is the ultimate reality. In him we can trust: he reveals that which has authority and that which must be believed. Moreover, a lot of things are true, but they are not the "truth" into which the Spirit guides us. The formula 2+2=4 is true, but the Spirit does not lead us into the truth of arithmetic. Instead, the Spirit guides us into the truth concerning Christ: he teaches us the saving realities of the Son of God.

A number of things qualify the Spirit to be the guide, the only guide. For one thing, the Holy Spirit is "the Spirit of truth" (v. 13). This is the third time that Jesus uses this name to refer to the Holy Spirit. "And I will pray the Father, and he shall give you another Comforter...even the Spirit of truth; whom the world cannot receive" (John 14:16–17). "But when the Comforter is come, whom I will send unto you from the Father, even the Spirit of truth, which proceedeth from the Father, he shall testify of me" (15:26). "Howbeit when he, the Spirit of truth, is come, he will guide you into all truth" (16:13).

If I introduced you to a man called "The guide of Limerick, Ireland," you would expect him to be an expert on Limerick: he knows its history, its geography, its people, and its culture. He knows every street: he knows Limerick like the back of his hand, we might say. The Comforter is the Spirit of truth: he knows the truth, he represents the truth, he speaks the truth, he promotes the truth, he defends the truth, and he loves the truth. The apostle writes about the Spirit, "[He] teacheth you of all things, and is truth, and is no lie" (1 John 2:27). Since he is God, the Spirit of truth is omniscient: he knows the deep things of God; and he knows, too, how to impart truth to creatures and how to enlighten the darkened minds of sinners, for he has perfect wisdom to apply the truth to the capacity of his hearers and to the needs of God's children. As the Spirit of truth he is intimately related to the God of truth and to Jesus Christ, who is truth incarnate: "I am the way," said Jesus, "the truth, and the life" (John 14:6).

In addition, the Spirit is the Spirit of Christ; he is that by virtue of Christ's departure and by virtue of his own coming. Take careful note of Christ's words, "Howbeit when he, the Spirit of truth, is come, he shall guide" (v. 13). The Spirit's guidance does not happen until after Jesus departs. As Jesus declared in verse 7, "If I go not away, the Comforter will not come unto you; but if I depart, I will send him unto you."

We need to understand further this idea of the coming of the Holy Spirit. Jesus makes a clear contrast in verses 12–13: "Ye cannot bear them now," and "When he…is come." Radical changes will occur between those two points in history. The difference is between circumstances before and circumstances after Christ's exaltation.

First, there will be a change in Jesus Christ. As Jesus speaks with his disciples in the upper room, he is not yet glorified or exalted. The cross lies before him, where he will accomplish our salvation by satisfying God's justice for our sins. The resurrection lies before him, in which he will seal our salvation. The ascension lies before him, in which he will present the finished work of our salvation to the Father, and in which he will receive honor and glory at the Father's right hand. These events cannot be overestimated in their importance for Jesus Christ, and they cannot be overestimated in their importance for us.

Moreover, there will be a change in the disciples because they will receive the Spirit. The eleven disciples could not yet understand these things in the upper room. Their comprehension of their Lord's person and work was limited. Their insight into the Scriptures was undeveloped. Jesus adapted his teaching to their weakness. "These things have I spoken unto you, being yet present with you. But the Comforter, which is the Holy Ghost, whom the Father will send in my name, he shall teach you all things" (John 14:25–26). "I have yet many things to say unto you, but ye cannot bear them now. Howbeit when he, the Spirit of truth, is come, he will guide you into all truth" (16:12–13). When the Spirit comes, the disciples will know the truth more deeply. Witness the insights that Peter enjoys after the crucifixion, death, resurrection, and ascension of Christ when the Spirit comes upon him and the other believers in the upper room.

But even more striking is that there is a change in the Holy Spirit, for he becomes, as the New Testament puts it, the Spirit of Jesus Christ. In his capacity as the Spirit of Jesus Christ he guides us into all truth. We must be very careful not to misunderstand this: when the Holy Spirit became the Spirit of Christ, his essence or being did not change. As the eternal, unchangeable, infinite third person of the Trinity, he cannot change. Nevertheless, the Bible does make a distinction between the Holy Spirit as the third person of the Trinity and the Holy Spirit as the Spirit of Christ. "But ye are not in the flesh, but in the Spirit, if so be that the Spirit of God dwell in you. Now if any man have not the Spirit of Christ, he is none of his" (Rom. 8:9). "And because ye are sons, God hath sent forth the Spirit of his Son into your hearts, crying, Abba, Father" (Gal. 4:6).

This change, if we might use that word, took place when Jesus ascended into heaven. Consider the words of John 7:39: "But this spake he of the Spirit, which they that believe on him should receive: for the Holy Ghost was not yet given; because that Jesus was not yet glorified." Since the word "given" is in italics, we know that the translators added it. Literally, John writes, "for the Holy Ghost was not yet." In other words, he was not yet the Holy Spirit of Christ, which is why believers did not yet receive him, and he was not yet the Spirit of Christ because Jesus was not yet glorified. He became the Holy Spirit of Christ when Jesus was glorified, as the apostle explains in John 7. Similar are Peter's words in Acts 2:33: "Therefore being by the right hand of God exalted, and having received of the Father the promise of the Holy Ghost, he hath shed forth this, which ye now see and hear." The Father gave Jesus the Holy Spirit at his ascension: he received the promise that is the Holy Spirit so that he could then pour out the Holy Spirit on his church on Pentecost.

In a certain sense, therefore, the Spirit became inseparably connected to Christ so that the Spirit now does the will of the exalted Jesus Christ. Christ sends the Spirit. Christ pours out the Spirit. Christ gives the Spirit. Before his exaltation Jesus Christ did not do this. The Spirit became the Spirit of Christ according to the will of the triune God. The Spirit is the reward that the triune God gave to Jesus Christ for enduring the cross and making perfect atonement and satisfaction for sin. The Spirit became the Spirit of Christ in order to glorify Christ, as he teaches in verse 14.

This explains the language of John 16:13–15. At first glance, the language is profound, and even strange. In verse 13 Jesus says, "He shall not speak of himself; but whatsoever he shall hear, that shall he speak." The Spirit shall not speak independently of Christ, for the Spirit has no ministry independent of Christ, and the Spirit speaks only what he shall hear from Christ. Those are profoundly mysterious words. In verse 14 we learn the origin of the truth that the Spirit speaks: "He shall glorify me: for he shall receive of mine, and shall shew it unto you." In verse 15 Jesus repeats, "He shall take of mine, and shall shew it unto you." The Spirit will speak of Christ, and the Spirit will never speak his own things in distinction from the things of Christ. Everything that the Spirit speaks will glorify Christ. In this way Christ speaks to his church by means of the Spirit.

Yet do not misunderstand: there is no subordination of persons in the Trinity. The Spirit does not submit himself to the Father or to the Son as their inferior. The Spirit is not dependent on the Father or the Son as a dependent creature because he is not a creature: he is the Creator, coequal God with the Father and the Son. The Spirit does not depend on the Father and on the Son, as if without them he has no access to the truth. The Spirit is omniscient and he perfectly knows the truth of God. Nevertheless, Jesus speaks of his glorification and exaltation, which glorification and exaltation are the good pleasure of the triune God. The triune God gives the Holy Spirit to Christ to be his so that the Holy Spirit serves the glory of the triune God by serving the glory of the exalted, incarnate Son Jesus Christ.

In fact, Jesus explains the divine channel by which the truth comes to us. Truth ultimately belongs to and comes from the Father. In verse 15 Jesus speaks of "all things that the Father hath." These "all things" are the truth or the "all truth" of verse 13. Moreover, truth is imparted from the Father to the Son, the incarnate Mediator. "All things that the Father hath are mine" (v. 15). They are Christ's because Christ is God and everything that belongs to God is his. They are Christ's also because God gives them to him. Jesus emphasizes here the intimate relationship between himself and his divine Father: the Father hides nothing from the Son, and the Son never acts independently of the Father.

Consider two profound passages in this regard. "All things are delivered unto me of my Father: and no man knoweth the Son, but the Father; neither knoweth any man the Father, save the Son, and he to whomsoever the Son will reveal him" (Matt. 11:27). "The Son can do nothing of himself, but what he seeth the Father do: for what things soever he doeth, these also doeth the Son likewise. For the Father loveth the Son, and sheweth him all things that himself doeth: and he will shew him greater works than these, that ye may marvel" (John 5:19–20). Consider those words for a moment. Let us say that an earthly father is working with his son on a project. Can he say what Jesus does here, that his son does whatever things he does? Does his son observe him and do exactly the same things, and is an earthly father able to show his son all things that he does, whether repairing something, making something, or programming something, and is his son able to comprehend all these things?

Jesus makes such astounding claims about himself. The Son sees the Father's work of creation and he does the same things. The Son sees the Father upholding all things by his providence and he does the same works. The Son even performs such works on the sabbath day, as his Father does: "My Father worketh hitherto, and I work" (John 5:17). The Son sees the Father giving life and he does the same things. In short, the Son sees, perceives, and understands everything that the Father does and he does the same.

Far from denying the divinity of Jesus, these words reveal the divinity, as well as the distinct personality, of the Son. In Romans 11:34 the apostle Paul asks, "Who hath known the mind of the Lord?" The answer is, of course, that no creature has known the mind of the Lord. However, Jesus not only knows the mind of the Father, for he dwells in the bosom of the Father, but he is also able to execute the decrees of the mind of the Lord, something that no creature could dare to say.

So the Father imparts truth to the Son; then the Son gives those things that concern himself and the truth to the Holy Spirit, or to express it differently, what belongs to the Father also belongs to the Son and therefore also belongs to the Spirit. Jesus says, "Whatsoever he shall hear, that shall he speak," and "He shall receive of mine," and "He shall take of mine" (vv. 13–15).

Finally, the Spirit guides us into all truth. But I repeat, this is revealed in deeply mysterious language: it does not in any way deny the equality of the Spirit. The Spirit is not dependent on the Son for truth, as if he would not know the truth without the Son telling him the truth. Scripture simply reveals that by virtue of the Son's exaltation, which is a reward for his humiliation, God has appointed this way in which to reveal truth to the church: from the Father, through Christ, by the Spirit, to us.

HIS ACTIVITY

What, then, does Jesus promise that the Spirit will do? He will guide the disciples into all truth. We must be careful not to misunderstand this promise. Christ does not promise omniscience. Only God is omniscient, and it is not possible for a creature to become omniscient and to know all truth in the absolute sense. It is certainly impossible for a creature exhaustively to know every divine reality. Even when the Spirit guides us into all truth, we only scratch the surface. Christ also does not promise infallibility. Only God is infallible and only his word, which the Holy Spirit inspired, is infallible. No Christian on his own, and no church council in a multitude of counselors, can claim infallible knowledge and understanding of the Scriptures. Christ also does not promise perfect, immediate understanding of the truth. The Spirit's guiding the church into all truth is a history-long process in which the church learns the truth little by little. In addition, the church makes many mistakes and fights against many errors along the way, but the end result is that the church is guided into all truth.

The disciples required this promise because the daunting task stood before them. They must preach the gospel to all nations and they must proclaim the truth, but as they sat around Jesus in the upper room they did not yet fully know the truth. They had a lot to learn. Therefore, Jesus promises a guide to teach them *all* truth.

The Spirit's guiding us into all truth involves a number of things:

he guides the disciples, he guides the church, and he guides the individual believer.

The Holy Spirit guided the eleven disciples (plus Matthias and Paul). He made them intimately familiar with the truth concerning Jesus, he gave them insights into the Old Testament Scriptures, and he enabled them to understand the significance of things that were inconceivable to them before the coming of the Spirit. By virtue of the Spirit's guiding, they understood the cross, the resurrection, and the ascension. By virtue of the Spirit's guiding, they understood the nature of the kingdom of heaven.

Then, the Holy Spirit guided certain of the disciples (apostles) and other associates of the apostles to write the New Testament Scriptures: he infallibly guided Peter, John, Paul, James, Jude, Matthew, Mark, and Luke. The result is the infallible Bible consisting of the Old Testament and the New Testament.

At the same time, the Holy Spirit guided the church, not an institution as such but the people of God, to recognize and believe the Scriptures. As Jesus puts it, his sheep heard his voice speaking in the Scriptures. They heard by virtue of the guiding of the Holy Spirit. The Spirit even guided church councils such as the one recorded in Acts 15.

Subsequently, the Holy Spirit guided the church over the centuries to define certain dogmas, such as, especially in her earlier years, the truth of the Trinity and the person and natures of Jesus Christ. The Holy Spirit enabled the church to develop the truth and to defend the truth against error. The Holy Spirit led the church through very dark days of persecution and apostasy. In everything, however, the Spirit preserved a people in the world who confess the truth.

Finally, the Holy Spirit guides the individual believer. The Holy Spirit works in the heart of every Christian to enable him to believe and to give him understanding of Scripture. He does not grant perfect understanding or immediate understanding, of course, but he enlightens our hearts and minds so that we know and love the truth as it is in Jesus. Therefore, we must be patient with one another in the church. Not everyone grasps the truth to the same degree, but the Spirit is working in every believer. This, too, is a reason for humility. Your grasp of the truth is not due to your superior intellect about which you might boast but is the fruit of the Spirit's gracious work in your heart. That is an incentive to pray when we read Scripture: "O Guide of all truth, enlighten me so that I know the meaning of thy Holy Word for Jesus' sake."

HIS PURPOSE

Jesus explains the purpose of this guidance in verse 14: "He shall glorify me: for he shall receive of mine, and shall shew it unto you." The Holy Spirit has one great purpose, therefore, which is to glorify Jesus Christ. There are two important indications that the Holy Spirit is working in a church: first, there is emphasis on the truth; and second, there is emphasis on Jesus Christ. Where you have mere emotionalism divorced from truth, where you have neglect of truth, and where you have the emphasis on the Spirit instead of on Christ, the Spirit is absent. That is the Spirit's work, after all: he takes the things of Christ, which are the things of the Father, and he makes them known to us. In so doing, he glorifies Christ.

How, then, does the Spirit glorify Christ? He does so by announcing (that is the meaning of "show") to the church and from the church to the world the great things concerning the person and work of Jesus Christ. He announces that Jesus Christ is the eternal God made flesh. He announces that Jesus Christ is the incarnate, virgin-born Savior. He announces the miracles, the parables, the teachings, and the works of Jesus Christ. He announces the sufferings, the atoning death, and the perfect satisfaction of Jesus Christ. And he announces the resurrection, ascension, and sitting of Christ at the right hand of God followed by the outpouring of the Spirit on Pentecost. He announces these things through the Scriptures read and preached. And he announces them in such a way that the world is reproved concerning them and the church with every believer is guided into the truth concerning them. Thus, Jesus is glorified: his perfections shine forth and we are glad.

Chapter 23

Jesus' Instruction About Two Little Whiles

(John 16:16–22)

16. A little while, and ye shall not see me: and again, a little while, and ye shall see me, because I go to the Father.
17. Then said some of his disciples among themselves, What is this that he saith unto us, A little while, and ye shall not see me: and again, a little while, and ye shall see me: and, Because I go to the Father?
18. They said therefore, What is this that he saith, A little while? we cannot tell what he saith.
19. Now Jesus knew that they were desirous to ask him, and said unto them, Do ye enquire among yourselves of that I said, A little while, and ye shall not see me: and again, a little while, and ye shall see me?
20. Verily, verily, I say unto you, That ye shall weep and lament, but the world shall rejoice: and ye shall be sorrowful, but your sorrow shall be turned into joy.
21. A woman when she is in travail hath sorrow, because her hour is come: but as soon as she is delivered of the child, she remembereth no more the anguish, for joy that a man is born into the world.
22. And ye now therefore have sorrow: but I will see you again, and your heart shall rejoice, and your joy no man taketh from you.

In the three chapters of the upper room discourse Jesus is interrupted only five times. In chapter 14 he is interrupted three times by three different disciples: in verse 5 by Thomas, in verse 8 by Philip, and in verse 22 by Judas, not Iscariot. On those three occasions, Jesus gives further instruction in response to their interruptions. In chapter 15 there are no interruptions, and in chapter 16 there are two further interruptions. In John 16:29–30 all the disciples interrupt him, while in this text some, probably most of them, interrupt him.

However, in this case the disciples do not actually ask a question: they merely desire to ask one. Instead, Jesus becomes aware of their private discussion and addresses himself to the question that they wanted to ask. These interruptions show the emotional state of the disciples: they are sorrowful, frightened, confused, perplexed, and troubled.

The interruption of the text concerns Jesus' mention of a "little while"' in verse 16. Jesus speaks of two short periods of time or two "little whiles." Jesus had mentioned the first "little while" before. Twice he had preached publicly about it. The first time was John 7:33–34, where we read, "Then said Jesus unto them, Yet a little while am I with you, and then I go unto him that sent me. Ye shall seek me, and shall not find me: and where I am, thither ye cannot come." The Jews misunderstood Jesus, wondering if he intended to go on a journey to teach the dispersed among the Gentiles (v. 35). The second time was chapter 12:35–36, where we read, "Then Jesus said unto them, Yet a little while is the light with you. Walk while ye have the light, lest darkness come upon you: for he that walketh in darkness knoweth not whither he goeth. While ye have light, believe in the light, that ye may be the children of light." The Jews responded to him in unbelief (v. 37).

In addition, Jesus had mentioned the "little whiles" twice in private conference with his disciples. The first time is in John 13:33, where Jesus says, "Little children, yet a little while I am with you. Ye shall seek me: and as I said unto the Jews, Whither I go, ye cannot come; so now I say to you." Peter especially objected to this statement of Jesus and demanded to be permitted to follow Jesus immediately. The second time is in chapter 14:19, where Jesus says, "Yet a little while, and the world seeth me no more; but ye see me: because I live, ye shall live also." Those words confused especially Judas, not Iscariot, in verse 22.

In John 16:16 Jesus raises the subject of the "little whiles" for the final time with more predictable confusion from the disciples. It is to this intriguing subject that we now turn.

WHAT THESE TWO "LITTLE WHILES" ARE

The heart of the text is that intriguing phrase "a little while" used seven times. The Greek word is simply *micro* and refers to anything small. When the reference is to time, as is the case here, the meaning is little or short. Jesus refers to two distinct, short periods of time. These two "little whiles" are easily distinguished: after the first little while the disciples will not see Jesus; but after the second little while they will see him again. "A little while, and ye shall not see me" (v. 16). That is a reference to the first little while. "And again, a little while, and ye shall see me" (v. 16). That is a reference to the second little while. In addition, these two "little whiles," or these two distinct short periods of time, are connected to Jesus' departure: "because I go to the Father" (v. 16).

You might think that Jesus' words are relatively straightforward, but they throw the disciples into confusion because they did not have a clue what Jesus meant. In fact, Jesus' words drove the disciples into hushed whispers as they discussed these words among themselves. You can picture the scene: Peter whispers to John, "Do you know what he means?" John shakes his head and asks his brother James, "Do you know what he means?" James expresses his bewilderment and asks Andrew, but Andrew does not know either. Not all the disciples were involved in this discussion. John writes, "Then said *some of* his disciples among themselves" (v. 17). However, even though not all the disciples participated in the discussion, not one of them understood the meaning of Jesus' words: "a little while."

They did not ask Jesus. John merely writes that they "were

desirous to ask him" (v. 19). They willed or wished to, but they refrained from doing so, probably because they were too embarrassed or ashamed to ask. Jesus, perceiving their confusion, takes the initiative and asks them in verse 19: "Do ye enquire among yourselves of that I said, A little while, and ye shall not see me: and again, a little while, and ye shall see me?" What we have here is confusion: the disciples say, "What is this that he saith?" and "What is this that he saith, A little while? we cannot tell what he saith" (vv. 17–18). And Jesus asks, "Do ye enquire among yourselves?" (v. 19).

Perhaps we might wonder about the disciples' confusion, for are Christ's words not easy to understand? He is talking, is he not, about his death and resurrection? He is talking, is he not, about his going away, the subject that has dominated this entire discourse? How, then, could they not understand? It is easy for us with hindsight and with the benefit of a complete Bible to know what Jesus meant. We know that Jesus died on the cross the day after he spoke these words. We know that Jesus rose again from the dead on the third day. We know that Jesus ascended into heaven forty days later. We know that ten days after the ascension Jesus poured out the Holy Spirit on Pentecost.

But the disciples knew none of these things: Jesus had mentioned them, but the disciples did not understand. They preferred to explain away painful realities rather than to take them to heart. Jesus could not possibly mean that he is literally going to be crucified and literally rise again from the dead, they thought. Surely, we should understand him figuratively and metaphorically. That was their attitude.

This is because the disciples were prejudiced against the truth. If a person has preconceived notions, he can understand words, but he cannot grasp the meaning of those words. In fact, his prejudice blinds him to the obvious meaning of the words. The disciples had their hearts set on the hope of an earthly Messiah and kingdom. They even expected positions of prominence in the Messiah's kingdom. They harbored the same prejudice that the people had. When

Jesus told the people that he must be lifted up (by which he meant the cross and future exaltation), the people said in John 12:34, "We have heard out of the law that Christ abideth forever: and how sayest thou, The Son of man must be lifted up? who is this Son of man?" It is striking that Jesus responds to them in these words, "Yet a little while is the light with you. Walk while ye have the light" (v. 35). There was no room in the disciples' theology for a Messiah who in a little while could not be seen, and then in a little while could be seen again. What kind of Messiah goes away from his people, disappears, and then becomes visible again?

If you have the wrong preconceptions, of course you will not be able to understand. The same is true with us. Be careful to avoid unbiblical prejudices. Do not allow such prejudices to blind you to the truth of God's word. Aim to read Scripture without preconceptions and seek the true meaning of the words. With the benefit of a completed Bible, we can unravel the mystery of Jesus' words here. In fact, they are not very mysterious at all. Nevertheless, they are instructive.

There are a number of possibilities in identifying the two little whiles. We begin with the first little while, for which there are two main candidates. "A little while, and ye shall not see me" (v. 16). The first possibility is the interval between Jesus' arrest and Jesus' death and burial. The second possibility is the interval between Jesus' arrest and Jesus' ascension. Both periods are short (a little while), either one day or forty days, and both periods of time end with Jesus disappearing from the disciples' sight. Either Jesus is buried in the tomb (and they do not see him) or he ascends into heaven (and they do not see him). Neither possibility violates any principle of Scripture. Neither possibility conflicts with any biblical doctrine, and both possibilities fit the context and the facts of the passage. However, as we shall see, one possibility fits better than the other.

For the second little while there are three main candidates. "And again, a little while, and ye shall see me" (v. 16). The first possibility is the interval between Christ's arrest and his resurrection. The second possibility is the interval between Christ's arrest and the day of Pentecost. The third possibility is the interval between Christ's arrest and his second coming on the last day of history. Of these three possibilities, the first and second are short, three days or fifty days, while the third possibility is long, already over two thousand years. Therefore, I reject possibility number three. It seems unlikely that the term "a little while" in this context could refer to two thousand years, although, of course, it is true that with the Lord a day is as a thousand years and a thousand years are as one day.

Sticking with the second little while, where the two remaining possibilities are the period between Jesus' arrest and his resurrection and the period between Jesus' arrest and the day of Pentecost, which one best fits all the facts? The view that the second little while refers to the period leading up to Pentecost is unlikely because the disciples did not actually see him with their physical eyes on that occasion. The seeing and not seeing in verse 16 are references to physical sight, not the spiritual sight of faith. Besides, Jesus adds something significant in verse 22: "I will see you again." Jesus did not see the disciples with his human eyes on Pentecost. On Pentecost the human eyes of Jesus, with the human nature of Jesus, were at the right hand of God, although of course the exalted Lord Jesus is, with respect to his divinity, omniscient. However, it seems simplest to interpret Jesus to mean that he and his disciples would see one another.

That leaves us with the second little while as a reference to the period between the arrest of Jesus and the resurrection of Jesus. If that is so, the first little while must be a reference to the period of time between Jesus' arrest and his death and burial. At that time the disciples did not see Jesus, but at his resurrection they saw him again. This fits with the world's reaction in verse 20: "The world shall rejoice." The world rejoiced at the death of Jesus (which was preceded by his arrest, trial, and crucifixion), but not at his ascension. The world did not believe that the resurrection or the ascension happened. Therefore, Jesus refers to two things: his death and resurrection. In a short while, in a matter of hours, Jesus will be taken from them, tried, condemned, and executed. They will not see him. Then a few days later he shall return to them in the resurrection. Then they shall see him again.

WHAT THESE TWO "LITTLE WHILES" MEANT FOR THE DISCIPLES

We might expect after the hushed discussion among the disciples, which Jesus interrupts in verse 19, that Jesus would simply say, "The two little whiles are my death and resurrection. When I die, you will not see me for a short time; and then you will see me when I rise again from the dead." But Jesus does not do that. Instead, he explains how the events involved in these two little whiles will affect them personally.

Generally, we should notice that Jesus did not have to spell it out because, first, they should have known; and second, they could not yet bear the truth. Therefore, Jesus spares them further details. In the synoptic gospels (Matthew, Mark, and Luke) Jesus referred to his death and resurrection on numerous occasions.

> 21. From that time forth began Jesus to shew unto his disciples, how that he must go unto Jerusalem, and suffer many things of the elders and chief priests and scribes, and be killed, and be raised again the third day. (Matt. 16:21)

> 22. And while they abode in Galilee, Jesus said unto them, The Son of man shall be betrayed into the hands of men:
> 23. And they shall kill him, and the third day he shall be raised again. And they were exceeding sorry. (Matt. 17:22–23)

> 17. And Jesus going up to Jerusalem took the twelve disciples apart in the way, and said unto them,
> 18. Behold, we go up to Jerusalem; and the Son of man shall be betrayed unto the chief priests and unto the scribes, and they shall condemn him to death,
> 19. And shall deliver him to the Gentiles to mock, and to scourge, and to crucify him: and the third day he shall rise again. (Matt. 20:17–19)

1. And it came to pass, when Jesus had finished all these sayings, he said unto his disciples,
2. Ye know that after two days is the feast of the passover, and the Son of man is betrayed to be crucified. (Matt. 26:1–2)

Nevertheless, the disciples did not understand these statements: "And they kept that saying with themselves, questioning one with another what the rising from the dead should mean" (Mark 9:10). Therefore, Jesus acts wisely and compassionately: he explains how these events will affect them, and he emphasizes the comfort that they will enjoy when these things have taken place. He also emphasizes the brevity of their sadness: it will be only a little while. What a compassionate Savior and Lord we have in Jesus Christ!

The first little while will be a time of great sorrow for the disciples. Jesus emphasizes that in verses 20–22, prefacing his remarks with a solemn, "Verily, verily." Jesus describes the disciples' grief in various ways. "Ye shall weep and lament" (v. 20). "Ye shall be sorrowful, but your sorrow shall be turned into joy" (v. 20). "And ye now therefore have sorrow" (v. 22). Sorrow or sorrowful is the most general word for sorrow: it refers to a deep sadness of the heart that a person might display. However, it can also be a hidden sorrow, a secret heartache that only the sorrowful person knows. We might translate it as *grief* or *grieve*. Often it refers to the response of one who has experienced the loss of someone in death. Weeping and lamenting are more specific manifestations of grief. The verb "weep" refers to audible weeping as a sign of grief or pain, while the verb "lament" is stronger: it refers to a loud wailing as a sign of intense grief.

Indeed, as Jesus indicates in verse 22, the sorrow of the disciples has already begun: "And ye now therefore have sorrow." But soon their sorrow will become even more intense to the point of loud weeping and lamentation. Of course it will, for in a few hours Judas Iscariot will arrive with his band of wicked men. Judas Iscariot will kiss Jesus in an act of base treachery and Jesus will be arrested. Moreover, Jesus will not even attempt to defend himself despite Peter's misguided efforts to defend Jesus at the point of a sword. Jesus, their beloved Master, will be taken from them, tried before the corrupt Sanhedrin, and then condemned by the ungodly Roman governor Pilate. Then Jesus will be taken, bloodied and beaten, to be crucified. At least one of the disciples—John—will witness him as he suffers on the cross. There is no way adequately to describe the horror that will fill the disciples' souls: the psychological trauma will be intense. In fact, if anything Jesus spares his disciples the gory, gruesome details.

Notice again Jesus' utter selflessness: "Ye shall weep and lament... ye shall be sorrowful...And ye now therefore have sorrow" (vv. 20, 22). But Jesus does not describe, never mind complain about, *his own* sorrow. Instead, Jesus is concerned about comforting and strengthening his disciples.

Jesus will soon enter his darkest hour: in Gethsemane he will sweat as it were great drops of blood in sorrow over "His inexpressible anguish, pains, terrors, and hellish agonies"[1] that will come upon him, but he does not mention this. Jesus will be cut off in death, but he does not mention what this will mean for him. Jesus will suffer under the wrath and curse of God and Jesus will be made sin, the object of God's avenging justice as he dies in our place to make full satisfaction for our sins, but he does not mention his sorrow or complain about it. Instead, Jesus focuses on the disciples' sorrow. The disciples should be comforting him, and in the garden an angel will strengthen him, but instead he comforts and strengthens them. Such selflessness! Such compassion! Such love!

However, not everyone grieved when Jesus died. In fact, the number of mourners, and they mourned behind closed doors for fear of the Jews, was very small. Only Jesus' closest disciples mourned his death. The world, says Jesus, "shall rejoice" (v. 20). As we have seen throughout the upper room discourse, the world is a reference to the wicked. It is not in this instance a reference to the whole world, nor is it a reference to all the wicked, but it is a reference to certain wicked people in Jerusalem who represent the world. The chief

1 Heidelberg Catechism A 44, in *Confessions and Church Order*, 100.

priests, Annas and Caiaphas, rejoiced; the Pharisees and Sadducees (with the exception of godly Nicodemus and Joseph of Arimathaea) rejoiced; the common people of Jerusalem who cried "Crucify him" in Pilate's courtyard rejoiced; and the Romans rejoiced.

The world was thrilled to get rid of and to kill Jesus: "Good riddance," they thought. What an example of the wickedness of man! The leaders of the false church and the leaders of the world rejoiced at the death of the Son of God! They rejoiced at judicial murder! They rejoiced at injustice! They delighted not in truth but in iniquity, and they were prepared to violate every principle of justice to secure the execution of Jesus.

Jesus illustrates the sorrowful experience of the disciples, as they move from sorrow to joy, with the example of a pregnant woman in verse 21. The illustration of a woman in travail or a woman in childbirth or labor is common in Scripture. Jesus describes the pain of such a woman as sorrow and anguish, where the word "anguish" is commonly translated as "tribulation." The word usually has the idea of being squeezed or placed under pressure. In childbirth, a mother squeezes the child out by means of a series of painful contractions, which intensify as the birth of the child draws nigh. Childbirth is, as many women can testify, extremely painful. However, it does not last for a long time. In most cases, labor pains last hours, not days. The pain is temporary, therefore, as was the pain of the disciples.

In addition, labor pains have a good purpose: they serve to bring a child into the world. In fact, they are necessary, for without them both the pregnant mother and the child would die. The same is true for the disciples' pain: the pains of Jesus' arrest, trial, death, and burial were necessary, and they served the disciples' salvation. Without these pains the joy of the resurrection could never have occurred.

The second little while will bring the disciples joy: "Your sorrow shall be turned into joy" (v. 20). "But I will see you again, and your heart shall rejoice, and your joy no man taketh from you" (v. 22). After three days of terrible misery, grief, sorrow, and shock, in which Jesus was dead and lay in the tomb, Jesus rose from the dead and appeared to his disciples. Their reaction to Jesus' resurrection when they saw him again was joy. Imagine their joy: the one whom they loved and who had died was alive.

The women found the tomb empty, which greatly puzzled and upset them. Peter and John saw the empty grave clothes in the empty tomb but could not understand the significance, although John at that time believed (John 20:8). Then Jesus appeared to them: first to the women, then to the ten disciples in the absence of Thomas, and then to the eleven disciples with Thomas. "[Jesus came] and stood in the midst, and saith unto them, Peace be unto you...Then were the disciples glad, when they saw the Lord" (vv. 19–20). If anything, the translation is too weak: "They rejoiced" is better. About the women we read, "And they departed quickly from the sepulchre with fear and great joy; and did run to bring his disciples word" (Matt. 28:8). Of course they rejoiced: he whom they loved was alive; his claim to be Messiah was vindicated; and death had not destroyed Jesus, which is what they had feared.

Return to the illustration of the pregnant woman in John 16:21: "As soon as she is delivered of the child, she remembereth no more the anguish, for joy that a man is born into the world." (By the way, the word "man" in verse 21 is not gender specific, but it simply refers to a human being: a pregnant woman rejoices also to receive a baby girl.) When a woman holds a newborn baby in her arms, she does not complain about the labor pains that preceded and even brought about the birth. Joy fills her heart, so much so that she forgets her former anguish. In addition, says Jesus, "Your sorrow shall be turned into joy" (v. 20) and "Your heart shall rejoice, and your joy no man taketh from you" (v. 22). There is a definite relationship between the anguish of childbirth and the joy of holding the newborn child: it is not only that one happens after the other, but rather it is that one turns into the other, one prepares for the other, and one is necessary for the other.

The same is true for the disciples: the horrors of Gethsemane, the events in Pilate's courtyard, and the cross of Calvary were transformed into the joy of resurrection morning. The horrors of the cross prepared for the joy of the resurrection and they were necessary for the joy of the resurrection. After the resurrection of Jesus, when the disciples saw him again, they felt lasting, everlasting joy. They experienced deep gladness of heart, gladness that transcended all circumstances, and joy that upheld them in all their trials. Yet a little while, and they would not see Jesus, but they would experience heart-rending sorrow; and yet a little while, and they would see Jesus again, and then their sorrow would be turned into joy!

WHAT THESE TWO "LITTLE WHILES" MEAN FOR US

What do these two little whiles mean for us? The answer is everything. The answer is eternal salvation. When you ponder these two little whiles, praise God for your salvation. In that first little while, when the disciples did not see Jesus, he purchased our salvation. The gospel is so simple and so beautiful: do we ever tire of hearing it? May God graciously forbid it!

When Jesus suffered and died, first at the hands of the wicked Sanhedrin, then at the hands of the wicked Romans, and finally at the hands of the righteous God, he suffered and died for our salvation. Jesus died for our sins. Jesus was crucified because we are sinners. Jesus died because we are proud, selfish, and greedy. Jesus died because we are disobedient to our parents, because we lie, because we gossip, because we backbite, and because we do not hallow the Sabbath. Jesus died because we do not love God as fervently as we ought and because we do not love our neighbor but love ourselves inordinately. The disciples did not see Jesus for a little while, and they did not understand, but while he was absent from them for only a few days, he purchased their salvation. He made full satisfaction to God for their sins, and for our sins, at the price of his blood. Every time that we sin, we must remember that: and we must turn from our sins in true sorrow and in faith trust in Jesus to cover our sins with his righteousness.

In that second little while, when the disciples saw Jesus again, he had already purchased our salvation. As the resurrected Lord he applies that salvation to us. The resurrection of Jesus filled the disciples with joy because it vindicated Jesus, proving without a shadow of a doubt that Jesus is the Christ and that he is the Son of God. He was, says Paul, "declared to be the Son of God with power, according to the spirit of holiness, by the resurrection from the dead" (Rom. 1:4). The resurrection proves that the sacrifice of Jesus was acceptable to the Father. By virtue of the resurrection Jesus gives us eternal life by the power of the Holy Spirit so that, whether we live or die, we enjoy salvation. Finally, the resurrection is the guarantee of our future resurrection.

Therefore, we thank God for the two little whiles. We thank God that Jesus departed for a little while in death, that he returned for a little while in the resurrection, that he departed in the ascension, and that he will return on the last day. We might have sorrow in this life, but even in the midst of sorrow no one can take away our joy. Our joy is in the resurrected Lord of our salvation.

Chapter 24

The Dawning of a New Day

(John 16:23–28)

23. And in that day ye shall ask me nothing. Verily, verily, I say unto you, Whatsoever ye shall ask the Father in my name, he will give it you.
24. Hitherto have ye asked nothing in my name: ask, and ye shall receive, that your joy may be full.
25. These things have I spoken unto you in proverbs: but the time cometh, when I shall no more speak unto you in proverbs, but I shall shew you plainly of the Father.
26. At that day ye shall ask in my name: and I say not unto you, that I will pray the Father for you:
27. For the Father himself loveth you, because ye have loved me, and have believed that I came out from God.
28. I came forth from the Father, and am come into the world: again, I leave the world, and go to the Father.

It is difficult for us to appreciate the changes that the eleven disciples experienced when they passed from the old dispensation into the new dispensation. Technically, the history recorded in the four gospels, and therefore the history recorded in John 14–16, took place in the Old Testament dispensation. We often think that the Old Testament ended with the book of Malachi or perhaps with the birth of Jesus the Messiah in Bethlehem. Certainly, the book named "the Old Testament" ended with Malachi, but the history of the Old Testament actually ended in the book of Acts with the day of Pentecost.

Although the church was not born on Pentecost with the outpouring of the Holy Spirit, since the church existed in the Old Testament, the church came to maturity or reached adulthood on that day. Paul explains that in detail in Galatians 3:23–4:7: in the Old Testament the church was like a child in his minority under the "tutors and governors" of the law (4:2), while in the New Testament the church is no longer under a schoolmaster (3:25) but has the freedom of the Spirit in Jesus Christ. This does not mean, however, that the New Testament church is not required to keep the law as a guide for thankful living, but she is free from the bondage, the condemnation, and the curse of the law.

In light of this we must understand that some of the characters in the New Testament Scriptures belong to the Old Testament dispensation. John the Baptist and his elderly parents, Zacharias and Elisabeth, lived and died in the Old Testament. Old Simeon and Anna in the temple lived and died in the Old Testament. Jesus Christ was an Old Testament Messiah ministering to an Old Testament people. He prepared the way for the New Testament and he brought the church into the New Testament, but his entire earthly ministry, including the discourse of John 14–16, took place in the Old Testament.

Other characters in the New Testament Scriptures actually belong to both dispensations. John the Baptist lived and died in the old dispensation, but the eleven disciples were born in the old dispensation, lived through the transition from the old dispensation to the new dispensation, and died in the new dispensation. We who have lived only in the new dispensation find that difficult to imagine, but we must understand it for a proper appreciation of the Scriptures.

When Jesus spoke to his eleven disciples in the upper room, the days of the Old Testament, which were the days of types and shadows, were drawing to a close, and a new day was dawning. We live in the New Testament dispensation, but the eleven disciples were about to enter it. Christ opened up that new day by his death, resurrection, and ascension. The eleven disciples would witness the cross, resurrection, and ascension; and they would be present at Pentecost.

In John 16 these important events were in the disciples' future, and they could not yet understand their significance. Jesus speaks of a new day: "in that day" (vv. 23, 26) and "the time cometh" (v. 25). In that day, the disciples' sorrows would be in the past and they would rejoice. That day would bring great changes, changes that we also enjoy.

GREATER ACCESS IN PRAYER

"In that day," says Jesus, "ye shall ask me nothing" (v. 23). The disciples were accustomed to asking Jesus, to asking him everything. A time was coming when they would ask Jesus nothing. The verb "ask" in verse 23a is not the same as the verb "ask" in verse 23b or in verses 24 and 26. In verse 23a ("Ye shall ask me nothing") the reference is to asking questions, asking for information, or asking about something. When someone seeks counsel or instruction, they ask in this sense. In verse 23b ("Whatsoever ye shall ask the Father"), verse 24 ("Hitherto have ye asked nothing...ask and ye shall receive"), and verse 26 ("At that day ye shall ask") the reference is to asking for something, or to seeking some benefit or blessing from God. The meaning therefore is this: "And in that day ye shall ask me questions about nothing" (v. 23a). Contrast that with verse 19: "They were desirous to ask him."

While Jesus was with them the disciples asked him in both senses. When they were confused, they asked him questions. When they were in need, they asked him for benefits, favors, and blessings. Here are a few examples: "Why then say the scribes that Elias must first come?" (Matt. 17:10). "Why could not we cast him out?" (v. 19). "Lord, how oft shall my brother sin against me, and I forgive him?" (18:21). "Behold, we have forsaken all, and followed thee; what shall we have therefore?" (19:27). They would not ask such questions in that day.

Here are some examples from the upper room discourse: "Lord, we know not whither thou goest; and how can we know the way?" (John 14:5). "Lord, how is it that thou wilt manifest thyself unto us, and not unto the world?" (v. 22). "What is this that he saith unto us, A little while, and ye shall not see me: and again, a little while, and ye shall see me: and, Because I go to the Father?" (16:17). Such questions will be unnecessary in that day. The disciples also asked Jesus for many things, but they did not pray to him or through him. That would soon change also.

Jesus' position will change. Therefore, in that day they shall ask Jesus nothing. Jesus looks forward to his future exaltation as the glorified Mediator. That is striking because in John 16 Jesus has not yet been crucified. Nevertheless, for Jesus his exaltation is as good as accomplished, because the cross will lead inevitably and infallibly to his resurrection, ascension, and sitting at God's right hand, which in turn will lead to the outpouring of the Holy Spirit. Jesus therefore is not concerned to describe the cross, something he never does in John 14–16, mainly because the disciples will not yet understand him, but is more concerned with assuring his disciples of the benefits that will accrue to them when he is exalted at the Father's right hand.

At the right hand of God in heaven Jesus will possess all power in heaven and on earth. He says so after his resurrection and just before his ascension in Matthew 28:18: "All power is given unto me in heaven and in earth." The New Testament is clear about the advantages to us: "Who is he that condemneth? It is Christ that died, yea rather, that is risen again, who is even at the right hand of God, who also maketh intercession for us" (Rom. 8:34). "Wherefore he is able also to save them to the uttermost that come unto God by him, seeing he ever liveth to make intercession for them" (Heb. 7:25). "And if any man sin, we have an advocate with the Father, Jesus Christ the righteous" (1 John 2:1). Jesus is our priest in a threefold sense: he offered himself as a sacrifice for our sins; he blesses us from heaven; and crucially, he intercedes for us so that the blessings obtained in his atoning work are applied to us.

We should understand that, lest Jesus' words in verse 26 confuse us: "I say not unto you, that I will pray the Father for you." Jesus is not denying his intercessory work, for of course Jesus will pray to the Father for us. Jesus prayed to the Father for Peter in Luke 22:32, and he prayed to the Father for the disciples and the whole church in John 17, but his intercession does not deny the Father's love for us. In other words, Jesus guards against a misunderstanding: it is not that the Father loves us *only because* Jesus prays for us. "The Father himself," says Jesus, "loveth you" (v. 27). Jesus does not need to persuade the Father to love us, for he already does, but Jesus' intercession is a matter of justice. The love of the Father is the source of the sending of Jesus and the source of the giving of Jesus. We must not doubt the Father's love any more than we would doubt Jesus' love.

The new thing is this: "Whatsoever ye shall ask the Father in my name, he will give it you" (v. 23). "Hitherto have ye asked nothing in my name" (v. 24). "At that day ye shall ask in my name" (v. 26). The new aspect is not asking the Father, but asking in Jesus' name, or praying in Jesus' name. The address of prayers in the New Testament age ("in that day" or "at that day") is the Father. This marks development in the practice and privilege of prayer. In the Old Testament the saints of God addressed him as Jehovah, the LORD, or as the God of Abraham, Isaac, and Jacob. Very few Old Testament saints addressed God as their Father. That name of God was relatively unknown. Although they viewed God as the Father of Israel or the Father of his people, they did not address him as "Our Father." During Jesus' public ministry Jesus taught believers, and especially his closest disciples, to pray, "Our Father, which art in heaven." But the new thing is prayer in Jesus' name. The disciples had not done that before.

But who is the Father? He is the triune God, the God and Father of our Lord Jesus Christ, the Father, the Son, and the Holy Spirit. The Father is not only the first person, but he is also the triune God. The God to whom Jesus prayed and to whom we also pray is the triune God. In John 8:54 Jesus said, "If I honour myself, my honour is nothing: it is my Father that honoureth me; of whom ye say, that he is your God." I have explained this before: the first person is the father of the second person in the Trinity, and the Father (the triune God) is the God and father of the mediator Jesus Christ. Jesus speaks of Father in the latter sense here. Christians pray thus: we pray to the triune God, whom we call Father, in the name of the Son, the mediator Jesus Christ, by the power of the Holy Spirit.

What, then, is it to pray in Jesus' name? Jesus' name is not a magic formula, but it is the revelation of the Son of God. In Acts 19:13 certain wicked Jews attempted to use Jesus' name as a magic formula to unlock spiritual powers: "We adjure you," they said, "by Jesus whom Paul preacheth." They were greatly humiliated as a result. The name in which we pray, or the name in which we ask petitions of the Father, is the name of the Lord Jesus Christ: he is the only savior from sin (Jesus); he is the anointed mediator and officebearer, the prophet, priest, and king (Christ); and he is the sovereign ruler and redeemer (Lord). The disciples did not yet pray in the name of the Lord Jesus Christ because he was not yet exalted on high. However, when he would be crucified, when he would rise from the dead, and when he would ascend and sit down at God's right hand, then, when he poured out the Spirit from on high, then they would ask in his name.

Jesus promises that petitions in his name will assuredly be answered: "Verily, verily, I say unto you, Whatsoever ye shall ask the Father in my name, he will give it you" (v. 23). When we ask in Jesus' name, we say, "Father, answer my prayer not because I come in my own name. I have no right. But answer because of Jesus. He is thy Son. His name carries weight with thee. Because I belong to him, answer me." When we ask in Jesus' name, we say, "As a sinner, I deserve to be cast out, but because Jesus died for me, hear my prayer: he makes me acceptable. He gives me access to thee. He is my advocate at thy right hand." Therefore, we ask only those things that are in harmony with his blessed name. We ask only for those things that please him and would glorify him.

Of course, there are limitations on our prayers. They are limited not because God cannot give, but because God is pleased to limit our prayers for his glory and our salvation. A godly parent does not give his children everything they want, even if they ask earnestly and sincerely. A godly father wisely refuses those petitions that would harm his children. In a much greater way, our Father is good and wise. Yet many Christians interpret texts like these as blank checks: fill in your desire and you will have whatever you want.

The rest of Scripture teaches certain requirements for acceptable prayer. Prayer must be in Jesus' name, even if the words "in Jesus' name" or "for Jesus' sake" do not explicitly appear. Prayer must be according to God's will because we do not pray according to our will, but according to his will (see 1 John 5:14). Prayer must be made in faith because one who prays in unbelief or doubting will not be heard (see James 1:6–7 and Mark 11:23–24). Prayer must be made with the right motivation because if we pray to satisfy our lusts we will not be heard (see James 4:3).

The point that must be stressed is this: a day was coming when the disciples would have, and the day has come when we already have, greater access in prayer. We have access to God through Jesus Christ (Rom. 5:2; Eph. 2:18), God accepts us in Jesus Christ (Eph. 1:6), and we have an advocate with the Father (1 John 2:1). Therefore, the disciples should not fret at Jesus' departure: greater days are coming. We should have great incentive to pray: we have greater access to God than any Old Testament saint enjoyed and any disciple before Pentecost knew. Then our joy shall be full.

GREATER KNOWLEDGE OF THE FATHER

The second great benefit of the new day promised in the text is greater knowledge of the Father. The revelation that the disciples enjoyed pre-Pentecost can be summed up in the word "proverbs." "These things have I spoken unto you in proverbs...I shall no more speak unto you in proverbs" (v. 25). A proverb is a form of figurative speech; it reveals something, but the truth is hidden behind figurative language. It is a dark or shadowy saying or a form of veiled speech. Jesus' teaching was almost exclusively delivered in the form of proverbs. We notice Jesus' parables. There is very little distinction between a parable and a proverb in the way that Jesus uses the word here. A parable is the throwing together of two or more ideas to teach something about the kingdom of heaven using earthly figures. A proverb is similar.

Even when Jesus was not actually speaking in parables, he used proverbial speech. Think of his sermon on the mount: it was full of proverbial speech. Think of his conversation with the woman at the well: he spoke of living water springing up into everlasting life. Think of his "I AM" sayings: these are proverbs. Such proverbial speech often confused and even offended the Jews, who exclaimed, "How can these things be?" Not even his disciples understood him much of the time.

Consider even his upper room discourse: he speaks in proverbs. He speaks of his Father's house: proverbial speech. He speaks of the vine and its branches: proverbial speech. He speaks of two little whiles: proverbial speech. The disciples did not understand his proverbs. Sometimes they asked him about them, but at other times they discussed his proverbs among themselves, not daring to ask him about the meaning.

Why did Jesus speak in such proverbs? Why not say, "I will die on the cross to make full atonement for your sins. I will rise again from the dead as proof that I am the Son of God with the power to grant eternal life to my people. I will ascend into heaven to be seated as the King. I will pour out the Holy Spirit. I will come again to judge the living and the dead"? Why not give a clear, comprehensive explanation of justification by faith alone? Why not give the same kind of systematic revelation of the gospel—the atonement, the resurrection, and regeneration, justification, and sanctification—as is found in the epistles?

There are two main reasons. First, the disciples could not yet understand or bear such direct truth: "I have yet many things to say unto you, but ye cannot bear them now" (v. 12). Second, the Spirit had not yet come: "Howbeit when he, the Spirit of truth, is come, he will guide you into all truth" (v. 13). "In that day ye shall ask me nothing" (v. 23). And recall Christ's words in John 14:20–21: "At that day ye shall know that I am in my Father, and ye in me, and I in you...And I will love him, and will manifest myself to him."

"But," promises Jesus, "the time cometh, when I shall no more speak unto you in proverbs, but I shall shew you plainly of the Father" (v. 25). The word "plainly" has the idea of freedom of speaking, unreserved speech, bold, open, frank speech, or speech with boldness or confidence. In other words, the time is coming when Jesus will hold nothing back. He will not have to speak of the Father under the figure of a rich landowner or husbandman, or a king, or a father with two sons (one prodigal and one self-righteous). He will not need to speak of sowers, seeds, and soils, or of fields, treasures, and pearls, but his speech will be plain. The reason for this will be the maturity of the disciples and the church: the coming of the Spirit marks the passage of the church from childhood to adulthood. A child is taught through pictures, while an adult can understand plain speech. That is the apostle's teaching in Galatians 3–4.

Remember Jesus will not speak to the disciples—and to the church—directly because he will no longer be with them. He will speak to them by the Spirit. Although the bulk of this plain speech took place on and after Pentecost, part of this plain speaking took place in the forty days after the resurrection and before the ascension. There is plain speech, for example, in Luke 24:25–27 on the road to Emmaus: "O fools, and slow of heart to believe all that the prophets have spoken: Ought not Christ to have suffered these things, and to enter into his glory? And beginning at Moses and all the prophets, he expounded unto them in all the scriptures the things concerning himself." There is more plain speech in verses 46–47: "Thus it is written, and thus it behoved Christ to suffer, and to rise from the dead the third day: and that repentance and remission of sins should be preached in his name among all nations, beginning at Jerusalem." But that plain speech, as plain as it is—certainly plainer than his speech before the resurrection—is not so much about the Father as it is about himself: "I shall shew you plainly of the Father" (v. 25).

That, indeed, is the work of Christ throughout the New Testament age: in the inspiration of the writers of the Bible, in the preaching of the gospel, in the guiding of the church into all truth, Jesus shows us plainly of the Father. The Father is God, the triune God, the God and Father of our Lord Jesus Christ. The book of Acts and the epistles, in which Christ by his Holy Spirit speaks to us plainly, teach us about the Father. They teach us who the Father is, they teach us the relationship of the Father to Christ, and they teach us the relationship of the Father to us. They do so in a far richer and clearer way than did Jesus during his earthly ministry.

In Romans 8:15 we learn about the Spirit of adoption by which we cry "Abba, Father." In Ephesians 2:18 we learn about the access that we have to the Father by the Spirit. In Philippians 2:5–11 we learn about the willing humiliation of Christ followed by his exaltation, which occurred "to the glory of God the Father" (v. 11). In James 1:17 we learn of the immutable or unchanging Father of lights. In 1 Peter 1:3 we learn of the mercy of our Father who has "begotten us again unto a lively hope by the resurrection of Jesus Christ from the dead." In 1 John 1:3 we learn about fellowship with the Father and with his Son Jesus Christ, as we walk in the light (vv. 6–7). That is just a small sample of texts about the Father.

In addition, the epistles contain comprehensive, systematic instruction about the Father: his name, his essence, his attributes, his persons, and his works. The apostles could not have written such things while they were in the upper room. Only in the day of plain speech, not in the day of parables, could they receive these things, understand these things, and communicate these things.

About one thing especially Christ speaks plainly: the Father's love. "At that day ye shall ask in my name: and I say not unto you, that I will pray the Father for you: for the Father himself loveth you, because ye have loved me, and have believed that I came out from God" (John 16:26–27). This is a dark saying or an example of veiled speech. What could Jesus mean? We have seen already what he did not mean. He does not deny his intercessory work at the Father's right hand. But he also does not intercede for us in order to make the Father love us.

The Son's intercession is not the cause of the Father's love. Rather the Son's intercession is the fruit of the Father's love. Because the Father loves us, he sent his Son. Because the Father loves us, he punished Christ on the cross in our place. Because the Father loves us, he raised Christ from the dead. Because the Father loves us, he set Christ at his right hand. Because the Father loves us, he gives us his Son to be our intercessor and advocate. And because the Father loves us, he gave the Spirit to Christ to pour out upon us. There can be no question about the Father's love for us: "The Father himself loveth you" (v. 27).

But what is the relationship between the Father's love for the disciples and the disciples' love for and faith in Jesus? Jesus says, "The Father himself loveth you, because ye have loved me, and have believed that I came out from God." That is a puzzling statement, which is clarified in the epistles. In 1 John 4:19 we read, "We love him, because he first loved us." God's love is first, therefore. Our love for the Father is always the fruit of his love for us.

Yet we need to say more about verse 27: it will not do simply to explain it away or to dismiss it as a dark, shadowy, proverbial saying. We should notice that the verb "love" in verse 27 is not *agape* but *phileo*. It is not quite accurate to say that *phileo* is a weaker form of love than *agape*, however. Jesus uses the same verb to describe the Father's love for the Son in John 5:20. The word emphasizes affection rather than the self-giving, sacrificial love that is the love of John 3:16 and many other places.

In addition, theologians distinguish between God's antecedent love, which is the love that moved him to redeem us from our sins, which is always *agape*; and God's subsequent love, which is God's love of affection for his children, which is *phileo*. The latter, God's subsequent love, is on the foreground here. God's subsequent love is sometimes called his love of complacency, which is the love with which he delights in and is pleased with his redeemed children. Of course, God delights in and is pleased with his children only because they are in Christ. Therefore, having redeemed us, he delights in us. The prophet Zephaniah exclaims, "The LORD thy God in the midst of thee is mighty; he will save, he will rejoice over thee with joy; he will rest in his love, he will joy over thee with singing" (Zeph. 3:17).

God loves (he has affection for or he expresses his subsequent love of complacency for) the disciples who love Jesus and believe in him. In fact, Jesus expresses it in words that we would hardly dare to employ: "For the Father himself loveth you, *because* ye have loved me, and have believed that I came out from God" (John 16:27). There is therefore a close and mysterious relationship between God's affection for his children and their love for Jesus and their faith in him.

Here is the sequence, if you will: God loves us, for his love is always first, since it, as it finds its source in the decree of eternal, unchangeable, unconditional election, is the "fountain of every saving good."[1] Subsequently or consequently, and by virtue of that love (that antecedent love), we love him and Jesus whom he has sent: "[We cleanse ourselves], and [render] grateful returns of ardent love to Him, who first manifested so great love towards [us]."[2] God then delights in us, as we love Jesus and believe in him, so that God is pleased when we love Jesus, when we show affection for him and delight in him, and when we believe in him. In that sense, Jesus uses the word "because," but we always remember that God our Father delights in us because our faith and love for Jesus are the fruit of his grace.

Jesus really teaches here something very similar to John 14:21: "He that hath my commandments, and keepeth them, he it is that loveth me: and he that loveth me *shall be loved* of my Father, and *I will love him*, and will manifest myself to him." The main difference between the texts is that one concerns the keeping of Christ's

1 Canons 1.9, in Confessions and Church Order, 157.

2 Canons 1.13, in Confessions and Church Order, 157.

commandments, while the other concerns our love for Jesus (which, of course, is always expressed in the keeping of God's commandments) and our faith in Jesus.

In summary: our love of Jesus and faith in him are not the cause of the Father's love for us, for the Father loves us eternally before we begin to love Jesus or believe in him. The Father's love for us is not conditioned upon or dependent upon our love of Jesus and our faith in him, for our love and faith are the fruit of his grace. Rather, the Father is pleased with our love of Jesus and our faith in him, and he delights in it (with a subsequent love of complacency) as the work of his grace. Jesus therefore does not have to convince the Father to love us as if by his redemption of us on the cross he will secure the Father's love for us or turn him from hating us: he has always loved us, it is because of his love that he sent Jesus Christ to be our Savior, and now (having redeemed us by the blood of the cross) his affection goes out to us and he delights in us as his affectionate, believing children.

BECAUSE OF THE SON'S COMING AND GOING

How will this new day dawn? How will greater access to the Father in prayer in the name of Christ and greater knowledge, even plain speech, about the Father be accomplished? The answer is found in verse 28. Verse 27 tells us what the disciples believed about Jesus: "Ye have...believed that I came out from God." Verse 28 reiterates that and elaborates upon it: "I came forth from the Father, and am come into the world: again, I leave the world, and go to the Father" (v. 28).

Jesus teaches us important truths in verse 28, which are really a culmination of everything that John has taught about Jesus in this fourth gospel. First, "I came forth from the Father" (v. 28). The same verb is used in both verse 27 and 28: "I came out" and "I came forth." The same origin of Jesus Christ is mentioned in verse 27 and 28: "out from God" and "from the Father." Where did Jesus of Nazareth, this man sitting in the upper room, come from? The answer is that he came from God. That does not mean that he is a creature of God or an angel sent from God, but that he is the Son of God. His origin indicates where he was before he came to earth: he was with God or with the Father in heavenly glory. "In the beginning was the Word, and the Word was with God, and the Word was God" (John 1:1).

Second, "I...am come into the world" (v. 28). This is a reference to the Incarnation: the Son's taking on our human flesh, or as John writes, "The Word was made flesh, and dwelt among us" (John 1:14). Because of the Incarnation the Son of God became visible, he walked and talked with his disciples, he performed miracles in their midst, and he sat with them in the upper room. But this one who had come into the world was no mere man, but the Son of the living God.

Finally, "Again, I leave the world, and go to the Father" (v. 28). Jesus Christ had finished his earthly ministry and was ready to leave the world and return to the triune God, whom he calls his Father. His departure to the Father would be difficult, although he spares the disciples the details, which would be clearer after his resurrection. He would die on the cross for the sins of God's people, he would rise again, and he would ascend and would pour out the Spirit.

By so doing he would usher in the new day: a day in which we will ask the Father in his name, and a day in which Jesus will no longer speak in proverbs but will speak plainly of the Father. Truly our fellowship is with the Father and his Son through the Holy Spirit purchased on Calvary's cross.

Chapter 25

The Disciples' Premature Enthusiasm

(John 16:29–32)

29. His disciples said unto him, Lo, now speakest thou plainly, and speakest no proverb.
30. Now are we sure that thou knowest all things, and needest not that any man should ask thee: by this we believe that thou camest forth from God.
31. Jesus answered them, Do ye now believe?
32. Behold, the hour cometh, yea, is now come, that ye shall be scattered, every man to his own, and shall leave me alone: and yet I am not alone, because the Father is with me.

Throughout the lengthy discourse of John 14–16 (almost three chapters or eighty-six verses) the eleven disciples have listened to Jesus, their beloved Lord and Savior. The words that he has spoken to them are spirit and life. They are profound, wonderful, comforting words. Undoubtedly, the disciples listened with rapt attention, only occasionally daring to interrupt him with questions or comments. There was so much to take in and so little time left to learn from the Master. Jesus is coming to the end of his instruction: soon he shall pray for them (in chapter 17) and then he shall lead them to Gethsemane, where he shall be taken from them.

Jesus has promised them great advantages in his imminent departure to the Father. Jesus has described in detail that spiritual fellowship that they enjoy, and that they will enjoy, with him by faith alone. Jesus has outlined the wonderful privileges and responsibilities that they have as his friends. Jesus has instructed them in detail about the ministry of the Holy Spirit, his ministry among them and in the world. Jesus has warned them about the persecution that will come upon them and has encouraged and comforted them with the promise of his gracious presence by the Holy Spirit.

Finally, Jesus has just encouraged his disciples with wonderful, comforting truths. He has promised a day when no more questions would be necessary, for the Spirit would lead them into all truth; he has promised the privilege of praying in his name; and he has promised a day of plain speech concerning the Father, rather than the proverbial speech with which he usually instructed them. The disciples are excited: now, finally, they have got it! But have they?

THE DISCIPLES' INADEQUATE CONFESSION

With considerable excitement the disciples exclaim in verse 30, "We believe that thou camest forth from God." What does this confession mean, and what have the disciples actually learned about Jesus? Certainly, the disciples have grasped something about the identity of Jesus of Nazareth, which goes beyond what the common people thought about him. A man like Nicodemus, for example, said, "We know that thou art a teacher come from God" (John 3:2). Nicodemus referred merely to the authority of Jesus' teachings, not to his divine origin. He did not view Jesus as heavenly (at least, not before he was converted). The multitude fed with bread and fishes exclaimed, "This is of a truth that prophet that should come into the world" (6:14). They had their eye on Deuteronomy 18:15–19, but they also did not view Jesus as heavenly.

Therefore, when the disciples say, "Thou camest forth from God," they confess the heavenly origin of Jesus of Nazareth: he is not a mere man. The disciples echo what Jesus said in verse 27: "Ye have loved me, and have believed that I came out from God," and they echo Jesus' own self-designation in verse 28: "I came forth from the Father." "We believe that thou camest forth from God." Earlier, the disciples had confessed, "We believe and are sure that thou art that Christ, the Son of the living God" (John 6:69). Although they echo Jesus' words, there is a question whether they truly understand them. The issue that they do grasp, however, is that Jesus is not from earth; he came from heaven. He is not merely human, but he is heavenly, and even divine.

The disciples echo only part of Jesus' words in verse 28. Their echo of Jesus' words therefore is incomplete, inadequate, and quite faint. Jesus' complete self-designation concerns four things, of which the disciples grasp—and therefore confess—only two. "I came forth from the Father." They confess Jesus' divine origin as the Son of God. Even then, they have a vague understanding of the relationship between Jesus and the Father. They say "God," not "Father." "I am come into the world." They confess that the heavenly, divine, otherworldly Jesus has entered the world. They see him before them, but they do not understand the Incarnation or the relationship of human and divine in him.

"Again, I leave the world." This made no sense to them, for how could Jesus, the Messiah, be leaving? Where would he go? How would he get there? And what would happen to them? They had not grasped that. "And I go to the Father." This, too, was a great mystery. Jesus had spoken of his Father's house of many mansions. Jesus had spoken of praying to the Father. Jesus had spoken of the Father's affection for them, but what did it mean to go to the Father? Where was this Father?

Why had the disciples not grasped this? It is because they had not grasped the cross: they did not understand the meaning or the necessity of the cross. The disciples had room in their theology, in their messianic expectations, for a Messiah who comes from God, for a glorious, even divine, Messiah, but they had no room in their theology for a Messiah who leaves the world again to return to heaven. They did not understand a Messiah who would suffer, who would be crucified, who would die, and who would be buried. Jesus had spoken to them of an hour when they would weep and lament, when the world would rejoice, and this had unsettled them.

It is not surprising to see the disciples omitting from their confession those aspects of the truth that they did not understand and that they disliked. We do the same: we tend to confess only those aspects of the truth that we understand, and especially those aspects of the truth that we like. We must confess the whole truth of God and we must seek to learn the whole truth of God. We must expect to hear from our preachers the whole truth of God and we must require from our ministers the whole truth of God. A truncated gospel simply will not suffice. When the Spirit came, he guided these eleven disciples from an inadequate confession to the whole truth of God.

What, then, is the reason for this confession, which despite its inadequacy was sincere and true? The disciples based their confession on two things.

First, the disciples are impressed by Jesus' knowledge. This is a common theme in the gospels: people are often impressed by Jesus' knowledge. His knowledge convinces people that he is the Messiah. When Jesus meets Nathanael for the first time, he says, "Before that Philip called thee, when thou wast under the fig tree, I saw thee" (John 1:48). In amazement, Nathanael cries out, "Rabbi, thou art the Son of God; thou art the King of Israel" (v. 49). When Jesus encounters the woman at the well of Samaria, he demonstrates knowledge of her sins, including knowledge of her five former husbands and her current sinful relationship. She calls to the men of her village, "Come, see a man, which told me all things that ever I did: is not this the Christ?" (4:29). Later in the chapter, we read, "And many of the Samaritans of that city believed on him for the saying of the woman, which testified, He told me all that ever I did" (v. 39). Even Peter after the resurrection appeals to Jesus' supernatural knowledge: "Lord, thou knowest all things; thou knowest that I love thee" (21:17). The supernatural knowledge, even omniscience, of Jesus impressed them.

We see that in two phrases in verse 30: "Now we are sure [or, we know] that thou knowest all things" and "[Thou] needest not that any man should ask thee." "By this," they conclude, "we believe that thou camest forth from God." The disciples were impressed because of what Jesus had said. They had been whispering among themselves in verses 17–18: "What is this that he saith unto us, A little while?" and before they could ask him the question that was on their minds, Jesus had exposed their question by reading their minds in verse 19: "Do ye enquire among yourselves of that I said, A little while"?

There is also a reference to verse 23: "In that day ye shall ask me nothing." Recall that the meaning of "ask" in verse 23a is to ask a question. The disciples had asked nothing: Jesus did not need to hear their question in order to answer it. He simply answered it because he knows all things. Because of this display of supernatural, even divine, knowledge, the disciples believed that Jesus came "forth from God."

Second, the disciples are excited about the promise of a new day characterized by clarity of revelation, and they conclude that the day in question has already arrived. In verses 23 and 25 Jesus promises a future day: "In that day ye shall ask me nothing...The time cometh, when I shall no more speak unto you in proverbs, but I shall shew you plainly of the Father." Instead of waiting patiently for that day and trying to grasp the meaning of Jesus' words in the present, the disciples think themselves to be in that day. "Lo, now speakest thou plainly, and speakest no proverb" (v. 29). Notice that the disciples use the word "now" and a verb in the present tense. The end of proverbs has arrived! The day of plain speech is here!

But the disciples are mistaken, which is typical of them. They are selective hearers, hearing what they want to hear, while they ignore the unpleasant aspects of Christ's teaching. They hear that Jesus has come forth from God, but they ignore that he is leaving again. They hear that a day of plain speech is coming, but they ignore the departure of Jesus that makes that day possible.

In verse 7 Jesus explained, "Nevertheless I tell you the truth; It is expedient for you that I go away; for if I go not away, the Comforter will not come unto you; but if I depart, I will send him unto you." In verse 13 Jesus explained, "Howbeit when he, the Spirit of truth, is come, he will guide you into all truth." In verse 25 Jesus promised, "The time cometh, when I shall no more speak unto you in proverbs, but I shall shew you plainly of the Father." Put those three truths together: Jesus speaks plainly because the Spirit comes, and the Spirit comes because Jesus departs in his death, resurrection, and ascension. Therefore, the disciples' conclusion is unwarranted: Jesus cannot yet speak plainly. Their misunderstanding shows that they have not reckoned with Jesus' cross and resurrection as necessary for the coming of the Holy Spirit.

Nevertheless, for all the inadequacy of the disciples' confession, it is the evidence of true, if undeveloped, faith. Jesus does not despise the embryo of faith in them. Jesus affirms the reality and genuineness of their faith in verse 27: "Ye have loved me, and have believed that I came out from God." He even prays about their faith in John 17:8: "For I have given unto them the words which thou gavest me; and they have received them, and have known surely that I came out from thee, and they have believed that thou didst send me." We should not despise weak, undeveloped faith. We should not despise one who does not yet know much about the Christian faith. If he has a teachable spirit, we should encourage him to learn. That is what Jesus does in his mercy toward his weak, but believing, disciples.

In addition, Jesus questions the disciples' faith, not the genuineness of their faith, not the sincerity of their faith, but the strength and resilience of their faith, in verse 31. "Jesus answered them, Do ye now believe?" Since in the original language there was no punctuation, we could translate Jesus' words as a question ("Do ye now believe?") or as a statement ("You do now believe") or even an exclamation ("Now ye do believe!"). It is really a combination of those ideas: Jesus affirms their faith in principle but warns them against self-confidence.

Jesus is in the habit of doing this: he generally does not encourage premature enthusiasm, cautioning would-be converts or believers to consider the implications of believing him or following him. In Matthew 8:19 a man cries out, "Master, I will follow thee whithersoever thou goest." Jesus warns him, "The foxes have holes, and the birds of the air have nests; but the Son of man hath not where to lay his head" (v. 20). Are you sure, he says, that you are ready to follow me? In Luke 14:26–27 he warns a multitude, "If any man come to me, and hate not his father, and mother, and wife, and children, and brethren, and sisters, yea, and his own life also, he cannot be my disciple. And whosoever doth not bear his cross, and come after me, cannot be my disciple." So here: "Do ye now believe?" Are you sure? Are you ready for the great trial that must come upon you? Your faith, such as it is, must be tested.

This has application to the church: do not become too quickly enthusiastic about a person's confession of faith. Wait and see. Be charitable, but a person's confession must be tested. How long will it take a professing Christian to understand the implications of confessing Christ? How long will it take for him or her to grasp the truth, the doctrines? Will he or she embrace the lifestyle required by the word of God, especially when it is costly? Will his or her faith endure when trials come? Or will he or she, may God forbid it, turn out to be a stony ground hearer with no root in Jesus Christ, as Jesus warns in the parable of the sower (Matt. 13:20–21)? Do you now believe? As Jesus said elsewhere, "If ye continue in my word, then are ye my disciples indeed" (John 8:31). If you do not continue, you show that you were not disciples of Jesus Christ.

CHRIST'S STARTLING PREDICTION

Jesus' next words are startling; therefore, he prefaces them with "Behold" (v. 32). These words are a development of some of Jesus' earlier predictions. So far Jesus has made some very unsettling predictions. In John 13:33 he announced his departure: "Little children, yet a little while I am with you. Ye shall seek me: and as I said unto the Jews, Whither I go, ye cannot come; so now I say to you." In verse 21 Jesus announced his betrayal by one of his disciples, who was later revealed to be Judas Iscariot: "Verily, verily, I say unto you, that one of you shall betray me." In verse 38 he warned of his denial by Peter: "Verily, verily, I say unto thee, The cock shall not crow, till thou hast denied me thrice."

Jesus now predicts the scattering of the disciples and their abandonment of him: "Ye shall be scattered, every man to his own, and shall leave me alone" (v. 32). It is not only that one of the disciples will betray Jesus: Judas shall actively, willingly, and treacherously deliver Jesus to his enemies. It is not even that Peter shall say three times with increased vehemence: "I do not know Jesus." It is that all the disciples, all eleven of them, shall forsake Jesus.

This happens because of a scattering of the disciples: the idea is of a wolf rushing into a flock of sheep with the result that the sheep run in every direction. The sheep in fear and panic abandon the shepherd and run for safety. Jesus explains this later in Matthew 26:31: "All ye shall be offended because of me this night: for it is written, I will smite the shepherd, and the sheep of the flock shall be scattered abroad." The sheep will not run away because the shepherd abandons the sheep—he never does that—but because the shepherd is smitten: he is arrested, tried, beaten, crucified, killed, and buried. This leaves the sheep in utter panic and bewilderment.

Moreover, this scattering of the sheep will happen very soon: "The hour cometh, yea, is now come" (v. 32). In fact, this scattering will occur this very night. As Jesus speaks these words, Judas Iscariot is making his way to the high priest. The high priest, the other priests, and the scribes are hurriedly preparing for Jesus' arrest, and they are scrambling to organize a trial at very short notice. Soon Judas will arrive at the upper room, but Jesus will have departed by then, so that Judas will lead the enemies of Jesus to Gethsemane. When Judas finds Jesus, he will kiss him with a treacherous, perfidious kiss to identify him to the mob of soldiers and officers; and Jesus shall willingly submit to their arrest.

What, then, will become of the disciples' confession of faith? "We believe that thou camest forth from God." Do you really, Peter? Where is your faith when three times you deny him? Do you really, John, James, Andrew, Philip, Thomas, Nathanael, and the others?

Where is your faith when in blind panic you run in every direction to avoid suffering with Jesus? Do you really believe when not one of you is willing to stand with Jesus in his darkest hour? Oh, do not boast of the strength of your faith when it has not been tested! And when it is tested, pray earnestly that God would strengthen you in the midst of trials and temptations. Left to yourself, you would fare no better than the eleven disciples, and you have not faced a trial as great as this!

Convicting about these words is the behavior of the disciples with respect to Jesus: the Lord emphasizes this. Literally, he says, "And me—*me*—ye shall leave alone." When Jesus is acting utterly selflessly, the disciples will act in utter selfishness. Jesus' chief concern in the upper room discourse is the disciples' comfort. He prepares them for the dark future that they must face when he dies. He emphasizes time and time again the advantages that they shall enjoy. He speaks to them as clearly as he can, making allowances for their capacity. Yet at the very end of the upper room discourse, they still have not grasped it.

Jesus' purpose is to have his disciples scattered in order to preserve them in salvation. Had the disciples not been scattered, they would have perished: the trial that Jesus must face would have been too great for them to bear. In John 18:8 Jesus selflessly gives his disciples room to escape and even to be scattered. He says to the mob, "I have told you that I am he: if therefore ye seek me, let these go their way." As it were, the shepherd offers himself to the wolf so that the sheep are spared. And so the disciples run, just as Jesus said.

Jesus behaves in this way so that he can accomplish the salvation of his sheep. Jesus willingly goes to the cross in order to make atonement for our sins. The terrible sins of Peter and the other ten—as well as our sins—must be paid for. Jesus must pay the price, which is death under the wrath and curse of God. It was wicked for the disciples, especially after their confession of faith, to leave Jesus alone. Jesus even feels the sting of it, for his friends abandon him, but it is also necessary, and Jesus willingly embraces abandonment for us.

Do not forget, either, that Jesus must be alone. He must be alone not only because his disciples cannot help him and because they must be preserved, for Jesus can lose none of the elect. He must be alone also because only Jesus can accomplish the salvation that God has promised. God withdrew all earthly support from Jesus when he bore our sin. In the garden of Gethsemane the disciples did not support Jesus: they fell asleep. God sent an angel to strengthen Jesus, who was under intense strain. In the garden, too, the disciples abandoned him: they fled in every direction. No man stood with Jesus at his trial before the Sanhedrin, during which time even Peter denied him. No man supported him at his trial before Pilate. And no man helped him when he was nailed to the tree on Calvary's hill.

Although a few disciples, including John, his mother, and some women, stood near the cross, they could do nothing to help him. Jesus did not call out to his mother to support him, John gave him nothing, and his followers did not give him even a drink of water when he hung on the cross. The Romans did not permit anyone to come near the cross to offer succor to the victims of crucifixion. Do not ascribe to anyone else a part, even the tiniest part, in the work of redemption. Jesus is the only savior, the only redeemer, and the only mediator. Jesus suffered alone: he bore the wrath of God alone, and no one helped him bear it; he suffered the curse of God, and no one helped him endure it; he paid the price of our redemption alone, and no one contributed to it. Only he, as the perfectly righteous Son of God in human flesh, was qualified to do it. Therefore, Jesus' doleful words are necessary: "Ye…shall leave me alone."

CHRIST'S UNWAVERING CONFIDENCE

Jesus adds an important qualifier in verse 32: "And yet I am not alone, because the Father is with me." All humans—especially the eleven disciples—shall abandon Jesus; they will flee. But Jesus trusts in one who will never fail him: the Father, the triune God, the one who sent him into the world to be the savior; and the one who will receive him into heaven when his work is completed.

The Father is with Jesus when Judas treacherously kisses him. The Father is with Jesus when the disciples flee from him. The Father is with Jesus when the Jews arrest him. The Father is with Jesus when Peter denies him. The Father is with Jesus when the Sanhedrin blaspheme him, condemn him, beat him, and spit in his face. The Father is with Jesus when Pilate tries him, when the soldiers make a crown of thorns for his head and scourge him. The Father is with Jesus when the Jews choose Barabbas instead of him. The Father is with Jesus when Pilate washes his hands of him. The Father is with Jesus when the Romans crucify him. Throughout the agonies of the cross the Father is with him. Even when the Father pours his wrath and curse upon Jesus, he is with him. "And yet I am not alone, because the Father is with me" (v. 32).

Yet a time is coming when even the comfortable sense of the presence of the Father will disappear from Jesus' consciousness. A time is coming when Jesus will not say, "And yet I am not alone, because the Father is with me," but "My God, my God, why hast thou forsaken me?" Was the Father with Jesus on the cross? Yes, he was, but only in his wrath and curse, as he pursued Jesus into hell in his justice and holiness. Jesus felt the pains of hell on the cross, although he did not go to the place called hell. On the cross, especially during the three hours of darkness, God was not present in his love and favor. In that sense, Jesus was, and knew himself to be, abandoned. And it was because of our sin! Jesus must be abandoned to God's wrath and curse so that he could make full satisfaction for our sins. Jesus must be abandoned to God's wrath and curse to pay for the disciples' cowardice. Finally, when the price was paid in full, he could say with confidence, "Father, into thy hands I commend my spirit."

The Heidelberg Catechism explains that phrase in the Apostles' Creed, "He descended into hell," thus:

> Why is there added, "He descended into hell"?
>
> That in my greatest temptations, I may be assured, and wholly comfort myself in this, that my Lord Jesus Christ, by

> His inexpressible anguish, pains, terrors, and hellish agonies, in which He was plunged during all His sufferings, but especially on the cross, hath delivered me from the anguish and torments of hell.[1]

Then the disciples would understand. Then, after the resurrection and ascension, they would know. Then they could say in sincerity, their faith tested and purified, "By this we believe that thou camest forth from God."

1 Heidelberg Catechism Q&A 44, in *Confessions and Church Order*, 100.

Chapter 26

Christ Overcoming the World

(John 16:33)

> 33. These things I have spoken unto you, that in me ye might have peace. In the world ye shall have tribulation: but be of good cheer; I have overcome the world.

These beautiful words mark the conclusion and the climax of the upper room discourse, which is Jesus' farewell to his disciples. These words are words of encouragement: "Be of good cheer." These words are affectionate words: they are words to eleven men whom Jesus dearly loves, men whose hearts are deeply troubled, men who in a short time will abandon Jesus, and yet men for whom Jesus will lay down his life on the accursed cross. These words are victorious words because they promise peace and victory to all believers.

These words are also Jesus' final words to his disciples about the world. The upper room discourse has included abundant instruction about the world. I summarize: in John 14:17 the world cannot receive the Spirit of truth because in verse 22 Jesus does not manifest himself to the world. In verse 30 the world has a prince, who is Satan or the devil, who has nothing in Jesus. In chapter 15:18 the world hates Jesus and Jesus' disciples. In verse 19 the disciples do not belong to the world because Jesus has chosen them out of the world. In chapter 16:2 the world will put the disciples out of the synagogues and kill them. In verse 8 the Spirit will reprove the world, leaving it without excuse for its unbelief, and in verse 11 the prince of the world is judged. In verse 20 the world will rejoice in Jesus' death, but its joy shall be short-lived because Jesus shall return after "a little while." Jesus' final word about the world is this: "In the world ye shall have tribulation: but be of good cheer; I have overcome the world" (v. 33). With those ringing words of victory Jesus ends his instruction and I end this book.

THE MEANING

Our first task is to define the world. The world is the society of ungodly men arranged under one head (Satan), united in their opposition to God. The world is a terribly dangerous foe of the church, and it operates in two ways.

The world begins its opposition to the church in the realm of temptation. The church is holy, while the world is unholy, and it wishes to corrupt the church. This was the case in the beginning when the church (Adam and Eve) faced the prince of the world, which is the devil. The very first weapon that Satan used against the church (Adam and Eve) was temptation. In temptation the world does Satan's bidding because it makes sin look attractive and beneficial, while it paints righteousness or holiness in an evil light. The world operates through its media, its entertainment, its advertising, and its propaganda. The world appeals to our flesh because it operates according to the principle of the flesh. God's word speaks of "having escaped the corruption that is in the world through lust" (2 Pet. 1:4) and warns of "the lust of the flesh, and the lust of the eyes, and the pride of life" (1 John 2:16).

The calling of the disciples (and of the church today) is to resist the world in its temptations, to say no to ungodly lusts, and to remain holy. When the world promotes lasciviousness, we live purely in holy wedlock or in single life. When the world promotes self-indulgence, we live in self-denial and in loving, devoted service to one another. When the world promotes materialism, greed, and covetousness, we live in contentment and temperance, as wise stewards of God's gifts. The world will see how the church lives, and it will increase its efforts to lure the church away from Christ, but we must steadfastly resist. When the world reviles the church for her holiness in devotion to Christ, the church must be holy still. When we are tempted, we remember that we have God's grace to enable us to endure: "For the grace of God that bringeth salvation hath appeared to all men, teaching us that, denying ungodliness and worldly lusts, we should live soberly, righteously, and godly, in this present world" (Titus 2:11–12). "This is the victory that overcometh the world, even our faith" (1 John 5:4).

Temptation, however, is only "Phase One" of the world's opposition. "Phase Two," which is the focus of verse 33, is tribulation: Jesus does not say, "In the world ye shall have temptation," but "In the world ye shall have tribulation." In fact, Jesus does not mention temptation at all in the upper room discourse, but his focus is on the hatred and the opposition of the world.

What, then, is tribulation? The word "tribulation" comes from a verb that means to press against or to apply pressure to someone or something. The verb is used in Mark 3:9: "And he spake to his disciples, that a small ship should wait on him because of the multitude, lest they should throng him." In Matthew 7:14 the verb is used as an adjective: "Narrow is the way, which leadeth unto life, and few there be that find it." The idea is of a way that presses against a person as he travels along it. Tribulation, therefore, is pressure.

When the world applies tribulation, the church feels pressure. The church feels as if she is being squeezed. The purpose of the tribulation is to make the church's place in the world narrow. Whatever pressure that the world applies to the church, to the disciples, or to you as a believer, to make you forsake Christ, is tribulation.

Tribulation comes in many forms, but the purpose of the world in tribulation is always the same: to make faithfulness to Christ difficult, to make obedience to God difficult, and to make holiness difficult. The world really does not care which method it uses: in fact, the world prefers to begin with less severe forms of tribulation, and then to ratchet up the pressure until the church succumbs; then and only then is the world satisfied. So the world begins with ridicule and scorn, then it progresses to threats and intimidation, and finally it progresses to physical forms of persecution, such as fines, imprisonment, torture, and death.

That was the world's method with the disciples. First, the world mocked: "These men are full of new wine" (Acts 2:13). Then the world threatened: "And they called them, and commanded them not to speak at all nor teach in the name of Jesus" (4:18). Then the world arrested, imprisoned, and beat the members of the church, especially her leaders: "And when they had called the apostles, and beaten them, they commanded that they should not speak in the name of Jesus, and let them go" (5:40). Finally, the world killed the disciples of Jesus: "Now about that time Herod the king stretched forth his hands to vex certain of the church. And he killed James the brother of John with the sword. And because he saw it pleased the Jews, he proceeded further to take Peter also" (12:1–3). At any time, if the disciples had stopped serving Jesus Christ, the tribulation would have ceased. "In the world," said Jesus, "ye shall have tribulation" (v. 33).

The same applies to us: if you want to be a faithful Christian, expect tribulation in the world. Expect opposition from friends, family, neighbors, and coworkers. Expect pressure from work: pressure to work on the Lord's day, pressure to promote ungodly causes, and pressure to agree with and participate in dishonest practices. Expect pressure from family to join a less faithful church or to abandon the church altogether. Expect pressure from family to live less strictly and in disobedience to God's commandments. Expect future persecution and opposition from the government when you insist on Christian doctrine and morality and when you teach them to your children. "Yea, and all that will live godly in Christ Jesus shall suffer persecution" (2 Tim. 3:12). "Blessed are they which are persecuted for righteousness' sake: for theirs is the kingdom of heaven" (Matt. 5:10).

The blessed truth of this text, one that Jesus wants his disciples to know before he departs from them, is this: "Be of good cheer; I have overcome the world" (v. 33). The world tried the same two "big guns" on Jesus Christ. When Christ came into the world, the world tempted Jesus and the world opposed and persecuted him.

The world began by tempting Jesus. As soon as Jesus began his public ministry with his baptism at age thirty, the devil, the prince of the world, tempted Jesus. The goal of the devil was simple: to cause Jesus to disobey his Father by turning him away from the path of the cross. The devil offered Jesus three attractive alternatives to the cross: turn stones into bread, leap from the pinnacle of the temple, and worship Satan to inherit the kingdoms of the world (Matt. 4). These temptations were the strongest allurements that the world had ever used. Multitudes of men and women had fallen when faced with much weaker temptations. The devil reserved his greatest temptations for Jesus Christ. Nevertheless, Jesus refused to yield to these temptations, answering each temptation in the same way, "It is written."

Although he departed from Jesus for a while, the devil persisted with his temptations until the very end. Satan tempted Jesus even when Jesus was on the cross. He tempted him to come down, but Jesus never yielded, not even for a moment, in order that we might be saved.

When temptations did not produce the desired results, the world applied greater pressure to Jesus. The devil, the prince of the world, applied pressure. The religious world, the false church, applied pressure. The pagan world of the Romans applied pressure. "Yield to us: we will reduce the pressure, but if you persist in your holy devotion to God, if you persist in teaching the kingdom of heaven, and if you persist in exposing us, then we will press down upon you to squeeze you and to crush you." The world attacked Jesus as soon as he was born: King Herod attempted to kill him. When Jesus appeared to his own people, they rejected him: they mocked him, they blasphemed him, and they afflicted him.

Jesus knew that the world's tribulation against him would only intensify. Already, the prince of the world was around the corner waiting to apply further pressure to Jesus. Satan had enlisted Judas, Herod, the Sanhedrin, Pilate, and the Romans to afflict Jesus. The pressure to deny God, to turn from the path of obedience, and to commit sin would be almost unbearable, and certainly unbearable for anyone less than the Son of God. Jesus said, "In the world ye shall have tribulation." He could equally—and even more accurately—have said: "In the world I [Jesus] shall have tribulation."

But Jesus is not afraid of the world as he speaks these words. Instead, he is triumphant: "Be of good cheer," he says. "I have overcome the world" (v. 33). To overcome something is to succeed in dealing with it so that it is no longer a problem or a threat. One overcomes an obstacle, for example. The Greek word means to have victory, to conquer, or to prevail. If Jesus overcomes the world, he has victory over the world. The world squeezed Jesus, but he was victorious over the world. The world applied pressure to Jesus, but he prevailed against it. The world fought against Jesus, but he conquered the world. In the battle between the world and Jesus the world was crushed, and Jesus emerged as the great victor. Thus is fulfilled the promise of Genesis 3:15: "And I will put enmity between thee and the woman, and between thy seed and her seed; it shall bruise thy head, and thou shalt bruise his heel." When Jesus bruised or crushed Satan's head, he overcame the world because Satan is the prince or the ruler of this world.

Do not misunderstand. Jesus did not overcome the world by forcing the world to accept him as king, by tyrannically subduing the world under himself, or by ending the world's power to tempt or to persecute the church. That kind of victory the unbelieving Jews would have welcomed and the disciples desired.

After Jesus overcame the world, the world still tempts us and still persecutes us. If anything, Jesus' victory over the world makes the world fiercer in its opposition to the church because Jesus' victory over Satan makes him even angrier and determined to inflict even more misery upon us. Jesus does not say, "Be ye of good cheer: in the world ye shall have no tribulation because I have overcome the world." We might almost expect that, but it would be a foolish expectation. Instead, Jesus says, "In the world ye shall have tribulation: but be of good cheer; I have overcome the world." Both are true: we have tribulation in the world, and Jesus has victory. Expect persecution, therefore, because Jesus has overcome the world. Expect opposition because the world is very angry at its defeat by Jesus. Expect opposition because the Spirit reproves the world concerning its own judgment. Remember verse 11: "Of judgment, because the prince of this world is judged."

Instead, Jesus defeats the world, Jesus overcomes the world, Jesus prevails against, is victorious against, and conquers the world by means of the cross. When Jesus seemed to be the weakest, then he overcame the world. When Jesus seemed to be in the world's power (betrayed by Judas, arrested by a Jewish and Roman mob, condemned by the Sanhedrin, manhandled by the Roman soldiers, rejected by the people, sentenced to death by Pilate, and finally crucified), Jesus was actually the victor or conqueror. When the devil seemed to have defeated Jesus, Jesus was actually crushing him.

Paul rejoices in this truth in Galatians 6:14: "But God forbid that I should glory, save in the cross of our Lord Jesus Christ, by whom the world is crucified unto me, and I unto the world." John rejoices in this truth in Revelation 5:5: "The Lion of the tribe of Juda, the Root of David, hath prevailed to open the book, and to loose the seven seals thereof." In verse 12 the angels, the beasts, and the elders in heaven sing, "Worthy is the Lamb that was slain to receive power, and riches, and wisdom, and strength, and honour, and glory, and blessing." The disciples did not yet understand, but what they viewed as his defeat—Jesus' death on the cross—was actually with the resurrection his victory over the world.

We might wonder: Why is this so? Why is the cross the victory over the world? Why did God choose such a strange instrument by which to defeat the world? The answer is simple: to defeat the world, Jesus destroyed sin. Sin, which is rebellion against God, is the power by which the world operates. Satan made the world the enemy of God by introducing sin into the world, and God judged the world with death and the curse. But Satan must not be allowed to enjoy any victory. God redeems his people from the power of the world by satisfying his own justice against sin. Jesus therefore became incarnate, suffered, and died in order to pay for the sins of God's people whom he redeemed out of the world. Otherwise, Peter, James, John, and the rest, and we too, must perish with the world. Moreover, Jesus redeems the world so that, although the ungodly perish, the world itself is saved, and God promises a new creation in which righteousness dwells.

Notice, too, the tense that Jesus uses: "I have overcome the world." Jesus speaks in the perfect tense. So sure is he of victory that he speaks as if it has already happened. Gethsemane, the trial before the Sanhedrin, the trial before Pilate, the cross itself, and death lie before him, but he sees them as already defeated foes. "I have already overcome the world." We must know the victory: we must be certain of it. The world must know it too: the world must repent, and if it does not repent, it is without excuse. Let the world tempt: Jesus Christ has overcome the world. Let the world mock and persecute: Jesus Christ has overcome the world. What a glorious truth!

THE FRUIT

In contrast with the tribulation of the world Jesus proclaims, "In me ye might have peace" (v. 33). Because Jesus has overcome the world, and because he has told us of his victory over the world, we have peace, which is the fruit of Christ's overcoming the world. Peace is a harmonious relationship with God. God is the God of peace; therefore, peace—true peace—is found in him.

The world seeks peace, but not true peace. The peace of the world is a false, counterfeit peace consisting in the absence of trouble for a time. The world's peace cannot last because it is not peace with God. If the world for a time is not at war, if for a time society is not in turmoil, if for a time the various factions in the world agree to some kind of ceasefire, if for a time bickering pauses in a family, or if labor disputes can be avoided for a time, then the world thinks that it has achieved peace, but it has not because the world is at war with God because of sin.

If peace is a harmonious relationship with God, and the world's war with God is because of sin, we can enjoy peace only when our sins are forgiven. This, then, is the relationship: on the cross Jesus paid for our sins, which is his victory over the world, and Jesus' victory over the world purchases peace for us. Since Jesus made full atonement for our sins, God has nothing against us. God's wrath does not burn against us because Jesus suffered God's wrath in our place. God does not curse us because Jesus was cursed with the curse of the law in our place (Gal. 3:13). God does not punish us for our sins because Jesus was punished for our sins in our place.

The result is peace, a harmonious relationship with God. "But now in Christ Jesus ye who sometimes were far off are made nigh by the blood of Christ. For he is our peace, who hath made both one, and hath broken down the middle wall of partition between us" (Eph. 2:13–14). "And, having made peace through the blood of his cross, by him to reconcile all things unto himself" (Col. 1:20). The world perishes in its sins under the wrath of God. The church made up of believers and their children lives in peace. We have peace because our sins are forgiven, and we have peace because we are reconciled to God: he loves us and we love him. No wonder Jesus said earlier, "Peace I leave with you, my peace I give unto you: not as the world giveth, give I unto you" (John 14:27).

There is more, because the disciples were not yet at peace; they did not yet enjoy peace. For one thing Christ had not yet purchased it, but more importantly their hearts were troubled and they were afraid. Therefore, Jesus says, "These things I have spoken unto you, that in me ye might have peace" (v. 33). The reference is to subjective peace. It is one thing to be at peace with God objectively since Christ purchased objective peace at the cross. But it is another thing to know peace, to enjoy peace, to experience peace, and to have the assurance of peace. That is subjective peace, which comes only through faith in Jesus Christ.

That is why Jesus refers to his words: "These things I have spoken unto you." Jesus expects the disciples to remember and to lay hold of his words—his instruction, his explanations, and his promises—and through faith in him to have peace. When we do not enjoy peace as we ought, when our hearts are troubled, the remedy is faith: remember what Jesus said, read the Scriptures, listen to the preaching of God's word, and embrace the truth by faith.

In a few hours, the disciples would be thrown into utter turmoil: they would know deep tribulation when the world would take their Lord away from them. When Jesus would return to them at the resurrection and they would believe, then they would enjoy peace. Peter would have precious little peace in the courtyard of the high priest's palace: he would be so frightened that he would deny Jesus three times. John would have precious little peace at Calvary: he would witness the horror of Jesus dying on the cross. The other disciples would have precious little peace when they fled from Jesus and hid behind closed doors for fear of the Jews. But the disciples would enjoy peace—precious, beautiful peace—when Jesus would return to them in the resurrection. Through faith they would embrace the peace of Jesus Christ, which is the peace of God, which passes understanding.

Thomas is another example: after the resurrection, he would not believe. While the other disciples enjoyed peace through believing, Thomas insisted on being gloomy. That gloom would oppress his soul for a whole week, while he lingered in unbelief concerning the resurrection. Jesus would then appear to Thomas, he would say, "Peace" (John 20:26), and Thomas would believe (v. 28). Or as Paul puts it, "Therefore being justified by faith, we have peace with God through our Lord Jesus Christ" (Rom. 5:1). "Now the God of hope fill you with all joy and peace in believing, that ye may abound in hope, through the power of the Holy Ghost" (15:13).

THE CALLING

The calling of the text is simply this: "Be of good cheer" (v. 33). The verb "to be of good cheer" is almost always found in the imperative, that is, as a command, in the New Testament. It is rendered in two different ways: mostly the translation is "Be of good cheer"; and twice the translation is "Be of good comfort." Often, the verb is used in connection with the miracles of Jesus. For example, Jesus says to the woman healed of the issue of blood, "Daughter, be of good comfort; thy faith hath made thee whole" (Matt. 9:22). Jesus says to his frightened disciples, as he comes walking to them on the water, "Be of good cheer; it is I; be not afraid" (14:27). The word therefore is intended to give encouragement to discouraged souls.

This being of good cheer was, of course, not the disposition of the disciples. The disciples' hearts were troubled (John 14:1) and they were afraid (v. 27). Sorrow filled the disciples' hearts (16:6) and they would weep, lament, and be sorrowful (v. 20); in fact, they had sorrow already (v. 22). Nevertheless, Jesus commands and encourages his disciples: "Be of good cheer. Stir yourselves up to lay hold of the comfort and peace that I give to you."

The reason for this good cheer is clear in verse 33: "Be of good cheer; I have overcome the world." Yes, the Christian life is hard, and even filled with tribulation. The world will squeeze us and put pressure on us, which we will find a very painful experience. Nevertheless, we must not fear, but we must remember this great truth: Christ has overcome the world; he has overcome the world's temptations and tribulations by the power of his cross. Therefore, our sins are forgiven and we have every reason to be cheerful, comforted, and courageous. In our Lord Jesus we shall have peace—he has told us so. Be of good cheer, then. Take heart. Be not discouraged. Our Savior has overcome the world.